Beyond the Band of Brothers

Women can't fight. This assumption lies at the heart of the combat exclusion, a policy that was fiercely defended as essential to national security, despite evidence that women have been contributing to hostile operations now and throughout history. This book examines the role of women in the US military and the key arguments used to justify the combat exclusion, in light of the decision to reverse the policy in 2013. Megan MacKenzie considers the historic role of the combat exclusion in shaping American military identity and debunks claims that the recent policy change signals a new era for women in the military. Placing the policy in a broader context, MacKenzie shows how women's exclusion from combat reaffirms male supremacy in the military and sustains a key military myth, the myth of the band of brothers. She traces the band of brothers myth from Freud to HBO in her critical analysis and history of the role of women in combat. This book will be welcomed by scholars and students of military studies, gender studies, social and military history, and foreign policy.

MEGAN MACKENZIE is a senior lecturer in the Department of Government and International Relations at the University of Sydney. Her research centers on gender and security. Her book *Female Soldiers in Sierra Leone: Sex, Security and Post-Conflict Development* (2012) included interviews with more than fifty female soldiers who participated in Sierra Leone's civil war.

Beyond the Band of Brothers

The US Military and the Myth that Women Can't Fight

MEGAN MACKENZIE

University of Sydney

CAMBRIDGE
UNIVERSITY PRESS

CAMBRIDGE
UNIVERSITY PRESS

University Printing House, Cambridge CB2 8BS, United Kingdom

Cambridge University Press is part of the University of Cambridge.

It furthers the University's mission by disseminating knowledge in the pursuit of education, learning and research at the highest international levels of excellence.

www.cambridge.org
Information on this title: www.cambridge.org/9781107628106

© Megan MacKenzie 2015

First published 2015

A catalogue record for this publication is available from the British Library

ISBN 978-1-107-62810-6 Paperback

Cambridge University Press has no responsibility for the persistence or accuracy of URLs for external or third-party internet websites referred to in this publication, and does not guarantee that any content on such websites is, or will remain, accurate or appropriate.

For Jason, with love

Contents

Tables

Acknowledgments

It is pure bliss to write the last sentence of a book. It is sweeter still to be able to reflect back on all the people who helped inspire, shape, and fuel this project. I'm afraid that words are least effective when attempting to say thank you. These acknowledgments reflect only a glimmer of the intense gratitude I feel.

I am indebted to the groundbreaking scholarship of many feminist international relations scholars, including Christine Sylvester, Carol Cohn, Cynthia Enloe, and Ann Tickner – whose work I continue to be inspired by. In particular, Cynthia Enloe encouraged me to keep pursuing questions about the peculiarity of excluding women from combat. I reread her work and relistened to her lectures online during the writing process, drawing on her insights into militarization and her infectious enthusiasm when I lost sight of the direction of the project.

The first pages of this book were written during weekly writing sessions with Teresia Teaiwa. I am profoundly thankful for the mentorship, friendship, patience, laughter, and intense conversations about militarization, war, and "real" soldiers Teresia shared with me. Thank you to Robbie Shilliam, Angela Fitzsimons, Gideon Rose, Charli Carpenter, Jacqui True, and Carol Harrington for their encouragement and feedback during early stages of the project. This book was greatly improved as a result of several exchanges with, and rounds of feedback from, Lene Hansen and Rebecca Adler-Nisson – thank you. I am grateful to have had the much-needed support of several fantastic research assistants over the past few years, including Marianne Bevan, Morgan Hanks, Aishwarrya Balaji, and Joshua Bird. A very special thanks to Alix Pearce for bringing passion, comic relief, and brilliant maturity to her role as primary research assistant. Thank you also to John Haslam at Cambridge University Press for his careful attention and support. I have benefited from the University of Sydney and the Australian Research Council in terms of institutional and funding support for this project. My colleagues at the University of Sydney have been incredibly generous in offering feedback, reading chapter drafts and grant applications, and attending two presentations of this work. Thank you in particular to Helen Irving, Anika Gauja, Ariadne Vromen, James Der Derian, Chris Hills, and Frank Smith. My colleague and good friend Christopher Neff deserves a special mention here; his insights, generosity, and passion helped sculpt and power this book from its beginnings.

I wrote this book during the first months back to work after giving birth to my son. This was not sensible, and it was only possible as a result of numerous forms of support. Thank you to my family and friends for their care, questions, and love. I would like to express heartfelt thanks especially to Amy Fung and Lisa King for helping me transition back to the academic world and to Linda Carnew for her role in making sleep, recovery, and writing possible during the last weeks. Thank you to Ira, for adding love, wonder, and insomnia to the process. Finally, but most importantly, I can say with absolute certainty that this book would not have been completed without the love and commitment of my husband Jason. Thank you for always believing in this book more than I did and for carrying it over the finish line in ways you may not even realize. This book was brought to you by love.

Introduction: myths, men, and policy making

From this day to the ending of the world,
But we in it shall be remember'd;
We few, we happy few, we band of brothers;
For he to-day that sheds his blood with me
Shall be my brother; be he ne'er so vile,
This day shall gentle his condition:
And gentlemen in England now a-bed
Shall think themselves accursed they were not here,
And hold their manhoods cheap whiles any speaks
That fought with us upon Saint Crispin's day.

Shakespeare, *Henry V*, 1598

The male combat unit lies at the heart of American military identity. The story of a group of men risking their lives to violently defend the United States has been a consistent national narrative. "Bands of brothers," "comrades in arms," and "a few good men" are examples of well-worn tropes that signal men's unique connection to one another and their ability to overcome extreme odds to protect the nation. According to military historian Martin van Creveld, war is "the highest proof of manhood" and combat is "the supreme assertion of masculinity."[1] In his Afghanistan war memoir, US Army Infantry Officer Andrew Exum described the infantry as "one of the last places where that most endangered of species, the alpha male, can feel at home."[2] These accounts of soldiering depict male troops as the natural and rightful protectors of society.

In contrast, women are often seen as potential spoilers to military culture. There are fears that the integration of women into the military – particularly into combat roles – "feminizes" and weakens

---

[1] Martin van Creveld, "Less Than We Can Be," 2.
[2] Andrew Exum, *This Man's Army* (New York: Gotham Books, 2005), 35.

the military. Stephanie Gutmann explains, "I do not think we could have a capable integrated combat arms without real androgyny, without real suppression of male and female qualities."[3] Such portrayals of the military imply that restricting women from the front lines of war is essential to national security. This rationale was at the heart of the combat exclusion – a US military policy designed to keep women from combat units. The policy was founded on the understanding that women were not natural soldiers, were physically inferior to men, and would ruin the bonds necessary for combat missions.[4]

For decades, the combat exclusion was heralded by Congress and the Department of Defense (DOD) as crucial for national security. At the same time, the all-male combat unit was lauded as the key component, or "the tip of the spear," of US military operations. In other words, American security was directly linked to male-only groups and to the exclusion of women from some military jobs. Given this, the Pentagon's announcement on January 24, 2013, that it was removing the combat exclusion came as a shock to many Americans and raised two questions: Why now? And what did the change mean? Although there are competing theories as to why the combat exclusion was removed, there is little understanding of how the combat exclusion survived for so long and the role it played in shaping military identity. The intense effort to keep women from combat roles, even in the face of evidence that women were already "doing the job,"[5] signals that the combat exclusion policy is an important site for understanding gender dynamics within the military.

This book is not a historical account of the combat exclusion or an evaluation of whether women should or should not fight in combat. It also does not predict whether the removal of the combat

---

[3] Stephanie Gutmann, *The Kinder, Gentler Military: Can America's Gender-Neutral Fighting Force Still Win Wars?* (Simon & Schuster, 2000), 272.

[4] As discussed in subsequent chapters, a number of other reasons are given for the combat exclusion, including concerns over privacy, sexual violence, and logistics.

[5] See Chapters 2 and 3 for more discussion on women's contribution to combat missions.

exclusion will produce positive or negative outcomes for women or for the US military. Instead, the book uses the combat exclusion as a vehicle for a broader analysis of military identity. The foundational argument of the book is that the combat exclusion in the USA has always been about men, not women. There are two pillars to this position. The first is that the combat exclusion was an evolving set of rules, guidelines, and ideas primarily used to reify the all-male combat unit as elite, essential, and exceptional. The second is that the combat exclusion was not designed in response to research and evidence related to women and war, but rather was created and sustained through the use of stories, myths, and emotional arguments.

In particular, the myth of the band of brothers shapes our understanding of what men and women can, and should do, in war. Specifically, the band of brothers myth conveys three key "truths." First, the myth casts the nonsexual, brotherly love, male bonding, and feelings of trust, pride, honor, and loyalty between men as mysterious, indescribable, and **exceptional**. Second, male bonding is treated as both primal and an **essential** element of an orderly, civilized, society. Third, all male units are seen as **elite** as a result of their social bonds and physical superiority; it is assumed that these qualities render them more capable of accomplishing military missions and defending the country compared to mixed-gender units. The physical differences between men and women are particularly emphasized and cited as evidence of women's inferiority. In other words, difference is equated with superiority. Moreover, combat units are treated as the most elite component of the military; as van Creveld put it, "warriors . . . occup[y] an elevated position on the social ladder."[6] As well as these three truths, the overarching message of the band of brothers myth is that the exceptional, elite, and essential characteristics of the male group depend on the exclusion of women.

In addition to developing and supporting this central argument, one of the broad objectives of this book is to contribute to debates

[6] van Creveld, "Less Than We Can Be," 3.

about the motivation and justifications for wars. The book offers a unique answer to the question "Why do we fight?"[7] Many analyses of the military-industrial complex focus on the economy and overlook the social and cultural justifications for perpetual militarization and war. Building on the work of gender scholars such as Aaron Belkin[8] and Cynthia Enloe,[9] I argue that the logic of war depends on the preservation of gendered stories and myths about "real" men, "good" women, and "normal" social order. One could call the constant perpetuation and dissemination of such gendered ideals a militarized-masculinity complex.

The all-male combat unit lies at the heart of gendered depictions of war, and the band of brothers myth serves as a linchpin to social and cultural justifications for war. The ideal of the heroic, brave, masculine, and mysterious all-male unit legitimizes male privilege within the military institution, represents war as "the ultimate expression of masculinity," and casts violence as a necessary political strategy. In turn, I argue that we fight because the myth of the band of brothers presents war as natural, honorable, and essential for social progress. Moreover, we fight because the band of brothers myth casts outsiders as inherent security threats and presumes that violence is the most efficient way of solving political problems. In light of these broader objectives, this book is not merely an account of the combat exclusion policy; rather, it uses the combat exclusion as a medium for unpacking

---

[7] For two interesting perspectives on this question, see Eugene Jareki's excellent documentary *Why We Fight*, which traces the military-industrial complex and the inability of governments or American citizens to detect or prevent the pattern of perpetual war, or what, in the film, Gore Vidal summarizes as "the United States of amnesia" [Eugene Jarecki, *Why We Fight*, Documentary, History, War (2005)]. In their book *Why They Fight: Combat Motivation in the Iraq War* (Strategic Studies Institute, U.S. Army War College, July 2003), Leonard Wong et al. make the case that cohesion, or the bonds between soldiers, is the primary motivation for combat soldiers.

[8] Aaron Belkin, *Bring Me Men: Military Masculinity and the Benign Façade of American Empire, 1898–2001* (New York: Columbia University Press, 2012).

[9] Cynthia Enloe, *Maneuvers: The International Politics of Militarizing Women's Lives*, 1st ed. (University of California Press, 2000). See also the lecture by Enloe, "Women and Militarization: Before, During and After Wars," for an excellent summary of the role of "good" women and "real" men in perpetuating wars ["Women and Militarization: Before, During, and After Wars" with Cynthia Enloe, 2012, http://www.youtube.com/watch?v=lfCktWyARVo&feature=youtube_gdata_player].

and unraveling one of the greatest – and most destructive – political myths: the myth of the band of brothers.

In addition to unraveling gender norms, this analysis provides an alternative perspective to those who laud the removal of the combat exclusion as a watershed moment. Using historical evidence, I will illustrate that it has been necessary for the US military to regroup and rebrand itself after almost every major military operation, particularly following the Vietnam War. Female soldiers are, and always have been, central to this rebranding and rewriting of history. Restricting women from combat units has served to confirm men's superior role in the military and reassure the public of the masculine identity of the military. This book traces the fluid and evolving stories and justifications associated with the combat exclusion throughout US military history. In doing so, it reveals a pattern in which women's exclusion from combat has been used to shape military identity, support militarization, and uphold male supremacy within the institution.

The removal of the combat exclusion is not a watershed moment and does not signal a new era for gender relations in the military. This characterization discounts women's historic contributions to combat operations – contributions that had been formally recognized in the form of combat badges and combat pay for years before the announcement. This characterization also overlooks ongoing sexism plaguing the institution, including a widely publicized yet largely unaddressed epidemic of sexual violence. Enthusiastic depictions of the combat exclusion policy change could be seen as part of a broader effort to revive a somewhat battered military image at the "end" of two largely unpopular wars, and in the face of ongoing scandals and criticism. This book demonstrates that the policy change did not mark the end of band of brothers narratives; rather, it served to recover and reshape the band of brothers myth, as well as military identity more broadly.

When seeking to understand the issues surrounding women and combat, a vast range of academic and nonacademic resources are available. In terms of nonacademic contributions, there are a number of monographs aimed at convincing readers that women should not be allowed in combat, or in some cases even in the military. These are largely polemics by former military staff – typically men – including *Co-ed Combat: The New Evidence That Women Shouldn't Fight the Nation's Wars* by Kingsley Browne[10]; Robert L. Maginnis' *Deadly Consequences: How Cowards Are Pushing Women into Combat*[11]; and *Women in the Military: Flirting with Disaster* by Brian Mitchell.[12] There are also several autobiographies and personal accounts of individual women's experiences of soldiering.[13]

In contrast to the polemics and individual features, there are excellent academic resources that examine the wider issues associated with gender and war,[14] gender and the military,[15] women's experiences of war,[16] violent women,[17] militarization,[18] women in

---

[10] Kingsley Browne, *Co-Ed Combat: The New Evidence That Women Shouldn't Fight the Nation's Wars*, 1st edition (Sentinel HC, 2007).

[11] Robert L. Maginnis, *Deadly Consequences: How Cowards Are Pushing Women into Combat*, 1st edition (Washington, DC: Regnery, 2013).

[12] Brian Mitchell, *Women in the Military: Flirting with Disaster*, 1st Edition (Regnery, 1997).

[13] Michele Hunter Mirabile, *Your Mother Wears Combat Boots: Humorous, Harrowing and Heartwarming Stories of Military Women* (AuthorHouse, 2007); James E. Wise Jr. and Scott Baron, *Women at War: Iraq, Afghanistan, and Other Conflicts* (Maryland: Naval Institute Press, 2011); Kirsten Holmstedt, *Band of Sisters: American Women at War in Iraq* (Stackpole Books, 2008).

[14] Carol Cohn, "Wars, Wimps, and Women: Talking Gender and Thinking War," in *Gendering War Talk*, edited by Miriam Cooke and Angela Woollacott (Princeton, NJ: Princeton University Press, 1993), 227–46; Carol Cohn, editor, *Women and Wars: Contested Histories, Uncertain Futures*, 1st edition (Cambridge, UK: Polity, 2012); Laura Sjoberg, *Gender, War, and Conflict*, 1st edition (Cambridge, UK: Polity, 2014).

[15] Melissa S. Herbert, *Camouflage Isn't Only for Combat: Gender, Sexuality, and Women in the Military* (New York: NYU Press, 1998), and Paige Whaley Eager, *Waging Gendered Wars: U.S. Military Women in Afghanistan and Iraq*, New edition (Farnham, UK: Ashgate, 2014).

[16] Christine Sylvester, *War as Experience: Contributions from International Relations and Feminist Analysis*, 1st edition (New York: Routledge, 2012); Sylvester, "The Art of War/The War Question in (Feminist) IR." *Millennium – Journal of International Studies* 33, no. 3 (June 1, 2005): 855–78; Chandra Talpade Mohanty, Minnie Bruce Pratt, and Robin L. Riley, editors, *Feminism and War*, 1st edition (London: Zed Books, 2008).

[17] Carol Cohn, *Women and Wars* (December 4, 2012).

[18] Cynthia H. Enloe, *Globalization and Militarism: Feminists Make the Link* (Rowman & Littlefield, 2007); Enloe, *Maneuvers: The International Politics of Militarizing Women's Lives*; Laura Sjoberg and Sandra E. Via, editors, *Gender, War, and Militarism: Feminist Perspectives*, 1st edition (Santa Barbara, CA: Praeger, 2010).

combat in other militaries around the world,[19] and women's participation in militant movements and terrorist activities.[20] Feminist scholarship on women, gender, and war has challenged mainstream perspectives on war by asking critical questions, providing alternative understandings of key concepts such as security and post-conflict, and employing unique and reflexive methods for studying war and its aftermath.

Despite these valuable feminist contributions to war studies, there is a noticeable absence of feminist scholarship focused on Western militaries. Among the few feminist analyses of American women and combat, liberal feminists often characterize the combat exclusion as an example of gender exclusion and discrimination. For example, Kathleen Jones argued, "The best way to insure women's equal treatment with men is to render them equally vulnerable with men," including within the military.[21] Some of those who lobbied to have the combat exclusion removed contended that the policy was a "gender-based barrier to service"[22] that created a "brass ceiling"[23] for women in the armed forces. From this perspective, the removal of the combat ban is a sign of improved gender relations within the military, an opportunity for women to advance their careers, and even potentially a catalyst for reducing the rates of sexual violence within the military.[24]

---

[19] See, for example, Maya Eichler, "Women and Combat in Canada: Continuing Tensions between 'Difference' and 'Equality,'" *Critical Studies on Security* 1, no. 2 (August 2013): 257–59; Orna Sasson-Levy, "Feminism and Military Gender Practices: Israeli Women Soldiers in 'Masculine' Roles," *Sociological Inquiry* 73, no. 3 (2003): 440–65.

[20] Miranda Alison, *Women and Political Violence: Female Combatants in Ethno-National Conflict* (London: Routledge, 2008); Margaret Gonzalez-Perez, *Women and Terrorism: Female Activity in Domestic and International Terror Groups* (New York: Routledge, 2008); Paige Whaley Eager, *From Freedom Fighters to Terrorists: Women and Political Violence* (Aldershot, UK: Ashgate, 2008); Swati Parashar, "What Wars and 'War Bodies' Know about International Relations," *Cambridge Review of International Affairs* 26, no. 4 (December 1, 2013): 615–30.

[21] Jones, 1984.

[22] Quoted in Mark Thompson, "Women in Combat: Shattering the 'Brass Ceiling,'" *Time*, accessed September 8, 2014, http://nation.time.com/2013/01/24/women-in-combat-shattering-the-brass-ceiling/.

[23] Ibid.   [24] Service Women's Action Network.

Debates on women's capabilities and the potential impact of removing the combat exclusion tend to focus on physical statistics, historical evidence of women's contributions to war, and the effect of the combat exclusion on the careers of women. Data about women's physical bodies and the "average" physical differences between men and women is deliberated and assessed ad nauseam in attempts to determine if women can or should serve alongside men. There have also been extensive discussions about whether women's essential nature, in particular their presumed sensitivity and propensity for weakness and emotional reactions, presents an obstacle to their ability to serve on the front lines. Although such reflections and resources have merit, they can close off space for broader critical reflections on militarization, military identity, and gender hierarchies. More specifically, such debates ignore the ways that gender is constructed within, and in relation to, the military. By examining the relationship of the combat exclusion to the male combat unit, this book provides a unique perspective on both the policy and the centrality of the band of brothers myth to US military identity.

WHY MYTHS?

Myths are typically defined in two ways. The first – *myth as fiction* – treats myth as an untruth, or something contradictory to "reality."[25] The second – *myth as symbolic* – depicts myth as stories or narratives that are widely known to particular communities and that explain, justify, or legitimize certain cultural beliefs and practices. The former understanding of myth is widely represented within the field of international relations (IR). There are a number of IR resources that use myth interchangeably with error or untruth, including titles such as "The Myth of 1648," "The Myth of the Autocratic Revival," and "The Myth of Post–Cold War Chaos." The second definition of myth – as

---

[25] For example, John McDowell described myths as narratives that are "counterfactual in featuring actors and actions that confound the conventions of routine experience" in "Perspectives" on "What Is Myth" in *Folklore Forum*, vol. 29, no. 2, 1998.

symbolic – remains relatively underexamined in IR. This definition treats myth as central to the way that social groups, including nations, identify themselves and make sense of the world around them.

In this analysis this second definition of myth is employed. I argue that myths matter to international relations (IR) and to foreign policy. They are not simply fables, stories, and untruths; rather, they are deeply embedded narratives that shape how we understand the world. Myths send explicit messages about appropriate, ideal, acceptable, and legitimate behaviors, identities, and practices. This analysis builds on a strong body of work examining how myths shape politics and identity. In his book *Political Myth*, Christopher Flood defines political myths as "ideologically marked narratives" that convey explicit norms, beliefs, ideologies, and identities.[26] Cynthia Weber's work is at the forefront of IR scholarship engaged with myths.[27] For Weber, the study of myths is not aimed at locating flaws or untruths, so that "more accurate" approaches to IR might be constructed. Rather, myths reveal the unstable and constructed nature of truths that are treated as "common sense" within the field. In other words, the objective is not to "abandon the myth" but to "abandon the apparent truths associated with the myth."[28]

MYTH AS SECURITIZING

Drawing on Weber's work, my objective in this book is to consider how the band of brothers myth shapes "truths" and "common sense" ideas associated with security and women's place in war. The analysis does not replace these truths with more accurate ones. Rather, it traces the origins of these ideas in order to destabilize them and to

---

[26] Christopher Flood, *Political Myth: A Theoretical Introduction* (Psychology Press, 1996).

[27] Cynthia Weber, *International Relations Theory: A Critical Introduction* (Psychology Press, 2005). Also, in their book on Harry Potter and international relations, Iver Neuman and Dan Nexon argue that myths "serve as the frame into which other phenomena are fitted and then interpreted." Daniel H. Nexon, *Harry Potter and International Relations* (Lanham, MD: Rowman & Littlefield, 2006).

[28] Weber, *International Relations Theory*.

create space for their critique and unraveling. Myths alone are certainly not capable of securitizing. However, myths are an essential element of the securitization process. Myths inform our understandings of international and social order, group identity, and appropriate norms and behaviors.

There is a particular gendered aspect to the relationship between myth and security. The "order" that is implicit to notions of peace and stability depends on multiple gender constructions, many of which can be traced back to myths. In particular, binaries such as disorder/order and insecurity/security largely stem from the gendered norms that myths evoke. For example, conjugal order is a term I developed in my 2012 book *Female Soldiers in Sierra Leone: Sex, Security and Post-conflict Development*. The term refers to the multitude of laws, rules, and social norms associated with the family and social order in particular contexts. It concluded that the myth of the nuclear family informed post-conflict security policies and defined female soldiers as a domestic "problem" rather than a security priority. By contrast, men were categorized as "real" soldiers and prioritized as security threats in the postconflict era. The term "conjugal order" helped illustrate how moments of insecurity or crisis are shaped in relation to peaceful, domestic order. This book examines how ideals of peaceful, weak, and vulnerable women help to define a hypermasculine military and are central to mythologies of the military and its bands of brothers. Building on existing work looking at emotions in international relations, this analysis also highlights the significance of, and the value placed on, emotion and "gut" feelings about the policy.

THE BAND OF BROTHERS MYTH

The band of brothers myth is another myth that shapes our understandings of order and security. The band of brothers myth refers to an all-male military unit, uniting to protect each other and defend their country. Although there have been references to "bands of brothers" for centuries, the band of brothers myth attained hegemonic status in relation to American military identity in the decades following the

Vietnam War. Using Flood's definition, the band of brothers is a myth and not just a narrative for two reasons. First, it is an established, well-known story that has substantial resonance and emotional purchase. Second, it conveys clear and consistent messages about natural order, the origins of society, legitimate behaviors, and ideal/heroic/or villainous identities. Particularly in the past fifteen years, "band of brothers" has come to represent and signal multiple ideals associated with the all-male combat unit.

The history of the band of brothers myth

The ideal of the all-male group dominating and protecting society can be traced back to the world of Charles Darwin and Sigmund Freud. Although the term "primal horde" is most associated with Freud, he borrowed from a reference Darwin made to "primitive hordes." According to Darwin, primitive hordes were prehistoric social formations. Darwin did not elaborate on how these groups were organized; instead, he used the term to signal the unknowable nature of ancient cultures. In *Totem and Taboo* (1912–1913a),[29] Freud explains how Darwin's work inspired him: "Darwin deduced from the habits of the higher apes that men, too, originally lived in comparatively small groups or hordes within which the jealousy of the oldest and strongest male prevented sexual promiscuity."

Adapting this reference, Freud developed a narrative surrounding primal hordes that largely drew on mythical ideals.[30] In simple terms, the primal horde is a story of the transition from the state of nature to early political, or organized, society. According to Freud, primitive societies were controlled by a single patriarch, who had exclusive access to power and to women within the social group. Driven by jealousy and sexual drive, a group of men band together

---

[29] Sigmund Freud, *Totem and Taboo* (Psychology Press, 1999).

[30] He maintained this idea and returned to it again in *Group Psychology and the Analysis of the Ego* (1921c), *The Future of an Illusion* (1927c), and *Civilization and Its Discontents* (1930a [1929]), and especially in his last book, *Moses and Monotheism* (1939a).

to kill the father and share the power that he once held. These men become united by their collective violence, their shared sense of guilt, and their newfound access to women. Freud's analysis ties the foundation of society and the birth of humanity to the formation of an all-male band of brothers. This unit propelled social groups forward from the chaos of primitive society because, "united," the all-male unit "had the courage to do and succeeded in doing what would have been impossible for them individually."[31]

Although Freud had strong critics who argued that this myth had no basis in reality and overemphasized a flippant comment made by Darwin,[32] the story of the primal horde reached iconic status. When discussing primal horde in a written exchange, Freud once said "Don't take this too seriously. It's something I dreamed up one rainy Sunday afternoon." Despite criticisms and his acknowledgment of its fleeting origins, Freud based much of his psychoanalytical theories on the narrative, and other scholars built on various aspects of the primal horde.[33] In turn, many elements to the story have become embedded in the social and political fabric of Western society and came to shape Western understanding of gender roles, family relationships, and the origins of political society.

Popular culture accepted and reinforced band of brothers narratives with enthusiasm, particularly following the Vietnam War. Into the 1990s, war movies shifted their attention from the politics of war, or the historical particularities of a battle, to stories of the bonds between male soldiers. In their analysis of combat movies, Rudy and Gates conclude, "The new Hollywood war film does not present a political war but a moral one – and the hero who fights them is the idealistic youth."[34] The authors go on to note that the dominant

---

[31] Freud, *Totem and Taboo*, 141–42.

[32] Paul Radin, 1929; Alfred Louis Kroeber, 1920.

[33] Géza Róheim, Claude Lévi-Strauss (1949); Eugène Enriquez (1967); Serge Moscovici (1981).

[34] Paul Rudy and Philippa Gates, "Sound Shaping and Timbral Justification in the 'Moral Realist Combat Film' *Black Hawk Down*," accessed February 5, 2014, http://oicrm.org/wp-content/uploads/2012/03/RUDY_P_CIM05.pdf, p. 2.

theme of this "new" type of war movie is "heroism defined through idealism, moral choice, and self-sacrifice in the interests of the brotherhood – the 'Army of One.'"[35] These war movies seem to treat war as merely the backdrop against which to portray brotherly bonding and relationships. In turn, military defeat or success is defined relative to the relationship between men and their capacity to support one another instead of the actual military mission. In doing so, *Black Hawk Down*, which had the tagline "Leave no man behind," can recast humiliating military loss as an achievement for the men who fought together on this mission. Sue Williams summarizes: "[*Black Hawk Down* is] an astonishing glorification of slaughter that makes the tragedy look like majestic triumph for the brotherhood of man, rather than a humbling defeat for the United States."[36]

One cannot discuss the present-day iconic status of the band of brothers in the United States without referring to the HBO television series of the same name. *Band of Brothers* chronicles one American paratrooper company, known as "Easy." It draws from Stephen Ambrose's 1992 book of the same name and features present-day interviews with actual veterans of the unit. The series aired shortly after September 11, 2001, to initial tepid ratings; however, the subsequent DVD set became the best-selling HBO series and the highest grossing TV-to-DVD release.[37] Through its dramatization of a "real" group of men during World War II, *Band of Brothers* came to encapsulate a deeper narrative and set of ideals associated with men, women, and American wars. In Debra Ramsay's analysis, she argues that the series has come to represent "totalizing narratives of World War II that provide primary mechanisms through which to understand the

---

[35] Rudy and Gates, "Sound Shaping and Timbral Justification."

[36] Philippa Gates and Paul Rudy, "Spectromorphology Hits Hollywood: Morphology, Objectification and Moral Messages in the Sound Design of 'Black Hawk Down." CEC 8.3. Accessed http://cec.sonus.ca/econtact/8_3/gates_rudy.html.

[37] Debra Ramsay, "Television's 'True Stories': Paratexts and the Promotion of HBO's Band of Brothers and The Pacific," *InMedia. The French Journal of Media and Media Representations in the English-Speaking World*, no. 4 (November 12, 2013), http://inmedia.revues.org/720.

war."[38] Ramsay outlines several specific messages the series reiterates for the public. The first is that war history can and should be "refracted through the memories of the ordinary soldier."[39] The second is that war battles constitute the "defining experience of the war."[40] Although only a small percentage of soldiers serve in front lines positions and face battle, war is represented as being "about" combat soldiers, their relationships with one another, and their man-to-man contests with the enemy.

The HBO series aside, today, particularly in the USA, the mention of "bands of brothers" evokes a generally accepted and consistent set of narratives linked to all-male units, male bonding, courage under fire, and the protection of the nation. The US military has woven this narrative into the way it talks about combat units. For example, the current Marine slogan "The Few. The Proud." draws directly from the King Henry V speech quoted earlier ("We few, we happy few, we band of brothers"). One of the slogans used by the Marines since 1883 is the Latin *Semper Fidelis*, which they define as "[what] distinguishes the Marine Corps bond from any other. It goes beyond teamwork – it is a brotherhood that can always be counted on. Latin for 'always faithful' ... It guides Marines to remain faithful to the mission at hand, to each other, to the Corps and to country, no matter what."[41] Finally, troop cohesion, which was largely defined as men's ability to trust each other and form social bonds, became "synonymous" with combat effectiveness following the Vietnam War.[42] Major Brendan McBreen explains, "Improving infantry cohesion is more important than any combination of doctrinal, organizational, training or equipment improvements."[43] Kingsley Browne describes the gendered nature of cohesion, and the problem women pose to it: "Men fight for many reasons, but probably the most powerful one is

[38] Ibid.   [39] Ibid.   [40] Ibid.

[41] http://www.marines.com/history-heritage/principles-values, June 9, 2014.

[42] Erin Solaro, *Women in the Line of Fire: What You Should Know about Women in the Military*, 1st edition (Berkeley, CA: Seal Press, 2006), 297–98.

[43] Maj. Brendan McBreen, "The Strength of the Wolf Is the Pack," *Marine Corps Gazette* 88 (February 2004): 2.

the bonding – 'male bonding' – with their comrades . . . Perhaps for very fundamental reasons women do not evoke in men the same feelings of comradeship and 'followership' that men do."[44] In turn, combat cohesion was heralded as essential to troop effectiveness, but was also defined largely as male bonding, which by definition excluded women from cohesion.[45]

In turn, aspects of the band of brothers myth became operationalized and accepted as common sense within the US military. It is important to note that although women have been consistently depicted as a threat to male bonding and combat cohesion, several other threats to all-male combat cohesion have been identified within the US forces at various times through history. In the 1930s, for example, African American men were seen as threats to cohesion. The institution characterized African American men as untrustworthy and naturally weaker than their white comrades. Similarly, the military justified its effective ban on gays and lesbians in the military until 2011 with the argument that openly serving homosexuals would weaken military cohesion. The band of brothers, then, is not simply a myth about an all-male unit; it is a myth about a white, heterosexual man and his nonsexual bonds with his comrades.

Band of brothers "truths"

As indicated earlier, the band of brothers presents all-male units as exceptional, elite, and essential. Although the details of the narrative may shift over time, the overarching messages remain constant. These include the depiction of male bonding as sacred and mysterious; the perception of a distinct front lines in warfare that is more dangerous than "rear" positions; the association of warrior spirit, unit cohesion, and courage under fire with all-male units; the characterization of all-male units, including Special Forces, as especially "hard core" as a result of their physical fitness and their undying commitment to

---

[44] Browne, *Co-Ed Combat* , 7.
[45] Combat cohesion is explored in greater detail in Chapter 5.

military missions; and the message that women must be excluded in order to maintain honor and order.

It seems obvious from the iconic name of the myth – band of brothers – that women are excluded; however, it is worth exploring in greater detail how messages attached to this myth require female exclusion. First, the myth requires the exclusion of women's physical bodies in order to establish the band of brothers. Second, the myth implies that sacred male bonding and relationships depend on the exclusion of women. Third, the myth associates positive group and national emotions such as pride, honor, trust, and loyalty with male-only groups. In turn, the myth links security and order to the establishment and valorization of all-male units as well as the exclusion of women from these units.

Applying band of brothers to the combat exclusion

It is possible to examine the combat exclusion and military identity in relation to the band of brothers myth through the use of discourse analysis. Bottici and Challand note that the "'work on myth' involves an analysis of the whole system of production-reception-reproduction."[46] The method most appropriate to such "work" is discourse analysis. Lene Hansen argues, "To understand language as *political* is to see it as a site for the production and reproduction of particular subjectivities and identities."[47] Discourse analysis, therefore, is a useful tool to use in evaluating the ways that myths influence, and are reproduced within, foreign policies and policy debates.

For this book, the discourse analysis centers on three major types of sources. The first includes official military reports, press briefings, government statements, and policies related to the combat exclusion. Second, news articles and opinion pieces from the

---

[46] Chiara Bottici and Benoît Challand, "Rethinking Political Myth: The Clash of Civilizations as a Self-Fulfilling Prophecy," *European Journal of Social Theory* 9, no. 3 (August 1, 2006): 315–36, p. 320.

[47] Lene Hansen, *Security as Practice: Discourse Analysis and the Bosnian War*, 1st edition (London: Routledge, 2006), 18–19. Emphasis in original.

following top US news outlets are included: the *Wall Street Journal*, *New York Times*, *Los Angeles Times*, *Washington Post*, *Chicago Tribune*, and *USA Today*. I chose these sources because they reach a broad readership across the USA and tend to appeal to different US demographics. I analyzed articles that included "women and combat" or "combat exclusion" published in 2012 and for the first four months of 2013. I chose this time frame because it illustrates the type of reporting, analysis, and debate that took place leading up to the policy change, as well as in the first few months after the combat exclusion was lifted. Finally, I analyzed comments on three online articles on the combat exclusion in order to provide a richer picture of public debates on the combat exclusion policy and the decision to remove it.

Discourse analysis is used to examine the history of, rationalization for, and the decision to remove the combat exclusion through the lens of the band of brothers myth. In Chapter 1, I provide an overview of the history of the combat exclusion within the USA to support the argument that the combat exclusion is an idea and a fluid set of discourses and stories. Chapter 2 builds on this argument, but focuses specifically on US operations in Iraq and Afghanistan. Here, I argue that these wars eroded any remaining enforceable rules associated with the combat exclusion and, because of the nature of the conflicts, largely rendered the distinction between combat and support roles irrelevant. Next, in Chapter 3, the key emotional arguments expressing opposition to women in combat are presented, followed by an analysis of how these positions relate to the band of brothers myth. The chapter aims to illustrate the way in which emotional positions inform, or are woven through, seemingly objective claims about women in combat, including conclusions about women's physical nature. From here, physical standards and combat cohesion are discussed as the main research-driven, objective reasons for excluding women from combat. Exploring each in depth, in Chapters 4 and 5, I demonstrate that arguments related to physical fitness and cohesion remain shaped and influenced by emotion and the band of brothers myth. Finally, in Chapter 6, online comments to three articles on the combat exclusion are examined in order to further illustrate the influence of myth and emotion within wider debates on the combat exclusion.

CONCLUSION

The band of brothers myth is a nodal point from which many military policies stem. The chapter sought to demonstrate the relationship between myth, policy, and national identity and to establish a methodology for evaluating this claim. The band of brothers myth requires the exclusion of women from the "heart" of warfare – the combat unit. The myth also requires and reproduces particular ideas about women, including the assumption that they are inherently different from men, that they lack the natural drive to fight, and that they spoil the bonding required to fight wars successfully. This book moves beyond questions of whether women "can" or "should" fight in combat. It is also skeptical of claims that removing the combat exclusion marks a new era for gender relations in the US military. Allowing women in combat is not a means to address gender discrimination and embedded gender hierarchies and norms within the institution. Instead of evaluating the potential impacts or limitations of removing the combat exclusion, this book asks how the combat exclusion has been used throughout military history to shape ideals of "good," "honorable," and "real" soldiers. If indeed the combat exclusion has always been about men and the band of brothers, the decision to remove the combat exclusion should also be treated as a signal of an effort to redefine and revive the masculine image of the military and create a new iteration of the band of brothers narrative.

The combat exclusion is a story we tell ourselves... about men

"The major social value of a military society is a warrior image, particularly a masculine warrior image."[1]

This chapter provides some context for the combat exclusion policy within the USA. It is not a comprehensive overview of the inclusion or exclusion of women in the US military throughout history.[2] Instead, there are three specific goals of this chapter. First is to demonstrate that the combat exclusion is a trope, made up of a fluid set of rules and stories, not a concrete policy that has restricted women from combat. Second is to show that policies designed to keep women from combat were designed arbitrarily – in the form of either political compromises, or reactions to political and historical events – rather than in response to evidence that women could not do the job. Third is to argue that the definition of combat itself is illusive: both "combat" and "the combat exclusion" are, in fact, constructed. This chapter illustrates that the ever-changing combat exclusion has reflected gender stereotypes, evolving political pressures, and historical events. Moreover, the combat exclusion itself is a story and a trope that has always been defined and constructed in relation to the band of brothers myth and the fantasy of the all-male unit.

In order to accomplish these goals, the chapter examines the evolving policies and regulations related to women in combat. Beginning with World War II and covering the time period up until the wars in Iraq and Afghanistan,[3] the following provides a context to the

---

[1] Dean H. Wilson and David C. Gillman, "The Integration of Women into a Male Initiation Right: A Case Study of the USAF Academy," quoted in Mitchell, *Women in the Military* , 44.

[2] Joshua S. Goldstein, *War and Gender: How Gender Shapes the War System and Vice Versa* (Cambridge University Press, 2001).

[3] Policy debates and changes associated with the combat exclusion during the wars in Iraq and Afghanistan are discussed in detail in Chapter 2.

evolution of the combat exclusion. It maps the various iterations of policies associated with the combat exclusion in order to demonstrate that there has never been a singular, clear, and enforceable combat exclusion policy. In addition to an overview of the political history of the combat exclusion, there is a discussion of various related court cases. The legal arguments reinforce the argument that the combat exclusion, although not an enforceable policy, was a powerful idea with significant political, bureaucratic, and legal influence. Finally, an analysis of the various interpretations of the combat exclusion within the forces, as well as an overview of the disparate definitions of combat within the services, support the overall argument that both combat and the combat exclusion have always been constructions defined in relation to a broader myth of the all-male combat unit, not a concrete policy designed to keep women from the front lines of war.

THE MILITARY EXCLUDES WOMEN TO PROTECT MEN

World War II and the return to normal

This section maps the major policies associated with the combat exclusion. One of the first formal policies limiting women from combat came at the end of World War II. During that war, approximately 330,000 women served in the American military.[4] In this period, women were required to fill largely administrative roles with the aim of leaving more men available for combat positions. Several auxiliary units (and interesting acronyms) were created for women. The Army housed the Women's Army Corps (WACs), while female units in the Navy were called WAVES (Women Accepted for Voluntary Emergency Services). Within the air force, women served as civilian aviators in the Women Airforce Service Pilots organization (WASP),

---

[4] Military Leadership Diversity Commission, Women in Combat: Legislation and Policy, Perceptions, and the Current Operational Environment (Arlington, VA: Military Leadership Diversity Commission, November 2010), https://www.hsdl.org/?view&did=716213.

and within the Marines, female units were called SPARS (inspired by the Coast Guard motto *Semper Pariatus*, or Always Ready).

At the end of the war, the military was faced with the dilemma of how to address this new cohort of women. As men returned home, women within the forces as well as those who had joined the labor force were encouraged to "return to normal" following the war. In other words, they were asked to return to more traditional domestic roles in society. Nearly 50 percent of the women who joined the labor force during the war left these roles by 1950.[5] The "Women's Armed Services Integration Act" was passed in 1948 in order to formalize the positions of remaining women within the military. This established a regular corps of women in all of the services.[6] The act also limited women to 2 percent of the total services and specified that only one female officer was permitted per ten enlisted women.[7] Finally, the act explicitly prohibited women from combat duties.[8]

The Women's Armed Services Integration Act was not a policy response to any particular problems associated with women's service. The rationale behind the act was that the war was over, and women's formal labor and military contributions were no longer necessary. The two main restrictions it placed on women, including establishing an overall limit on the percentage of women and prohibiting them from combat roles, were part of an overall national effort to "return to normal" following the war. This was also part of a broader effort to reestablish traditional gender roles: returning men were encouraged to get married; the nuclear family was heralded as an

---

[5] Claudia Goldin, "The Role of World War II in the Rise of Women's Work," National Bureau of Economic Research, no. 3203 (December 1989), http://www.nber.org/papers/w3203.pdf?new_window=1.

[6] Lucinda J. Peach, "Women at War: The Ethics of Women in Combat," *Hamline Journal of Public Law and Policy* 15 (1994): 199.

[7] John Cushman, "History of Women in Combat Still Being Written Slowly," *New York Times*, February 9, 2012, http://www.nytimes.com/2012/02/10/us/history-of-women-in-combat-still-being-written-slowly.html?ref=us.

[8] For an excellent overview of the history of women in the US military, see Judith Stiehm, *Arms and the Enlisted Woman* (Temple University Press, 1989), and Jean Bethke Elshtain and Sheila Tobias, editors, *Women, Militarism, and War* (Rowman & Littlefield, 1990).

essential element of the American dream; and women were encouraged to manage the home and raise children. Women were expected, and encouraged, to return to their roles as wives and mothers in order to facilitate economic growth and reestablish the social order. These policies reinforced the perception that women's newfound roles, both within the military and in the domestic labor force, were temporary and exceptional byproducts of the war. The fantasy of the all-male combat unit was also reinforced through these policies; they formalized the ideal that men were the "real" soldiers during the war and would continue to be the primary and rightful protectors of the nation.

Vietnam

The next major policy shift related to women and combat came as a result of the Vietnam War. Seven thousand women served in the US Army during the Vietnam conflict. Most women served as nurses[9] or within the WACs, completing tasks that focused on communications, supply, and administration.[10] Although women were not permitted to serve in infantry units, many faced front line conditions equal to those of male troops. For example, hospitals were prime targets during wartime, "which meant that all personnel working or being treated in them were in combat."[11] During the Vietnam War, there were eight female casualties, one of which was determined to be the result of combat.[12]

The 1948 Women's Armed Services Integration Act was repealed in 1967 in response to the need to expand the forces to support the war in Vietnam. This eliminated restrictions specifying that

[9] Heather Marie Stur, *Beyond Combat: Women and Gender in the Vietnam War Era* (New York: Cambridge University Press, 2011), 107.

[10] Col. Bettie J. Morden, "The Women's Army Corps during the Vietnam War" (Vietnam Women's Memorial), 1, accessed January 22, 2014, http://www.vietnamwomensmemorial.org/pdf/bmorden.pdf.

[11] Stur, *Beyond Combat*, 107.

[12] National Center for Veterans Analysis and Statistics, "America's Women Veterans: Military Service History and VA Benefit Utilization Statistics" (November 23, 2011), 1, http://www.va.gov/vetdata/docs/specialreports/final_womens_report_3_2_12_v_7.pdf.

women could make up only 2 percent of the enlisted force and 10 percent of officers, and removed the combat restriction outlined in this
act. However, women continued to be formally banned from combat
roles throughout the war.[13] In addition to the repeal of the Armed
Services Integration Act, several other changes encouraged women to
join the US forces during this period[14]:

- In 1969 the Air Force Reserve Officers Training Corps (AFROTC) were
  opened to women[15]; in 1972 the Reserve Officer Training Corps were
  opened to women[16]; and, in 1975 the three service academies also
  began accepting female applicants.[17]
- Conscription ended in 1973, and the All Volunteer Force (AVF) was
  established.[18]
- The Army launched a recruitment campaign targeted specifically at
  women following the end of conscription.
- A 1974 decision changed the age requirement for women enlisting to
  match that of male enlistees.
- In 1977, Congress moved to clarify the definition of "combat" and
  requested the DOD to submit recommendations indicating ways that
  roles for women might be expanded in the armed services.[19]
- In order to boost troop numbers, the Women's Army Corps was
  dissolved and integrated into the Army in 1978.[20]

Partially because of these changes, there was a significant increase of
women serving on active duty. The numbers of women grew from less

---

[13] David F. Burrelli, "Women in Combat: Issues for Congress," May 9, 2013, 1, http://
www.fas.org/sgp/crs/natsec/R42075.pdf.

[14] For an extensive list of policies and "firsts" for women in the US military, please
see Women in Military Service for America Memorial Foundation, "Highlights in
the History of Military Women" (Women in Military Service for America Memorial
Foundation, n.d.), http://www.womensmemorial.org/Education/timeline.html.

[15] Ibid.   [16] Ibid.   [17] Burrelli, "Women in Combat: Issues for Congress," 2.

[18] Military Leadership Diversity Commission, *Women in Combat: Legislation and
Policy, Perceptions, and the Current Operational Environment.*

[19] Ibid.

[20] Stur, *Beyond Combat: Women and Gender in the Vietnam War Era*, 218.

than 1 percent of the active duty force in 1972,[21] to nearly 8 percent in 1980.[22]

In addition to specific policy changes in this period, there were broader social and cultural changes that encouraged women to join the US military. Deindustrialization and the introduction of the Equal Rights Amendment resulted in a marked increase in women in the labor force between 1976 and 1986.[23] Though the growing feminist movements were often anti-war and anti-military, they critiqued traditional gender roles, providing support and encouragement for those women who chose a career in the military.

Post-Vietnam

Following the establishment of the AVF in 1973, it became clear that despite the increasing number of women joining the forces, all would remain prohibited from combat. It was during this period that the term "combat exclusion" readily came into use in reference to this restriction. In 1988, with approximately half of all positions within the US forces open to women, the DOD decided to formalize a combat exclusion. It established what came to be known as the "Risk Rule."[24] This policy permitted the exclusion of women from any role, combat or non-combat, "if the risks of exposure to direct combat, hostile fire or capture were equal to, or greater than, the risk in the units they supported."[25] These confusing and "rather subjective criteria"[26] required an assessment of both perceived risk and comparative risk of any particular role. The rule specified that "risks of exposure to direct combat, hostile fire, or capture are proper criteria for closing non-combat positions or units to women, providing that the type,

---

[21] Ibid., 2.

[22] National Center for Veterans Analysis and Statistics, "National Center for Veterans Analysis and Statistics: Selected Research Highlights" (December 2010), 3, www.va.gov/vetdata/docs/quickfacts/reports-slideshow.pdf.

[23] Howard N. Fullerton Jr, "Labor Force 2006: Slowing Down and Changing Composition," *Monthly Labor Review* 120 (1997): 31.

[24] Burrelli, "Women in Combat: Issues for Congress," 2.   [25] Ibid., 2.

[26] Ibid., 3.

degree, and duration of such risks are equal to or greater than that experienced by combat units in the same theater of operations."[27] In many ways, this rule broadened the restrictions for women, leaving their exclusion open to an interpretation of risks associated with particular roles.[28]

The Risk Rule reinforces the position that the combat exclusion is a trope rather than a formal policy. The Risk Rule was meant to establish a formal combat exclusion law; however, it did not specify particular positions that were closed to women, instead requiring that positions be restricted based on perception, interpretation, and comparison of an incredibly subjective concept: risk. In turn, the rule muddied the waters when it came to the combat exclusion, leaving room for different interpretations of what constituted risk, and which positions might place women at risk. Amid this confusion, the rule provided one obvious point of clarification: it served to perpetuate the perception that it was men, not women, who were fulfilling the "riskiest" roles in war. Furthermore, it generated a general perception that women were not on the front lines of war, and that men were the primary protectors of the nation. In sum, the Risk Rule complicated the formal restriction of women from combat roles, but clarified the misperception that women were excluded and protected from combat.

Similar to the Armed Forces Integration Act, the Risk Rule was not a specific policy created in response to a particular problem. The rule was not created in response to indicators that women were not able to fill combat roles, examples of women failing to complete their jobs, proof that women were distracting men from accomplishing military missions, or research showing that women required protection from combat. Instead, the policy was designed to formalize the *idea* of the combat exclusion established by the AVFs.

---

[27] Military Leadership Diversity Commission, *Women in Combat: Legislation and Policy, Perceptions, and the Current Operational Environment*, 2.

[28] Cushman, "History of Women in Combat Still Being Written Slowly."

Into the 1990s with the Persian Gulf War

An unprecedented 41,000 US female troops participated in the Gulf War, suffering fifteen female casualties.[29] Although it is not possible here to recount the history of the war, or all of the respective contributions of women, it is important to note that the conflict is seen as "a watershed for women in the US military."[30] Images of women leaving for war, stories of their contributions, and statistics regarding injuries of women in combat inspired renewed dialogue and debate about their place in the military. During this period, several important policies were changed in relation to women in combat. The National Defense Authorization Act of 1992 and 1993 lifted the limits on the assignment of women to combat aircraft in the Air Force, the Navy, and the Marine Corps.

This act also established the Presidential Commission on the Assignment of Women in the Armed Forces, which was tasked with reviewing the role of women in the military, with attention to women in combat.[31] At this time, Congress also acknowledged that all service members, including women, were "at risk" during war. In turn, there was renewed debate about the relevance of the Risk Rule. The results of the commission included somewhat confusing recommendations, including a call for the maintenance of the combat exclusion, combined with a declaration that "no person who is best qualified should be denied access on the basis of gender to an assignment that is open to both men and women."[32] In other words, it endorsed the existing Risk Rule and recommended that women be allowed to serve in positions for which they were qualified – provided that this did not include combat roles.[33]

One of the reasons offered by the commission for keeping the combat exclusion was that female soldiers were more likely to be

---

[29] National Center for Veterans Analysis and Statistics, "America's Women Veterans: Military Service History and VA Benefit Utilization Statistics," 1.

[30] Lella Jacinto, "The Cost of Women in Combat," ABC News (2014), http://abcnews.go.com/International/story?id=79646&page=1&singlePage=true.

[31] Ibid. [32] Burrelli, "Women in Combat: Issues for Congress," 3–4. [33] Ibid.

captured and raped in war, and that this might negatively impact public morale: "Female Prisoners of War, no matter what the treatment they received, would have a far more demoralizing effect on the American public than similar treatment of male prisoners."[34] It is difficult to substantiate this two-part claim regarding first, women's vulnerability, and second, the public's reaction to women's capture or rape. Two women were held as prisoners of war during the Persian Gulf War, and the only reported cases of rape or sexual assault against female soldiers were committed by fellow US soldiers.[35]

In terms of public opinion, a poll was conducted at the request of the commission to determine public support for the combat exclusion. The poll found that 47 percent of respondents opposed the exclusion, with 44 percent supporting it.[36] The results were heralded as evidence that "Americans favor offering women the right to volunteer, or to choose."[37] Despite indications that the public was largely in favor of women's increased roles in the US military, Retired Army General Henderson argued that the results were shaped by military victory euphoria unrepresentative of "true" shifts in opinion, saying, "If you get a different international involvement that doesn't turn out as happily (as the Persian Gulf War), public opinion will turn rapidly."[38]

While the Persian Gulf War prompted new public dialogues and perceptions of the contributions of women during war, the

---

[34] Cynthia Nantais and Martha F. Lee, "Women in the United States Military: Protectors or Protected? The Case of Prisoner of War Melissa Rathbun-Nealy," *Journal of Gender Studies* 8, no. 2 (1999): 188.

[35] Kang et al. found that internal sexual harassment rates for men and women went up during this military operation. Reported rates of sexual harassment in 1995 were 46 percent for women and 8 percent for men; in 2002 these numbers were 24 percent and 3 percent, respectively. Han Kang et al., "The Role of Sexual Assault on the Risk of PTSD among Gulf War Veterans," *Annals of Epidemiology* 15, no. 3 (March 2005): 191–95.

[36] Melissa Healy, "Poll Finds Split over Women's Combat Role: Military: 47% Oppose Ban, While 44% Back It. Public Sentiment Will Be a Key in Determining Future Duties," *Los Angeles Times* (September 12, 1992), http://articles.latimes.com/1992-09-12/news/mn-276_1_public-sentiment.

[37] Ibid. [38] Ibid.

DOD clung to the combat exclusion. Mirroring previous formal reports and policies, the commission relied on ideas and perceptions to justify the combat exclusion. In this case, the commission focused on fear of the hypothetical threats that female prisoners of war (POWs) might face, and concern over potential public reaction to female POWs. Note the emphasis on emotion, such as fear, and the reliance on possible threats and reactions, instead of available evidence related to both possibilities. The commission ultimately reaffirmed the Risk Rule despite a complete lack of evidence suggesting that the public was indeed apprehensive about female POWs, and in the face of contradictory evidence indicating that the public was in fact generally supportive of enhancing the role of women in war. The result was that the combat exclusion policy remained founded on, and supported by, subjective beliefs and judgments.

Combat Definition and Assignment Rule

Largely as a result of the continued confusion and varied interpretations of the Risk Rule, in 1994, then Secretary of Defense Les Aspin established new criteria for both the definition of combat, and women's exclusion from combat. This came in the form of a memorandum entitled "Direct Ground Combat Definition and Assignment Rule."[39] The memorandum was designed to provide clarity in relation to Direct Ground Combat (DGC) units. The declared purpose of the change was to expand opportunities for women, and assurances were made that no roles previously opened to women would be closed as a result of the rule. The memorandum made two specific recommendations concerning the existing combat exclusion. First, the memorandum declared that all service members should be eligible for positions for which they qualify, but it stated that women should be excluded from roles within units below the brigade level

---

[39] United States General Accounting Office, *GENDER ISSUES: Information on DOD's Assignment Policy and Direct Ground Combat Definition* (Washington, DC, October 1998).

whose primary mission is direct ground combat. Second, individual services were permitted "to impose further restrictions on the assignment of women where the Service Secretary attests that the costs of appropriate berthing and privacy arrangements are prohibitive; where units and positions are doctrinally required to physically colocate and remain with direct ground combat units that are closed to women; where units are engaged in long range reconnaissance operations and Special Operations Forces missions; and where job related physical requirements would necessarily exclude the vast majority of women Service members."[40] In turn, the individual services were able to propose additional limits on women's participation in the name of cost, proximity to combat and Special Forces, and physical requirements.

This simple, two-page memorandum became the foundation for the combat exclusion for nearly twenty years. A number of reasons were given for the changes it offered and for sustaining the combat exclusion more broadly.

Specifically, the DOD provided the following list of six reasons for sustaining the combat exclusion:

1. A lack of congressional support for women in combat.
2. A lack of public support for women in combat.
3. Women's lack of support for the involuntary assignment of women to direct ground combat units.
4. Potential problems related to physical strength and living conditions.
5. Women would not contribute to the readiness and effectiveness of combat.
6. The lack of need for women in combat due to a sufficient number of men.[41]

The following section unpacks this list of reasons for sustaining the combat exclusion, which supports the overall objective of this chapter to demonstrate that the combat exclusion is not a concrete policy, but a trope that is largely motivated by, and focused on, emotions,

[40] Ibid.   [41] Ibid.

images, and myths of the band of brothers. Interestingly, the first three reasons listed here all emphasize how people "feel" about the combat exclusion. The DOD is acknowledging that it has created and reaffirmed a policy based on public, congressional, and women's apparent preferences.

To further support the rationale behind the memo, the DOD referenced a 1992 poll Roper Poll,[42] which was conducted in association with the Presidential Commission on the Assignment on Women. Evidence from this poll indicated that approximately 57 percent of US service members supported the current policy restricting women from combat. A 1997 RAND Corporation study,[43] conducted at the request of DOD, also found that there was a lack of support among women service members when it came to the involuntary assignment of women to combat roles. However, it should be noted that this same study also found that the majority of women service members supported opening up combat roles to women; they just did not support the involuntary assignment of women to combat.

The Roper Poll also found that the public was largely split in terms of opinions related to women in combat. Specifically, almost exactly 50 percent of the 1500 adults who were asked said they supported the current policy restricting women from combat assignment. In sum, at this time, a slight majority of US service members opposed women in combat, most women supported opening combat positions to women, and the public was split in terms of its support for women in combat. In turn, the claim that there was no public support for women entering combat is not entirely truthful. In fact, there was hardly a widespread call for women to be included or excluded from combat from within the forces, from female service members in particular, or from the general public.

The fourth reason for sustaining the combat exclusion also centers on emotion, namely fear. General references to physical standards

---

[42] Healy, "Poll Finds Split over Women's Combat Role."

[43] Margaret C. Harrell and Laura L. Miller, "New Opportunities for Military Women," Product Page (1997), http://www.rand.org/pubs/monograph_reports/MR896.html.

and living conditions demonstrated a fear of the possible effects of allowing women to serve in combat roles. There are no references to specific physical requirements associated with combat that women had consistently failed to meet. Nor was there any guidance given as to how potential changes to living conditions would necessarily be a negative for the military. Arguments related to women, physical standards, and living conditions in combat are detailed in subsequent chapters.

Finally, the last two arguments for excluding women from combat fall into what I call the "we do not need them" category. This position emphasizes that women are not needed because, first, they will not increase the effectiveness of combat units, and second, there are enough men. There is no argument to be made that women will decrease military effectiveness, nor is there an explanation for why a surplus of male candidates is an appropriate reason to exclude female candidates, for combat or any other roles. In turn, these are not in fact reasons for excluding women, but a justification of the status quo.

The 1994 memorandum was meant to clarify the guidelines surrounding the combat exclusion, replacing the vague Risk Rule with a seemingly more specific and concrete set of guidelines. However, the direct combat memorandum further complicated the combat exclusion, not least because each of the services were required to specify how they would implement the assignment policy. As a result, from 1994, each of the services developed their own assignment policies for women. This meant that for decades, the combat exclusion was applied and interpreted in disparate and inconsistent ways across the Army, Navy, and Air Force. Allowing each of the services to determine their own implementation plan and set out exceptions for the combat exclusion guidelines meant that there was ample room for interpretation.

(Re)defining combat

Another source of confusion associated with the 1994 memo stemmed from the definition of combat. Although combat, and combat roles, seem like they should be easily and clearly defined, the definition of combat has varied over time and across the services within the US military. The memorandum offered its own definition of combat, but failed to acknowledge or address the fact that each of the individual services already had their own, different definitions of combat. The memorandum defined combat as "engaging an enemy on the ground with individual or crew served weapons, while being exposed to hostile fire and to a high probability of direct physical contact with the hostile forces personnel. Direct ground combat takes place well forward on the battlefield while locating and closing with the enemy to defeat them by fire, maneuver, or shock effect." It is important to note the emphasis on "ground combat" and direct, "man to man" contact with enemy forces.

The definition offered in the memorandum contradicted the one used by the Army at that time. The Army defined direct combat as "[e]ngaging an enemy within individual or crew served weapons, while being exposed to direct enemy fire, a high probability of direct physical contact with the enemy/s personnel, and a substantial risk of capture. Direct combat takes place while closing with the enemy by fire, maneuver, and shock effect in order to destroy or capture the enemy, or while repelling the enemy's assault by fire, close combat, or counterattack."[44]

The Military Leadership and Diversity Commission (MLDC) noted the significance of these disparate definitions, particularly in the fact that the Army added the requirement for "substantial risk of capture" and "repelling the enemy's assault." The DOD emphasizes the exclusion of women from units whose "primary mission" is direct ground combat, whereas the Army prohibits women from units whose "routine mission" involves direct combat. MLDC has indicated that the slight difference in semantics mattered in terms of operations on the ground in Iraq and Afghanistan where there were "military units

---

[44] Quoted in Scott Mills, *Women in the Army – Review of the Combat Exclusion Policy* (U.S. Army War College, March 24, 2011), 5.

that have routinely participated in combat, although combat was not their primary mission."[45] MLDC also outlined that the references to "enemy," "hostile fire," "forward," and "well forward" used in both definitions were outdated and did not capture the modern nature of warfare in Iraq and Afghanistan: "[t]he enemy is no longer clearly and consistently identifiable, and all units are essentially exposed to hostile fire. Additionally, the spatial concepts of forward and well-forward are inappropriate and lacking to convey the complexity of operations such as those in Iraq and Afghanistan."[46]

The purpose of comparing these two definitions of combat is not to debate what "real" combat is. Instead, these two definitions demonstrate that although combat is something that is constantly discussed within the military and by the general public, there is in fact no singular or static definition of "combat." Even within the US military there are disagreements and disparate definitions of combat. This is important for a discussion of the combat exclusion policy. If the very understanding of combat is fluid and changing, any policy designed to prevent women from participating in combat will be as illusory as the definition itself.

Cynthia Enloe[47] has encouraged a feminist reflection on the definition of combat. Although definitions of combat may vary, she argues that all definitions of combat focus on limited types of violence, ignoring the multiple forms of violence that women, men, and children "combat," or face, during war. This includes domestic violence, sexual violence perpetrated by fellow soldiers, and drone or cluster bomb attacks. It is worth noting her reflections at length:

> Combat, in other words, is an activity narrowly reserved for only those occasions when there is a two-sided militarized violence, in which both sides are ready for the violence and equipped with

---

[45] Military Leadership Diversity Commission, *Women in Combat: Legislation and Policy, Perceptions, and the Current Operational Environment*, 2.

[46] Ibid., 3.

[47] Cynthia Enloe, "Combat and 'Combat': A Feminist Reflection," *Critical Studies on Security* 1, no. 2 (2013): 260–63.

weapons. That is, "combat" is reserved for those occasions when each actor is fully aware that he/she is an armed adversary, each anticipates the violence to come, and each is armed to respond to that violence. "Combat" is commonly imagined to be a place where men can prove their manhood. However, given these conventional – and official – criteria for violence to be recognized as "combat," one might argue that "combat" is for sissies.

Here, Enloe encourages us to recognize the variations in the way combat is defined. Further, she asks us to reflect on the paradox between the understanding of combat as the most risky, violent, and dangerous role, and the reality of the multiple types of violent activities associated with war, which, because of their unexpected, unauthorized, and unprotected nature, require extreme perseverance, bravery, and endurance.

In addition to the narrow emphasis of "combat" definitions and their variation across service branches, these definitions have been criticized for being out of touch with the reality of modern warfare. Depicting combat as something that takes place "well forward" on the battlefield with soldiers having to "engage" or "close in" on the enemy to "defeat them by fire, maneuver, or shock" provide almost no guidance as to which particular military roles "count" as combat. Instead, what these definitions of combat provide is an image and a story of combat. It reaffirms the fantasy of combat as a "man to man" clash and gun battle conducted across defined battle lines. In doing so, it ignores countless depictions of modern war and counterinsurgency war as an activity that has no battle lines, is conducted by various groups both uniformed and ununiformed, and is waged using multiple forms of technology, including drones, air attacks, improvised explosive devices (IEDs), and suicide bombers.

The US military has long acknowledged the changing nature of warfare and the extinction of "front" and "rear" battle lines. The 1998 US General Accounting Office Report on Gender Issues was critical of the definition of combat offered within the 1994 memorandum.

It noted that battlefields are not necessarily linear and gave examples of recent military operations, including in Somalia and Bosnia, which "involved nonlinear situations that lacked well-defined forward areas."[48] According to the report, "on a nonlinear battlefield, close operations can take place throughout the entire area of military operations, rather than just at the forward areas."[49] In sum, the definition of combat offered by the DOD was conflicted and outdated in 1994. By the time the combat exclusion was lifted in 2013, the definition was relevant only in its ability to sustain a particular myth of "combat" as a battle of brothers.

From trope to legal precedent

There are several court cases that have both been impacted by and come to shape the combat exclusion, though perhaps none as significant as *Rostker v. Goldberg*, 1981.[50] The case was brought forward following President Carter's decision to reinforce the draft in 1980, through the enactment of the Military Selective Service Act. Congress reacted strongly against calls to extend the draft to women and called for the Military Selective Service Act law to apply only to men. *Rostker v. Goldberg* involved several men who challenged the constitutionality of this law.

The case was initially filed in the district court. This court ruled that "the Act's gender-based discrimination violated the Due Process Clause of the Fifth Amendment."[51] However, this decision was overturned when the case reached the Supreme Court, which ruled 6–3 in favor of women's exclusion from the draft. The Court

---

[48] United States General Accounting Office, *GENDER ISSUES: Information on DOD's Assignment Policy and Direct Ground Combat Definition.*

[49] Ibid.

[50] For an excellent overview of gender jurisprudence in relation to the American military's combat exclusion policy, see Angela Rollins, "Act Like a Lady!: Reconsidering Gender Stereotypes and the Exclusion of Women from Combat in Light of Challenges to 'Don't Ask Don't Tell,'" *Southern Illinois University Law Journal* Winter (2012).

[51] *Rostker v. Goldberg,* 435 U.S. 57 (U.S. Supreme Court 1981).

found that "[t]he District Court, undertaking an independent evaluation of the evidence, exceeded its authority in ignoring Congress' conclusions that whatever the need for women for noncombat roles during mobilization, it could be met by volunteers, and that staffing noncombat positions with women during a mobilization would be positively detrimental to the important goal of military flexibility."[52]

The understanding that women were not available for combat roles was the primary motivation behind the Court's decision. It was determined that "since the purpose of registration is to develop a pool of potential combat troops,"[53] women could be excluded from the draft "simply because they were ineligible for combat positions."[54] In their decision, the judges of the Supreme Court quoted from the Senate Armed Services Committee: "The principle that women should not intentionally and routinely engage in combat is fundamental, and enjoys wide support among our people. It is universally supported by military leaders who have testified before the Committee... Current law and policy excluded women from being assigned to combat in our military forces, and the Committee reaffirms this policy."[55]

The Supreme Court ruling was important for several reasons. First, it established that a male-only draft was constitutional and not in violation of the Equal Protection Clause of the Fifth Amendment. In many ways, the concerns raised regarding women's equal rights and protections were sidelined. The message was that women and men were not equal within the military as a result of the combat exclusion. At the time, the American Civil Liberties Union (ACLU) described the decision as "damag[ing] the cause of women's rights."[56] Second, the Court took the position that the primary purpose of the draft is to recruit combat soldiers. This is interesting because military operations require a vast array of soldiers, and generally in war, less than

---

[52] Ibid.   [53] Decision p. 79, quoted in Rollins, "Act Like a Lady!"   [54] Ibid.

[55] Decision, p. 77, quoted in ibid.

[56] Linda Greenhouse, "Justices, 6–3, Rule Draft Registration May Exclude Women," *New York Times* (June 26, 1981), sec. U.S., http://www.nytimes.com/1981/06/26/us/justices-6-3-rule-draft-registration-may-exclude-women.html.

10 percent of troops are involved in combat operations. As a result, this ruling reinforced "combat" roles and activities as privileged and protected. Finally, and perhaps most significantly, the decision served to reinforce the combat exclusion and establish substantial legal precedent for what was, as I argued earlier in this chapter, largely a fluid, unenforceable idea. As a result, the case justified gender discrimination, venerated combat as essential to military identity, and elevated the combat exclusion from a fluid idea and policy to the cornerstone of an important legal precedent.

Rostker v. Goldberg continues to be significant thirty-three years later. It is referred to within current discussions of the constitutionality of the draft and debates over whether women should now be included in the draft. To fully comprehend the impact of the case, it is worth tracing some of the cases in which *Rostker v. Goldberg* was referred to as a precedent.

One such example was a 1988 case against the Army. In the case, which was promptly dismissed, Vivian Lewis sued the military when her application to the Army was rejected because she held a GED[57] and no other qualification. The lawsuit challenged the constitutionality of the Army's policy of accepting men with only GED qualifications, but not women.

The combat exclusion was central to the Court's decision to dismiss the case, because the "wide disparity in number of male and female recruits needed, caused by female combat exclusion policy, enabled Army to set higher enlistment standards for women and obtain requisite number of recruits was reasonably relevant and necessary to national defense and violated neither due process nor equal protection either on its face or as applied."[58] This decision is significant because it demonstrates that the combat exclusion formed the basis for future decisions that allowed for preferential treatment of

---

[57] GED stands for General Educational Development and is a standardized set of tests that individuals must pass in order to certify that they have high-school level academic skills.

[58] *Rostker v. Goldberg*, 435 U.S. 57 (U.S. Supreme Court 1981).

men over women. Rollins summarizes, "The court found it reasonable for the Army to set higher standards for women, because it needs fewer women than men due to the combat exclusion of women."[59] Again, the combat exclusion was used as justification for the unequal treatment of women, even with regard to something quite separate from combat operations, namely, educational requirements.

The constitutionality of the Military Selective Service Act, and the provision that only men were required to register for the draft, was challenged again in the 2003 court case *Schwartz v. Brodsky*. The plaintiffs of the case were four male college students and one female high school senior from Massachusetts, all between the ages of 17 and 20. The defendants were the Director of the US Selected Service System during the George W. Bush Administration, and the Attorney General of Massachusetts.[60]

Similar to earlier cases, the four plaintiffs argued that the Selective Service Act was unconstitutional because it violated the Equal Protection Clause of the Fifth Amendment. The plaintiffs pointed out a major contradiction to the law. Men who were not eligible to enlist in the military, because of a disability, for example, were still required to register for the draft, while "[c]onversely, all women, no matter their fitness or ability to serve in the armed forces, are excluded from registration."[61]

The complaint noted that as of 2003, 91 percent of positions within the military were open to women and that the military was an active employer of women. The case further argued that unlike women, men faced fines and might be ineligible for certain jobs, benefits, and scholarships if they chose not to register for the draft.[62] The case was lodged and then dismissed in the District Court of Massachusetts. The decision to dismiss was based on the combat exclusion. The court ruled:

---

[59] Rollins, "Act Like a Lady!," 4.
[60] *Rostker v. Goldberg*, 435 U.S. 57 (U.S. Supreme Court 1981).
[61] Ibid.   [62] Ibid.

Military Selective Service Act (MSSA) did not violate men's equal protection rights under Due Process Clause by requiring only men to register with Selective Service System, even if women were permitted to serve in virtually all military units; purpose of MSSA was to facilitate draft of combat troops, and women remained ineligible to serve in units whose primary mission was direct ground combat.[63]

The court cited *Rostker v. Goldberg* in its ruling. Here again, the combat exclusion was used to justify unequal treatment with reference to registering for military service. Furthermore, the precedent of not requiring women to register was cited as justification for their continued exclusion from registering.

A case similar to *Schwartz v. Brodsky* was brought by a group of plaintiffs in 2009. *Elgin et al. v. United States* saw several plaintiffs argue that the Selective Service Act was unconstitutional because it prevented men from gaining federal agency employment if they were not registered for the draft. Again, the plaintiffs cited the Equal Protection Clause as the foundation for their case. The plaintiffs also argued that rationale behind the *Rostker v. Goldberg* decision was outdated, given the evolving roles of women in the US forces. They noted the increased presence of women in the forces and argued that women should not be excluded from the draft.

Similar to earlier cases, the judge's decision to dismiss the case and reaffirm the constitutionality of the male-only draft rested on the combat exclusion for women. The judge declared that "[a]lthough women are now permitted to serve in certain positions related to combat settings, the scope of their combat participation does not yet approach that level permitted for male military personnel."[64] Despite twenty years of evidence of the changing nature of women's contribution to the military and evidence of women's participation in combat

[63] Ibid.   [64] Ibid.

activity, the survival of the combat exclusion provided justification for upholding the Selective Services Act. Thus, in many ways *Rostker v. Goldberg* not only validated the combat exclusion, it extended the influence of the policy and idea. The unequal treatment of women, in terms of educational requirements and requirements to register, were justified on the basis of the combat exclusion.

This overview of selected court cases demonstrates how the idea of the combat exclusion came to represent "real" restrictions for women, in terms of the types of jobs they could attain and opportunities for promotion, as well as educational levels and requirements to register. The combat exclusion and the exclusion of women from the draft were used to justify each other. This "exclusion loop" served to reaffirm the ideal of the combat band of brothers, and men as the primary protectors of the nation.

CONCLUSION

This chapter detailed the history of the female combat exclusion *as an idea*. It highlights policy changes and reactions from the end of World War II to the beginning of the wars in Afghanistan and Iraq. I show how the tenuous and befuddling sets of policies associated with the combat exclusion were primarily the product of political image concern, emotional reactions to the idea of women in combat, and efforts to sustain the icon of the all-male combat unit. Included in the analysis is a call for a critical reflection on the fragile definitions of combat. Finally, the chapter illustrated that, through various court cases, the idea of the combat exclusion was married to the fantasy of the all-male draft in order to reconfirm and reinvent the all-male combat unit despite growing evidence of women's involvement and contribution to war.

The combat exclusion is often understood as a concrete policy, designed as a result of differences between men and women. It is seen as a policy created to protect both male and female troops, and the American public, by promoting and ensuring troop effectiveness. The purpose of this chapter was to contrast the fluid and changing nature of the combat exclusion policy to this ideal of a fixed and essential military policy. From efforts to restrict the roles of women after World War II, to vague definitions of risk, to outdated definitions of combat, the combat exclusion has always been understood in relation to broader military fantasies and ideals, including the "return to normal" post World War II, the ideal of combat as the "riskiest" and most dangerous military role, belief that support for the war depends on the exclusion of women from combat, and, the perception of men as the primary protectors and "ideal" soldiers within the US military.

2   The disintegration of the combat exclusion in Iraq and Afghanistan

As Chapter 1 illustrated, the combat exclusion has always been a fluid idea evolving over time. It is argued in this chapter that the wars in Iraq and Afghanistan extinguished any remaining practical applicability of the combat exclusion, rendering it a catchphrase rather than an enforceable policy. This chapter examines the modern history of the combat exclusion policy. In doing so, it continues to contrast the "reality" of women's contributions to war to the "fantasy" of the all-male combat unit. This chapter also outlines the context for subsequent chapters, which consider the rationale behind the decision to remove the combat exclusion and the depiction of this decision as a watershed moment. The chapter points to the efforts to sustain the combat exclusion during the Iraq and Afghanistan wars, despite evidence indicating it was unenforceable, unnecessary, and potentially detrimental to the security of soldiers. Evidence of women contributing to combat operations was routinely met with political efforts to reinforce the perception that women were not in combat. This chapter illustrates that during the wars in Iraq and Afghanistan – which saw the disintegration of front lines and the removal of most of the mechanisms available to keep women from the so-called front line – the efforts to sustain the myth of the all-male combat unit became increasingly desperate and, at times, absurd.

Three central arguments drive the chapter. First, the nature of military operations, and the assignment and contribution of women in both wars, made the combat exclusion unenforceable. The realities of insurgency warfare in Iraq and Afghanistan have rendered

This chapter draws on Megan H. Mackenzie, "The Pentagon Still Needs a Facelift," *American Review* (May 2013).

divisions between front lines and rear units irrelevant. Women were consistently part of hostile military operations; bureaucratic division between combat and support units did not shield women from the reality of military operations. Moreover, the US military has made several policy and structural changes that have served to remove the final thread holding the combat exclusion in place. In turn, the changing nature of conflict in Iraq and Afghanistan has seen the death of the combat exclusion.

Second, although the practical obstacles to women participating in combat have disintegrated, the myth and idea of the combat exclusion persist and are being constantly revived. While women were being assigned to, and were serving in, hostile operations, politicians, the DOD, and the media made intense efforts to reframe women's contributions as exceptional. Consequently, the combat exclusion remained a bureaucratic obstacle for women seeking to apply for promotion based on their combat experience, or for roles that required acknowledging their combat experience. Therefore, the idea that women were not on the front lines has survived, both on paper and within public rhetoric.

The third central argument is that the January 2013 announcement should be analyzed through the lens of the band of brothers myth. Ideals associated with the band of brothers became increasingly untenable, as US soldiers were increasingly associated with human rights abuses, sexual violence, and various scandals. Reversing the combat exclusion policy at the end of these wars might be viewed as part of an effort to redefine the military in the face of these crises. This chapter asks if the removal of the combat exclusion was used as a means of both reshaping and recovering the band of brothers myth.

To support these arguments, this chapter draws on operational evidence from the wars in Iraq and Afghanistan, various policy changes related to the combat exclusion, court cases centered on women in combat, and media portrayals of women in both wars. The first section begins with an outline of several policy changes during the Iraq and Afghanistan wars, which whittled away the foundation of the combat exclusion. The next section reviews the nature of modern warfare and the contribution of women in Iraq and Afghanistan. This is used to demonstrate that the combat exclusion was not only outdated and unenforceable, but also detrimental to national security. Through a discussion of the military's all-female Lioness and Female Engagement Teams (FETs), the third section highlights the hypocrisy of the military assigning women to combat operations while, at the same time, claiming to be enforcing a combat exclusion. The final section includes a brief review of two major lawsuits filed against the military during this period. It reiterates that while the combat exclusion threatened women's security and job opportunities, it did not prevent them from risking their lives and contributing to both wars.

OPERATIONAL REALITIES

No battle lines, no front lines

War tends to be idealized as man-to-man combat, with those working in supporting roles safely behind the front lines. This depiction, although always slightly romantic and unrealistic, is today a complete myth. The combat exclusion depends on an antiquated conception of war having strict battle lines and "front" lines; without these lines and boundaries, the exclusion of women becomes impossible. The disintegration of these boundaries not only makes a combat exclusion unenforceable, it calls into question the broader historical understanding of combat, as well as the hierarchical prioritization of combat as an exclusive role. Despite the changing nature of warfare, for the entirety of the Iraq War and the majority of the Afghanistan war the US military insisted on sustaining a combat exclusion policy based on the ideal of distinct battle lines and combat units. Women were presumed to be spatially separate from the "front" lines, where combat activity was meant to take place.

There is widespread consensus on the changing nature of modern military operations. Warfare in both Iraq and Afghanistan has been described as irregular[1] and "characterized by guerrilla fighting in urban war zones with no clear front lines."[2] Pentagon spokeswoman Eileen Lainez summarized the impact of these changes for combat operations, saying "the nature of today's conflicts is evolving; there are no front lines in Iraq and Afghanistan."[3] Hannah Fischer, an Information Research Specialist working on US military casualty statistics, reiterated this position, declaring "the Iraq insurgency obliterated conventional battle lines."[4]

For women, the disintegration of boundaries between combat and non-combat positions resulted in "unprecedented levels of combat exposure for female service members."[5] Congressional statistics from 2001 to 2009 indicate that there were 102 and 14 female military deaths[6] in Operation Iraqi Freedom and Operation Enduring Freedom, respectively;[7] by 2013 a reported total of 152 US female troops died in Iraq and Afghanistan.[8] The US military had recognized the changing nature of warfare and had been including women in combat training since 2003, when the Army altered its basic

---

[1] John A. Nagl and Brian M. Burton, "Dirty Windows and Burning Houses: Setting the Record Straight on Irregular Warfare," *Washington Quarterly* 32, no. 2 (2009): 91–101.

[2] Amy E. Street, Dawne Vogt, and Lisa Dutra, "A New Generation of Women Veterans: Stressors Faced by Women Deployed to Iraq and Afghanistan," *Clinical Psychology Review* 29, no. 8 (December 2009): 685–694 (686).

[3] Ed O'Keefe and Jon Cohen, "Most Americans Back Women in Combat Roles, Poll Says," *Washington Post*, March 17, 2011, sec. Politics, http://www.washingtonpost.com/wp-dyn/content/article/2011/03/16/AR2011031603861.html.

[4] Hannah Fischer, *United States Military Casualty Statistics: Operation Iraqi Freedom and Operation Enduring Freedom*, March 25, 2009.

[5] Street, Vogt, and Dutra, "A New Generation of Women Veterans," 686.

[6] Military deaths are typically defined as the death of a service member as a result of war or war-related operations.

[7] Fischer, "United States Military Casualty Statistics."

[8] Roulo Claudetta, "Defense Department Expands Women's Combat Role" (US Department of Defense, January 24, 2013), http://www.defense.gov/news/newsarticle.aspx?id=119098.

training procedures in order to ensure that all soldiers were pre-
pared for irregular warfare. These training procedures were altered in
response to growing recognition within the US forces that the nature
of warfare in Afghanistan and Iraq meant that a distinction between
combat and non-combat roles could not be sustained: "women were
working alongside war fighters, taking hostile fire – even in the
role of designated support forces."[9] In addition, women were officially given combat pay – or hostile fire/imminent danger pay – in
acknowledgment that they were regularly under threat in combat
situations.

By January 2013, more than 280,000 women had served in Iraq
and Afghanistan: hundreds of those have received Combat Action
Badges, and scores have been given combat pay in recognition of their
work in hostile operations.[10] Among the women who died in Iraq, 78
percent of the deaths were categorized as "hostile," indicating that
women are indeed putting their lives at risk in war. The military
has formally acknowledged and rewarded women for their combat
contributions: a 2007 RAND report indicated that hundreds of female
Army members have received a Combat Action Badge,[11] and Sergeant
Leigh Ann Hester and Specialist Monica Lin Brown have received
Silver Stars – one of the highest combat military decorations – for
their contributions to Iraq and Afghanistan, respectively.

The increasingly untenable paradox was that while the US military sustained the combat exclusion, it reported on women's deaths
in hostile operations, distributed combat pay to some women, and
officially recognized some women for their valor and contribution to
combat operations. This demonstrates that the combat exclusion survived simply as an idea; it prevented women from being part of the

---

[9] Anne W. Chapman, "Mixed-Gender Basic Training: The U.S. Army Experience,
1973–2004" (Library of Congress Cataloging-in-Publication Data, 2008), 161.

[10] "Military to Ease Rules on Women in Combat," USATODAY.COM, http://
www.usatoday.com/news/washington/story/2012-02-08/war-women-pentagon/
53017764/1.

[11] Margaret C. Harrell et al., "Assessing the Assignment Policy for Army Women,"
Product Page (2007), http://www.rand.org/pubs/monographs/MG590-1.html.

war narrative, relegating them to the fictitious "support roles," and it was a formal obstacle for those women seeking promotion based on their combat experience. Mark Thompson summarizes the situation: "The wars in Afghanistan and Iraq essentially placed [women] on the front lines, without getting the combat credentials often needed for promotions."[12]

Another factor that made the combat exclusion irrelevant was the cooperation of the US military with other global forces that allowed women in combat. Both the Iraq and Afghanistan missions relied on contributions from coalition militaries – several of which allowed women on the front lines. There are approximately fifteen militaries around the world that allow women to participate in combat roles, including Canada, New Zealand, Norway, Denmark, Finland, France, Germany, Netherlands, Poland, Sweden, Australia, Israel, Eritrea, Lithuania, and Romania. Of these, all but Israel and Eritrea contributed troops to either the Iraq or Afghanistan missions. Given the globalization and integration of defense forces with different policies on women and combat, it is unclear how it was possible, or why it would be useful, to enforce women's exclusion from combat in Iraq and Afghanistan. Moreover, it is perplexing that the US military grappled with questions about whether women could serve on the front lines at the same time as they worked alongside militaries that had integrated women into the combat arms with success. Thus, although the USA was willing to accept coalition support from various forces, it seemed unprepared to observe any lessons learned from them regarding the integration of women.

Policy disintegration and battle line erasure
From the beginning of the Iraq and Afghanistan wars, in 2001 and 2003, respectively, there were several policy changes that impacted both the idea and the formal restrictions associated with the combat exclusion. This is a tumultuous period in the history of the

---

[12] Thompson, "Women in Combat: Shattering the 'Brass Ceiling.'"

combat exclusion. Efforts and policies to exclude women from combat have changed every few years, largely as a result of, or in reaction to, political pressure or events. The changes were almost tit-for-tat, with proponents of women in combat making headway, only to have conservative responses roll back those advances or reestablish restrictions. Constructing a clear understanding of the military's shifting and unraveling policies related to women in combat in this period is, therefore, a challenge. Several changes and amendments involved opaque language and terms, such as "colocation," "attached," and "forward support companies." For nonmilitary (and even military) experts, the result is a confusing, jargon-filled set of bullet points related to women in the military. This section presents a basic overview and primer to the changes, as well as an analysis of their impact on women in the forces.

In 2004, the Army decided to alter the size of its units, moving from larger divisional-sized units to smaller, "more agile" brigade formations. "Forward support companies" (FSCs) were created in the process. FSCs were designed to provide logistical support to battalions. The language used to describe them became iconic military jargon; the units were designed to be "embedded," "attached," and "collocated" with infantry and armor battalions. In other words, these FSCs were in the same locations, providing support to infantry and armor units. They faced the same threats as their nodal units; however, FSCs were not officially classified as combat units. Instead, they were described as "colocation" and "attached" to combat units. This rhetoric sustained a perceived division between "support" and "front line" units. However, in practical terms, the distinction had disintegrated, placing both FSCs and combat units in the same insecure places at the same insecure times.

While women were excluded from combat units, they were permitted to be assigned to FSCs. This change in the unit structure and assignment policies opened up approximately 168 positions previously closed to women, including mechanic and supply specialist roles. This change also effectively allowed thousands of women to work in the same arena as infantry and armor units. Steve Griffin explains:

> This may seem like a bureaucratic word game to non-military types, but to professional soldiers the difference is obvious. In essence, it means that combat units can't 'own' female soldiers, but they can accept them on 'loan' from other, non-combat units. Due to ever-changing needs on the battlefield, this is the administrative loophole that military commanders have been using to fill critical gaps in their ranks since the onset of these wars.[13]

Put plainly, women's inclusion in FSCs placed them directly alongside infantry and armor units – they were now officially assigned to "the frontline." Thus, even if one ignored the changing nature of war and the decline of traditional forms of battle, women were now part of the so-called tip of the spear in military operations. In its definition of combat, the DOD emphasizes the location of combat as being "well forward on the battlefield." FSCs were assigned to operate alongside combat units, rending them just as "forward" as their attached units.

There was widespread recognition that these changes placed more women in harm's way during the Iraq and Afghanistan wars. The policy of attaching women to combat units, therefore, came to be seen as "verbal contortions,"[14] effort to "stretch gender boundaries,"[15] and a means of "going around the non-combat rule"[16] without formally recognizing the actual contributions of women to military operations. The Center for Military Readiness lamented that the changes resulted

---

[13] Steve Griffin, "Fighting for Gender Equality on the Battlefield; At War," *New York Times*, January 31, 2012, https://global-factiva-com.ezproxy2.library.usyd.edu.au/aa/?ref=NYTB000020120131e81v008n9&pp=1&fcpil=en&napc=S&sa_from=.

[14] "Women in War Zones Take Risks but Don't Reap Rewards," *USA Today*, December 12, 2012.

[15] Fischer, *United States Military Casualty Statistics*.

[16] Petula Dvorak, "Will We One Day Mourn Female Combat Veterans?," *Washington Post*, May 29, 2012, http://www.highbeam.com/doc/1P2-31456233.html.

in the Army "bending, breaking, redefining, or circumventing the rules on women in or near direct combat."[17]

As described in the Introduction, evidence of women's involvement in combat consistently provoked political reactions, including attempts to reverse the changes or at least control the perception that women were in combat. Perhaps in an effort to reclaim the steadily disintegrating ideal of the all-male combat unit, Duncan Hunter, then chairman of the House Armed Services Committee, and John McHugh, then Military Personnel Subcommittee chairman, co-sponsored an amendment to the 2006 Defense Authorization Bill. "The Hunter Amendment," as it became known, called for the codification of DOD regulations related to women in all services, and specifically asked that Congress be notified if the services planned on changing the role of women in operations. This meant that over a decade later, the 1994 memo regarding women in combat was formally put into law, and Congress was given "more proactive control over assignment policies government units involved in ground combat."[18]

The declining relevance of the combat exclusion inspired further official calls for a review of the policy from both conservatives and proponents of women in combat. In early 2011, the MLDC recommended that the DOD remove combat restrictions because of the limitations they placed on career opportunities for women.[19] The commission's report identified the exclusion as a "structural barrier" for women, noting that the policy limits women's career paths and assignment options. Although the total number of positions closed to women in the US Army is relatively low at 7.3 percent, the

[17] Elaine Donnelly, Center for Military Readiness, quoted in "GOP Retreats on Women-in-Combat Bill," *Washington Times*, accessed July 24, 2014, http://www.washingtontimes.com/news/2005/may/26/20050526–121729–8305r/.

[18] Ann Scott Tyson, "Amendment Targets Role of Female Troops," *Washington Post*, May 19, 2005, sec. Politics, http://www.washingtonpost.com/wp-dyn/content/article/2005/05/18/AR2005051802094.html.

[19] "From Representation to Inclusion: Diversity Leadership for the 21st-Century Military (Final Report)" (United States, Military Leadership Diversity Commission, 2011), https://www.hsdl.org/?abstract&did=1139.

commission found that "exclusion from these occupations has a considerable influence on advancement to higher positions"[20] and that eliminating the exclusion was essential to "removing barriers and inconsistencies, to create a level playing field for all service members who meet the qualifications."[21] In May 2012, Senator Kirsten Gillibrand introduced the Gender Equality in Combat Act, a bill designed "to require a report on implementation of a termination of the ground combat exclusion policy for female members of the Armed Forces."[22]

Partially as a result of these growing pressures, in 2012, the DOD announced more than 14,000 "new" combat-related jobs for women serving in the Army.[23] Although this was seen by some as a defining moment for women in the military, many experts and critics argued that the DOD was now merely officially recognizing roles women had been filling informally for years. The announcement meant that roles within FSCs, which had previously been defined as "collocated" but not formally assigned to battalions, were now classified as combat roles. In turn, to a large extent, roles women were already filling were now classified officially as combat roles. One expert concluded that the recent policy changes merely "reflect what's been happening for the past 10 years of war in Iraq and Afghanistan."[24] Thus, while the headlines read "Pentagon to Ease Restrictions on Women in Combat,"[25] the reality was that the Pentagon had simply eased its definition of combat roles.

---

[20] Ibid., 67.   [21] Ibid, xvii.

[22] Kristen Gillibrand, "Gender Equality in Combat Act" (Senate of the United States, May 2012).

[23] "Women in Combat: Army to Open 14K Jobs, 6 MOSs," *Army Times*, accessed July 10, 2012, http://www.armytimes.com/news/2012/05/army-to-open-14000-jobs-6-mos-women-in-combat-050212/; Karen Parrish, "DOD Opens More Jobs, Assignments to Military Women" (U.S. Department of Defense, February 9, 2012), http://www.defense.gov/news/newsarticle.aspx?id=67130.

[24] "Women at War: Pentagon Is Easing Its Job Limits | World News | The Guardian," January 23, 2008, http://www.guardian.co.uk/world/feedarticle/10086205.

[25] David S. Cloud, Washington Bureau, "Pentagon to Ease Restrictions on Women in Combat," *Los Angeles Times*, February 9, 2012, http://articles.latimes.com/2012/feb/09/nation/la-na-pentagon-women-20120209.

Regardless of whether the May 2012 changes recognized existing contributions or opened new positions for women, it reignited debates surrounding women in combat and inspired a swath of subsequent policy changes. These changes were a catalyst for a continuous stream of new policy revisions, reviews, and relaxed restrictions related to women and combat. For example, in early 2012, the Army announced that six combat support military occupational specialties would be open to women.[26] In April 2012, the *Marine Corps Times* announced that, for the first time ever, women will enroll and train as infantry combat officers.[27] In June 2012, Cicely Verstein officially became the first woman in a combat support role when she signed up to be a Bradley Fighting Vehicle systems maintainer.[28] By the end of 2012, these changes had left the combat exclusion very much hanging by a thread.

Lioness and Female Engagement Teams: women assigned to battle

As the combat exclusion policy was being whittled away through administrative changes, women were increasingly being placed on the front lines on special assignments with the Lioness program in Iraq and the FETs in Afghanistan.[29] In the initial stages of the Iraq War, the military determined that women were needed to assist

---

[26] Sean O'Melveny, "Army Announces First Woman in Combat Support Role," Text, *Stars and Stripes*, n.d., http://www.military.com/daily-news/2012/07/03/army-announces-first-woman-in-combat-support-role.html.

[27] "USMC 4-Star: Women to Attend Infantry School," *Marine Corps Times*, accessed July 16, 2012, http://www.marinecorpstimes.com/news/2012/04/marine-corps-women-infantry-combat-dunford-amos-041812/.

[28] O'Melveny, "Army Announces First Woman in Combat Support Role."

[29] Lawrence V. Fulton et al., "Policy Implications for Female Combat Medic Assignment: A Study of Deployment and Promotion Risk," *Armed Forces & Society* (November 3, 2011; Lizette Alvarez, "G.I. Jane Breaks the Combat Barrier," *New York Times*, August 16, 2009, sec. US, http://www.nytimes.com/2009/08/16/us/16women.html; Holmstedt, *Band of Sisters*; Keally McBride and Annick T. R. Wibben, "The Gendering of Counterinsurgency in Afghanistan," *Humanity: An International Journal of Human Rights, Humanitarianism, and Development* 3, no. 2 (2012): 199–215; Stephanie K. Erwin, "The Veil of Kevlar: An Analysis of the Female Engagement Teams in Afghanistan" (Thesis, Monterey, California: Naval Postgraduate School, 2012), http://calhoun.nps.edu/mgmt/handle/10945/6792.

combat units in conducting searches on Iraqi women and inside Iraqi homes. To fulfill this need, units composed of approximately 20 women, called Lioness Teams, were created in 2003.[30] The teams accompanied combat units in order to conduct searches and to train other Iraqi women on searching techniques.[31] Because of the nature of their work, these female-only teams "routinely engaged in combat."[32] In recognition of the risk that Lioness Team members could face, women who volunteered for the program received training that included language skills, martial arts, and conflict resolution training.[33]

Drawing from the Lioness model, from 2009 the US military created several Female Engagement Teams in Afghanistan. FETs were designed to be "attached" to infantry or combat units to "engag[e] local populations to ascertain information on civil-society needs and problems, address security concerns, and to form links between the populace, the military and the interagency."[34] In the first year of their operation alone, FETs conducted more than seventy short-term search and engagement missions.[35] Following the positive response of the first FET in Afghanistan, the organizer of the initial FET, Capt. Matt Pottinger, campaigned for an expansion of the FET program to all Afghan provinces.[36] Between 2010 and 2011, permanent teams were established within the US Army, Marines, and Navy, and in that same

---

[30] Kelly Von Lunen, "Female Engagement Teams Built Trust in Iraq," *VFW, Veterans of Foreign Wars Magazine* 99, no. 6 (March 1, 2012): 28.

[31] Drawing from this program, "Iraqi Women's Engagement Teams" (IWETs) were created in 2004; however, the Lioness Program remained much more well-known.

[32] Service Women's Action Network, "Women in Combat," March 2011, http://servicewomen.org/media/publications/#factSheet.

[33] Ibid.

[34] "Army Marine Integration Volume III: Observations, Insights, and Lessons" (Center for Army Lessons Learned, July 2011), https://call2.army.mil/toc.aspx?document=6695& filename=/docs/doc6695/11–35.pdf. P15.

[35] Andi Allen, Gina Ladenheim, and Katie Stout, "Training Female Engagement Teams: Framework, Content Development, and Lessons Learned" (Center for Army Lessons Learned, July 2011), http://usacac.army.mil/cac2/call/docs/11–35/ch.3.asp.

[36] Anna C. Coll, "Evaluating Female Engagement Team Effectiveness in Afghanistan," Wellesley College Digital Scholarship Archive, 2012, http://repository.wellesley.edu/cgi/viewcontent.cgi?article=1068&context=thesiscollection.

period Jordan, Britain, Norway, and Sweden established FETs.[37] As of July 2014, each Brigade Combat Team and Provincial Reconstruction Team in Afghanistan was meant to have an accompanying FET.[38]

Although searching civilian homes and female Afghans remains central to the function of FETs, the mission of these teams has been extended to reflect counterinsurgency (COIN) priorities. This includes an emphasis on "the population . . . as the key battleground in the competition between insurgent and counterinsurgent."[39] FETs were central to the growing perception that military operations needed to win the "hearts and minds" of the Afghan people in general, and the "support of Afghan mothers and daughters" in particular.[40] Acknowledging and respecting local gendered customs was seen as key to this objective. FETs were, in turn, essential for respecting the cultural norms that prevented men from conducting searches and, therefore, a tool for building relationships and trust within the local population.[41] The FET program was "designed to allow access to half of the population which normally would have been denied due to cultural sensitivities."[42] In fulfilling these objectives, each member of a FET is given cultural training before becoming part of the team.[43]

According to the Army, the FET do not "have a combat function, but if found in a hostile situation they are trained to react appropriately."[44] Given the role of FETs within the broad objectives

---

[37] Transcript of DoD Blogging Roundtable, December 2010, 6; FET USMC presentation, 2.

[38] Coll, "Evaluating Female Engagement Team Effectiveness in Afghanistan."

[39] Ibid., 2.

[40] US Marine Corps, "Timeline: Engaging Afghan Women on the Front Lines," US Marine Corps, n.d., http://www.marines.com/history-heritage/timeline?articleId=TIMELINE_FEMALE_TEAMS#2000.

[41] Christopher McCullough, "Female Engagement Teams: Who They Are and Why They Do It," October 2, 2012, http://www.army.mil/article/88366/.

[42] Allen, Ladenheim, and Stout, "Training Female Engagement Teams," 15.

[43] Tyra A. Harding, "Women in Combat Roles: Case Study of Female Engagement Teams" (United States Army War College, 2012), www.dtic.mil/docs/citations/ADA561195.

[44] Ida Irby, "'FET' to Fight: Female Engagement Team Makes History," April 18, 2013, http://www.army.mil/article/101111/.

of the COIN paradigm, they undertake a range of tasks, including distributing medical and school supplies, sitting and talking with Afghan women, visiting schools or hospitals, providing access to clean drinking water, and leading community discussions on topics such as hygiene, childbirth, or breastfeeding.[45] Although the primary mission of FET is presented as communication, or drinking tea with locals, Capt. Kelly Hasselman, a FET commander, notes "all Soldiers can find themselves on the frontline."[46] Carey Lohrenz, the first female F-14 Tomcat fight pilot in the US Navy, reaffirmed this argument, stating "Female Engagement Teams . . . constantly put [women] in the direct line of fire."[47] Gen. Richard Mills, then commander of the Marines in Helmand also acknowledged that FETs were "out on the point of the spear many times."[48]

In July 2010, FETs were temporarily withdrawn from their roles after members of Congress expressed concern that they were violating the combat exclusion rules. As a result of the review, women were told they could not participate on foot patrols "primarily intended to hunt and kill the enemy." Furthermore, their stay on combat bases was restricted to a maximum of 45 days. The results of this arbitrary and awkward rule were summarized by the *New York Times* feature: "To fulfill the letter but hardly the spirit of the guidelines, the female Marines now travel from their combat outposts every six weeks for an overnight stay at a big base like Camp Leatherneck, then head back out the next morning."[49]

The expansive mandate of FETs, combined with the decision to assign an FET to each combat-focused brigade-level team, resulted in a further blurring of the combat and support distinction in

---

[45] Coll, "Evaluating Female Engagement Team Effectiveness in Afghanistan."

[46] Irby, "'FET' to Fight."

[47] Carey D. Lohrenz, "Time for Some Fearless Leadership," *Time*, January 20, 2013, http://nation.time.com/2013/01/30/time-for-some-fearless-leadership/.

[48] Elisabeth Bumiller, "For Female Marines, Tea Comes with Bullets," *New York Times*, October 2, 2010, sec. World/Asia Pacific, http://www.nytimes.com/2010/10/03/world/asia/03marines.html.

[49] Ibid.

Afghanistan. Despite this, and ample evidence that women in FETs were operating in hostile environments, intense efforts were made to sustain the idea that FETs were separate from combat operations and contributing different skills: "While the FETs are believed to undermine the insurgency and contribute to security, they were not created to help counterinsurgent forces fight the enemy directly."[50] The trope "tea as a weapon"[51] became readily associated with FETs, creating the impression that these women were largely sitting down with Afghan women and building relationships. A *New York Times* feature on FETs contrasted the objectives of tea drinking and combat operations. The headline of the feature was "For Female Marines, Tea Comes with Bullets," with the leading line reading, "They expected tea, not firefights."[52] The article captures the tension between perceptions of FETs and their actual, everyday operations in Afghanistan. It presents women in FETs as those "who have been closer to combat than most other women in the war... [they have] had to use real weapons in a tougher fight than many expected."[53]

In practice, the imaginary line between counterinsurgency operations, focused on winning hearts and minds, and direct combat was impossible to sustain during ground operations. Lizette Alvarez argues that female troops in both Iraq and Afghanistan "have done nearly as much in battle as their male counterparts: patrolled streets with machine guns, served as gunners on vehicles, disposed of explosives, and driven trucks down bomb-ridden roads."[54]

In further effort to sustain the idea of the combat exclusion, women in FETs are not given the same training as combat soldiers despite combat exposure, potentially placing them at risk. John Wilson summarizes the situation:

> A practical example of the problems associated with the burden of proof required to determine who "is engaged in combat with the

---

[50] Coll, "Evaluating Female Engagement Team Effectiveness in Afghanistan," 15.
[51] Bumiller, "For Female Marines, Tea Comes with Bullets."
[52] Ibid.   [53] Ibid.   [54] Alvarez, "G.I. Jane Breaks the Combat Barrier."

enemy" can be found with the U.S. Army's Lioness Program in Iraq. Despite a U.S. DoD policy banning women from direct ground combat, U.S. military commanders have been using women as an essential part of their ground operations in Iraq since 2003 . . . Against official policy and at times without the training given to their male counterparts and with the firm commitment to serve as needed, these dedicated young women have been drawn on to the front lines to some of the most violent counter insurgency battles in Iraq.[55]

Colonel Ellen Haring reiterated the façade of women as merely providing support, and not requiring combat training. She concludes: "[Women] go into these units with a lack of training, and they are at greater risk without that training . . . So yes, women are unofficially in combat, through the back door and without the training they need."[56]

The Lioness Program and the FETs operating in Iraq and Afghanistan illustrate the powerful effort to maintain the perception of the combat exclusion, as well as the ridiculous and often dangerous means necessary to sustain this idea. Ignoring or downplaying the daily threats that these female-only teams faced, and equating the teams to cultural ambassadors of the military, belittles and ignores the various roles these teams have fulfilled. Moreover, the restrictions placed on the teams in order to follow the rules of the combat exclusion, such as traveling every 45 days, defied logic and placed these women and the rest of the troops at risk. Finally, presuming that women would not be in direct combat meant that the military did not offer female-only teams the same training as combat units, again, putting them, and their fellow soldiers, at an unnecessary risk.

---

[55] John Wilson, *Compensation Owed for Mental Health Based on Activities in Theatre Post-Traumatic Stress Disorder Act* (US Government Printing Office, 2009), 5, http://www.gpo.gov/fdsys/pkg/CHRG-111hhrg49911/pdf/CHRG-111hhrg49911.pdf.

[56] Dvorak, "Will We One Day Mourn Female Combat Veterans?"

LEGAL CHALLENGES

The following section profiles two court cases filed during the Iraq and Afghanistan wars. The cases are important because they challenge the legality of the combat exclusion, and, in doing so, they demonstrate the structural barriers it created for women operating in Iraq and Afghanistan. Basic details of the case, as well as an overview of the plaintiffs and their experience, reiterate the argument that the combat exclusion did not prevent women from fighting alongside men, but it limited their ability to apply for jobs, attain training, and receive recognition for this work.

Baldwin, Haring v. Panetta

Command Sergeant Major P. Baldwin & Colonel Ellen L. Haring v. the Hon L. Panetta, the Hon. J. McHugh, Lieutenant General T.P. Bostick & the Hon. T.R. Lamont was the first lawsuit to directly challenge the combat exclusion.[57] The suit was raised in May 2012 through the Molly Pitcher Project,[58] a program led by Professor Anne Coughlin at the University of Virginia School of Law. The plaintiffs challenged the constitutionality and legality of excluding women from combat solely on the basis of sex, and argued that their Fifth Amendment rights were violated by the combat exclusion policy.[59]

The case is distinct from previous Fifth Amendment challenges in that it cites US military operations in Iraq as both indication of the changing nature of combat and evidence of women's contribution to combat zones and roles. The Plaintiffs characterized the combat exclusion as arbitrary, irrational, and a largely ignored or unenforced

---

[57] Prior lawsuits mentioned in Chapter 1 focused on the constitutionality of the male-only draft, as well as the separate entrance requirements for men and women in the military.

[58] The express aim of the Molly Pitcher Project is to "open the profession of combat arms to women on an equal basis to men." Prof. Coughlin quoted in University of Virginia School of Law, "Students, Professor Help File Lawsuit on Behalf of Plaintiffs Seeking to Overturn Military Ban on Women in Combat," University of Virginia School of Law, May 24, 2012, http://www.law.virginia.edu/html/news/2012_spr/combat_exclusion.htm.

[59] *Baldwin et al. v. Panetta et al.* (District of Columbia District Court 2012).

policy. In supporting this position, the plaintiffs pointed to the contradicting definitions of the combat exclusion offered by the DOD and the Army, noting that "there is little consensus on either the goals and 'spirit' of the DoD and Army Policies, or the actual 'letter' of the Policies themselves."[60] The plaintiffs referenced the Marines' Lioness program and combat support teams in arguing that the combat exclusion policy is consistently ignored or undermined in current military practice. They also pointed to weaknesses in the argument that women should be excluded from combat based on physical standards. The plaintiffs reminded the court that no specific criteria for physical standards exist in relation to the combat exclusion, making it impossible to argue that women fail or succeed in meeting these standards.[61]

The plaintiffs included Command Sergeant Major Jane P. Baldwin, a decorated soldier with deployments to South Korea, Germany, and Iraq. Baldwin argued that her career opportunities had been limited by the combat exclusion because she was prevented from applying for positions that she was qualified for, and had the relevant experience to undertake, because they were "combat-coded posts."[62] A second plaintiff, Colonel Ellen L. Haring, served for twenty-eight years within the US military as a platoon leader, commander, executive officer, bridge commander, and an associate professor at Army's Command and General Staff College. Haring specified instances in which the combat exclusion limited her opportunities, including an instance when a position was given to a lower-ranking male colleague with combat experience over her. In a public statement related to the case, she explained, "combat arms are seen as the bread and butter of the military . . . When you're excluded from them, you're not treated equally. You're not valued equally. You're marginalized."[63]

---

[60] Ibid.   [61] Ibid.

[62] University of Virginia School of Law, "Students, Professor Help File Lawsuit."

[63] Kate Wiltrout, "Suffolk Reservist Sues over Ban on Women in Combat," *Virginian-Pilot*, May 25, 2012, http://hamptonroads.com/2012/05/army-reservist-assigned-suffolk-sues-pentagon-over-combat-exclusion.

In September 2012, the Pentagon moved to dismiss the lawsuit, citing presidential and congressional entitlement to "substantial deference...in areas of military expertise."[64] When Panetta announced the end of the combat exclusion in 2013, this case was still pending. As of January 2014, the case was still open after several extensions. Despite the lifting of the combat exclusion, the plaintiffs have fought for extensions because "the military has yet to explain how it will allow senior women to cross over into branches from which they were previously excluded."[65]

Hegar et al. v. Panetta

In November 2012, just a few months after the *Baldwin & Haring v. Panetta, McHugh, Bostick & Lamont* case was filed, another legal case was filed questioning the constitutionality of the combat exclusion. *Hegar et al. v. Panetta*, supported by the ACLU, alleged that the combat exclusion was an illegal and discriminatory policy. Each of the plaintiffs had served "in combat in our nation's theatres of war" but had faced limitations and discrimination due to the combat exclusion.[66] The first plaintiff was Major Mary Jennings Hegar, who had served three tours in Afghanistan. Her military background included service in the Air Force, training as a pilot with the Air National Guard in 2004, and then Survival, Evasion, Resistance and Escape (SERE) training for her missions as a medevac pilot in Afghanistan. SERE instruction included weapons training, grueling physical challenges, and "physically and mentally arduous tasks"[67] largely seen as preparation for possible combat operations. As a medevac pilot, Hegar operated in the line of fire; in 2009, after her aircraft was shot down in Afghan territory, she safely landed the helicopter, returned fire, and carried out a rescue operation. In recognition for

[64] David Zucchino, "Female Soldiers Fight Pentagon in Court for Combat Positions," *Los Angeles Times*, October 11, 2012, http://articles.latimes.com/2012/oct/11/nation/la-na-women-combat-20121012.

[65] Ibid.   [66] Ibid.

[67] *Hegar et al. v. Panetta* (California Northern District Court 2012).

her contribution to the operation, Major Hegar received the Purple Heart and the Distinguished Flying Cross with a Valor Device.[68] The awarding of this medal raised questions and caused controversy, as only those who participate in direct combat are meant to receive it.

The court case notes that "Despite Major Hegar's SERE training, her success as a combat pilot, and her recognized valor in ground combat, the combat exclusion policy bars her categorically from competing for certain combat positions."[69] Perhaps most significantly, Major Hegar chose to end her career with the Air National Guard primarily because she felt she was not able to advance her career further as a direct result of the combat exclusion. She summarized the contradictions and impact of the combat exclusion policy, saying:

> The policy creates the pervasive way of thinking in the military and civilian populations that women can't serve in combat roles, even in the face of the reality that servicewomen in all branches of the military are already fighting for their country alongside their male counterparts. They shoot, they return fire, they drag wounded comrades to safety, and they engage with the enemy, and they have been doing this for years.[70]

The second plaintiff, Staff Sergeant Jennifer Hunt, had been deployed to both Iraq and Afghanistan, where her role as a civil affairs specialist included assisting combat troops in search missions. While colocating with combat troops, Hunt was exposed to the same conditions as male combat soldiers. Hunt received a Purple Heart after suffering injuries when the military vehicle she was traveling in was hit by an IED in Iraq. The ACLU case specified that although Hunt operated under the same conditions as combat troops, she was not given the same combat-specific training as her male counterparts. It

---

[68] Ibid. [69] Ibid.

[70] Major Mary Hegar Jennings, "Women Warriors Are on the Battlefield. Eliminate Outdated, Unfair Military Combat Exclusion Policy," American Civil Liberties Union, November 27, 2012, https://www.aclu.org/print/blog/womens-rights/women-warriors-are-battlefield-eliminate-outdated-unfair-military-combat.

is argued that this exposed both Hunt and her colleagues to unnecessary risk. Hunt noted in an interview, "The shrapnel that tore through the vehicle that day didn't stop because I'm a female."[71] In addition, Hunt's formal exclusion prevented her from applying for military positions for which she had unofficial experience, yet lacked "official" recognition. Therefore, "the combat exclusion policy put Staff Sergeant Hunt at a disadvantage in her chances for career progression compared with male soldiers."[72]

Captain Alexandra Zoe Bedell, the third plaintiff to the case, was deployed to Afghanistan twice as an officer in the Marine Corps. Despite graduating in the top 10 percent of her class from The Basic School, Bedell's options were limited within the forces as a result of her sex. She became a Logistics Officer because she was not able to pursue her first choice, which was any "combat arms military occupations specialty."[73] Captain Bedell took on a leadership role within the FET program beginning in 2009. According to the lawsuit, "[t]he combat exclusion policy interfered with Captain Bedell's ability as Officer-in-Charge of the FET program to fulfill her mission of providing support to combat and counterinsurgency operations."[74]

As indicated earlier, one of the central issues associated with the combat exclusion policy was the need for female soldiers to return to base every 45 days in order to fulfill the "temporary" requirement of the colocation policy.[75] In an interview, Bedell described the everyday reality for those working within the FET program, saying:

> They wore the same gear and they carried the same weapons (as male Marines). And if the unit was attacked, my Marines fought back with the Marines. They returned fire. They looked for additional shooters – everything that the men did . . . The combat

[71] Craig Whitlock, "4 Women Sue Over Pentagon's Combat-Exclusion Policy," *Washington Post*, November 28, 2012, http://global.factiva.com.ezproxy1.library.usyd .edu.au/aa/?ref=WP00000020121128e8bs0001c&pp=1&fcpil=en&napc=S&sa_ from=.

[72] *Hegar et al. v. Panetta* (California Northern District Court 2012).

[73] Ibid.   [74] Ibid.   [75] Ibid.

exclusion policy does not recognize this reality. Instead, it creates a complex and dangerous set of rules, which prevent commanders from making the best choices when deciding how to fight.[76]

Like Hunt, Bedell left active duty in part because of the combat exclusion policy and the limitations it placed on her prospects for career advancement.

The fourth plaintiff was active duty First Lieutenant Colleen Farrell, who also served in a leadership capacity with FETs in Afghanistan. While under her command in Afghanistan, three teams of female Marines were awarded Combat Action Ribbons for "receiving and returning fire."[77] Farrell also noted the challenge that the combat exclusion policy, particularly the requirement to return to base every 45 days, posed for her in her daily operations in Afghanistan.[78]

The ACLU lawsuit contends that the combat exclusion policy has resulted in the plaintiffs being "denied the official recognition they need to advance their careers"[79] as their roles in combat are not acknowledged. Furthermore, it notes that this lack of recognition perpetuates the impression that women do not contribute as much as men to war, inspiring further discrimination. As of January 2014, the ACLU was in the process of opposing the Pentagon's request that the case be dismissed. The grounds for extending the case are detailed on the ACLU website, which states that despite the official removal of the combat exclusion policy, "the Department of Defense has continued its policy of excluding women from even applying for, much

---

[76] Transcript, National Public Radio, Interview with Larry Abramson on *All Things Considered*, November 27, 2012.

[77] Ibid.

[78] It should be noted that a fifth plaintiff to the case was the Service Women's Action Network (SWAN). SWAN's mission is "to transform military culture by securing equal opportunity and freedom to serve without discrimination, harassment or assault; and to reform veterans' services to ensure high quality health care and benefits for women veterans and their families." They were included as a plaintiff because they argued that much of their modest resources are directed at addressing the harmful consequences of the combat exclusion policy, rather than its overall mission.

[79] *Hegar et al. v. Panetta* (California Northern District Court 2012).

less serving in, tens of thousands – we believe about 200,000 – of combat positions, solely because of their gender. Inexplicably, the military continues to run all-male schools and training courses, including prestigious leadership schools like Ranger School, that women can't even apply to."

These two cases demonstrate the impacts of the combat exclusion for individual female soldiers serving in Iraq and Afghanistan. The cases reinforce the position that there are no front lines, and that the military's own policy of "attaching" women placed them directly alongside infantry units. The cases put a face to the policy, illustrating the types of contributions women made to the wars, as well as the logistical and bureaucratic obstacles the policy has posed for them. Again, this illustrates the paradox surrounding the combat exclusion. In one sense, the military was willing to acknowledge that women "were there," in hostile operations in Iraq and Afghanistan, awarding them honors and giving them combat pay in recognition of this service. Yet, the military also attempted to sustain the argument that women were not on the front lines, by preventing them from attaining promotions, or, in some cases, compensation for their contributions to combat operations.

HOW DO YOU CHANGE A POLICY THAT DOESN'T EXIST?

The combination of the unraveling of the policies associated with the combat exclusion, increased evidence of women's contributions to the wars, and high-profile cases calling the combat exclusion illegal should have made the decision to remove the combat exclusion obvious. However, the Pentagon's January 24, 2013, announcement to lift its ban on women in front line combat roles came as a surprise to many. For years, Congress and the DOD had justified the exclusion as essential to national security. The Center for Military Readiness, a conservative nonprofit think tank that focuses on personnel policies of the US military, had argued that women's inclusion in combat would dilute entrance standards, provoke greater rates of sexual tension and harassment, and unnecessarily place troops at risk. Less than a year earlier, when then–Pentagon press secretary George Little announced the 14,000 "new" combat-related jobs opened to women, he made it clear that infantry and direct combat roles would remain off-limits.

This begs two questions: what motivated the decision to remove the combat exclusion, and how do you remove an exclusion that didn't exist? The following section explores these questions. I consider whether the announcement is an indication of a military identity crisis at the end of two hugely unpopular and largely unsuccessful wars. By 2013, the ideal of the band of brothers had been severely tainted, with multiple military scandals, an epidemic of posttraumatic stress disorder (PTSD) and suicide, and an epic sexual violence scandal. The "removal" of the combat exclusion might be viewed as a distraction and a publicity "release valve" for a military embroiled in a public relations crisis. It detracted attention from other scandals and re-created the image of the band of brothers from an all-male unit, to a new, more equal and inclusive family.

The purpose of this section is not to make the case as to whether Iraq and Afghanistan were "just" military operations or to provide an extensive analysis of various scandals, including the sexual violence epidemic in the US military. This section highlights the possibility that the decision to remove the combat exclusion was, once again, all about men and preserving military identity. I argue that there are at least four factors that undermined the positive association between band of brothers and "ideal soldiers," bravery, and successful warfare: growing awareness of sexual violence within the military; the epidemic of suicide within the ranks of US soldiers; and several scandals, including prisoner abuse at Abu Ghraib, and video and images of soldiers urinating on the corpses of deceased Taliban men.

It is difficult to know the precise impact of these issues and events on public morale and perceptions of US soldiers and military operations. However, I argue that they all contribute to a generalized unease with the band of brothers myth and trope. Bands of brothers were increasingly and repeatedly associated with unauthorized violence – sometimes perpetrated against their own comrades and civilians – dishonorable and illegal behavior, military failures, and military trauma. This is not to say that all US soldiers were dishonorable or failures; rather, it is to say that the easy association between bands of brothers and pure, military success and glory was called into question and became more difficult to sustain. For example, whereas cohesion and bonding was once depicted as essential to the success of all-male units, it was now associated with the sort of groupthink and complicity that leads to Abu Ghraib prison abuse and the perpetration – and coverup – of sexual violence within the ranks.

The full scope of the sexual violence epidemic within the military cannot be detailed here, but it is worth noting the scale of the problem in order to consider how it might affect the band of brothers myth – particularly the ideal of men as natural protectors of women. According to the Department of Veterans Affairs, almost half of women who served in Iraq and Afghanistan were sexually harassed, and one in four were sexually assaulted. Other research shows that between 20 and 40 percent of women serving in the US military experienced rape or attempted rape during their military careers; this is despite the fact that the DOD estimates that approximately 80 percent of incidents are not reported.[80] What these statistics mean is that "[w]omen serving in the U.S. military today are more likely to be raped by a fellow soldier than killed by enemy fire in Iraq."[81] Further statistics on sexual abuse in the military are staggering. Since DOD began collecting statistics on reported sexual assaults, the numbers have increased from 1700 in 2004 to 3374 in 2012 – that is, the equivalent of more than 9 reported sexual assaults a

[80] Jacque Wilson, "Unplanned Pregnancies May Be on Rise in Military," January 24, 2013, http://edition.cnn.com/2013/01/23/health/unplanned-pregnancies-military/.

[81] "Sexual Assault in Military 'Jaw-Dropping,' Lawmaker Says," CNN, July 31, 2008, http://edition.cnn.com/2008/US/07/31/military.sexabuse/.

day.[82] Aside from causing mass insecurity for women and men within the forces, sexual violence costs the military in terms of medical treatment, lost work hours, and loss of cohesion and trust. There is also research indicating that sexual assault causes military sexual trauma (MST), which can trigger PTSD. In her work on the cost of sexual violence in the armed forces, Christine Hansen summarizes the impacts:

> Sexual trauma and combat exposure appear to be strong risk factors for PTSD within the military community. The trauma denoted as military sexual trauma (MST) has implications for the physical and mental health of the survivor, disability assessment within the Veterans' Health Administration, and transition from military to civilian life. Although MST may occur less frequently than actual war trauma, the sexual trauma has a great impact on the symptoms of PTSD. Women veterans reporting a history of sexual assault are nine times more likely to have PTSD . . . Health care utilization and cost of services is higher among women reporting an assault while on active duty. The study concludes that women veterans with MST are more likely to have PTSD. The results also suggest that they are receiving fewer health care services with implications for public health policy.[83]

Sexual violence within the ranks of the US military has received increased attention over the past decade. A documentary film, *The Invisible War*, focused on the issue and garnered significant acclaim and attention, including an Oscar nomination. In March 2013, a Senate Armed Forces Committee hearing was held on the subject. During the hearing, various experts and victims argued that the military continues to promote and protect perpetrators while it silences victims.

---

[82] US Commission on Civil Rights, *Sexual Assault in the Military, Statutory Enforcement Report* (Washington, DC, September 2013), http://sapr.mil/public/docs/ research/USCCR_Statutory_Enforcement_Report_Sexual_Assault_in_the_Military_ SEP2013.pdf.p. 5.

[83] Christine Hansen, "A Considerable Sacrifice: The Costs of Sexual Violence in the US Armed Forces," *The Baldy Centre for Law and Social Policy*, no. Military Culture and Gender (September 15, 2005), 5.

The military justice system was described as ineffective and in need of a major overhaul.

Finally, alongside general negative trends in sexual violence over the past two decades, there have also been larger scandals that have garnered significant public attention. Large sexual violence scandals have been all too common within the US military. This includes the 1991 "Tailhook" scandal[84] and the 1996 Aberdeen scandal.[85] Although there were several sexual violence scandals during the Iraq and Afghanistan wars, the Lackland scandal stands out as one of the most damaging to the US military's image. Between 2009 and 2012 at the Lackland Airbase in Texas, sixty-two trainees were identified as victims of assault or improper conduct perpetrated by thirty-two instructors.[86]

All this provides a brief snapshot of the broad and complex set of issues associated with sexual violence within the military. What is interesting for this analysis is how the increased statistics and growing attention to the issue have undermined several of the ideals associated with the band of brothers myth. In particular, assumptions that men cannot suppress their natural instinct to protect women and that the military requires all-male units to achieve its national security objectives – in other words, to protect the nation – become untenable. The sexual violence scandals indicate that men clearly are able to suppress their "urge" to protect women and in fact may not have an inherent

---

[84] This scandal saw men and women assaulted on a mass scale during a Navy convention. Eighty-three women and seven men were assaulted, and 117 officers were implicated in the assaults. Office of the Inspector General, Tailhook 91: Part 2, Events at the 35th Annual Tailhook Symposium (Washington DC: US Department of Defense, February 1993), http://hdl.handle.net/2027/mdp.39015029525204, 1–1.

[85] This scandal involved more than twelve instructors charged with sex crimes and led to a flood of reports of sexual assault across the services as a sexual assault hotline was set up. Jackie Spinner, "In Wake of Sex Scandal, Caution Is the Rule at Aberdeen," Washington Post, November 7, 1997, http://www.washingtonpost.com.

[86] James Risen, "Former Air Force Recruit Speaks Out about Rape by Her Sergeant at Lackland," New York Times, February 26, 2013, sec. U.S., http://www.nytimes.com/2013/02/27/us/former-air-force-recruit-speaks-out-about-rape-by-her-sergeant-at-lackland.html.

drive to protect them or their interests. Moreover, surely the security of women within the military is part of our understanding of national security. If nearly half of female service members can expect to face sexual violence or rape, this is an indication of an insecurity crisis.

The Abu Ghraib prisoner abuse scandal was one of the most damaging scandals of the Iraq War. Early on in the war, US military personnel seized control of this notorious Iraqi prison. As early as January 2004 it was reported that between October and December 2003, members of the US military had been involved in "numerous incidents of sadistic, blatant, and wanton criminal abuses... inflicted on several detainees."[87] These abuses were investigated and detailed by Major General Antonio Taguba in a report that was later leaked by New Yorker reporter Seymour Hersh.[88] The reported abuses included: "positioning a naked detainee on a MRE Box with a sandbag on his head, and attaching wires to his fingers, toes and penis to simulate electric torture," "a male MP guard having sex with a female detainee," "sodomizing a detainee with a chemical light," "beating detainees with a broom handle and chair."[89] There is no doubt that the images associated with this scandal propelled it into spotlight in dramatic ways. Several images – including the "hooded man" and the image of Lynndie England holding a leash tied to a prisoner – are widely recognized and iconic images representing a dark aspect of the history of the Iraq War.

For the purposes of this analysis, the impact that this scandal had on military identity is important to note. The US government attempted to cast the prisoner abuse as the work of "a few bad apples," yet there was widespread evidence that the shocking

---

[87] Antonio Taguba, "The 'Taguba Report' on Treatment of Abu Ghraib Prisoners in Iraq" (FindLaw, January 19, 2004), http://news.findlaw.com/cnn/docs/iraq/tagubarpt.html#ThR1.8.

[88] It should be noted that Amnesty International's Dr. Abdel Salam Sidahmen, at the time Deputy Director of AI's Middle East Program, was also key to raising awareness of prisoner abuse at the time. Joseph Darby was a reservist in the military police who reported abuse to his superiors in January 2004, leading to an internal investigation.

[89] Ibid. MRE: Meal, Ready to Eat; MP, military police.

torture tactics had been systematically used and authorized from within the military chain of command. A report published in November 2008 by the US Senate Armed Services Committee found that the abusive tactics seen in prisons such as Abu Ghraib were part of the interrogation practices that were circulated through the CIA in early 2002.[90] The perpetrators of the Abu Ghraib abuse referred to this report when justifying their actions. The suspended head of the prison, Janis Karpinski, told CBS, "These soldiers didn't design these techniques on their own . . . we were following orders." She also added that her team were merely scapegoats: "scapegoat is the perfect word and it's an understatement."[91] The Pentagon certainly treated the scandal as isolated: only one soldier – Charles Graner – was imprisoned,[92] whereas four of five top officers overseeing prison policies and operations were cleared of any wrongdoing.[93]

This tension between the "few bad apples" narrative and the "just following orders" narrative has implications for how the public sees the band of brothers. Despite the treatment of this scandal as isolated, it evoked broader questions about the nature of operations in Iraq and the justness of intervention activities in the country. Over time, "Those pictures unfortunately became symbolic, emblematic of all the troubles that the U.S. faced in the last four years of the Bush administration, particularly given its war in Iraq."[94] Most importantly, the idea that soldiers justified such grave abuse as "following orders" tainted the ideal of the band of brothers as inherently

---

[90] Committee on Armed Services, Inquiry into the Treatment of Detainees in US Custody, Committee Findings (Washington, DC: United States Senate, November 20, 2008), http://www.armed-services.senate.gov/imo/media/doc/Detainee-Report-Final_April-22-2009.pdf.

[91] Michelle Levi, CBS News, April 22, 2009, "Abu Ghraib Head: We Were Scapegoated," accessed May 12, 2014, http://www.cbsnews.com/news/abu-ghraib-head-we-were-scapegoated/.

[92] Daniel Nasaw, "Report Vindicates Soldiers Prosecuted over Abu Ghraib Abuses, Lawyers Say," *The Guardian*, April 23, 2009, sec. World news, http://www.theguardian.com/world/2009/apr/22/abu-ghraib-iraq-torture-senate.

[93] Ibid.

[94] http://edition.cnn.com/2009/WORLD/meast/05/18/detainee.abuse.lookback/index.html?iref=24hours

noble and brave. In an interview following the scandal, the infamous Lynndie England was interviewed about her part in the abuse. She maintained that the abuse was "like nothing" and that her and her fellow soldiers had simply been "following orders." Such representations associated the band of brothers with groupthink and soldiers ignoring their own conscience in the process of blindly following orders.

Another scandal that exemplified the "bad apples" versus "groupthink" narrative came in January 2012. At the time, a video began circulating across the internet of US Marines urinating on the corpses of Taliban fighters in the Helmand province of Afghanistan. The video was apparently taken on July 27, 2011.[95] Almost immediately after its release, the military condemned the video and characterized the incident as isolated. Then–Defense Secretary Leon Panetta reportedly told Afghan officials that "the conduct depicted in the footage is utterly deplorable, and that it does not reflect the standards or values American troops are sworn to uphold."[96]

One of the highest-ranking Marines in the video was Staff Sergeant Edward Deptola. He admitted to "dereliction of duty for desecrating remains, posing for photographs with corpses and failing to properly supervise junior Marines"; however, his lawyer claimed he had been punished enough by the publicity and that this was an "isolated mistake by a well-regarded Marine."[97] In the end, Deptola received a reduction in rank due to a pretrial agreement.[98] US Marine Staff Sergeant Joseph W. Chamblin also had a pretrial agreement; he pleaded guilty and faced a rank reduction and a $500 fine. Two other

---

[95] Adam Gabbatt, "US Marines Charged over Urinating on Bodies of Dead Taliban in Afghanistan," *The Guardian*, September 25, 2012, sec. World News, http://www.theguardian.com/world/2012/sep/24/us-marines-charged-dead-taliban.

[96] http://www.nytimes.com/2012/01/13/world/asia/video-said-to-show-marines-urinating-on-taliban-corpses.html?pagewanted=all&_r=0

[97] http://www.theguardian.com/world/2013/jan/17/us-marine-admits-urinating-on-taliban-corpse

[98] "Corps: Urination Video Was 1 of 12 Marines Made," *Marine Corps Times*, accessed May 15, 2014, http://www.marinecorpstimes.com/article/20130116/NEWS/301160308/Corps-Urination-video-1-12-Marines-made.

soldiers involved in the incident, whose names were not released, received "non judicial punishment after pleading guilty."[99]

Again, there were tensions between claims that the incident was unrepresentative, deplorable, and isolated and efforts within government and by the soldiers to justify their actions. The cavalier attitudes of the soldiers both within the video and during subsequent interviews undermines the claim that this incident was uncharacteristic and an outlier. In the video, one of the marines says "Have a good day, buddy" as he urinates on the corpse. In 2013, when Staff Sergeant Joseph Chamblin was interviewed about his role in the incident, he stated, "These were the same guys that were killing our family, killing our brothers . . . do I regret doing it? Hell no."[100] Moreover, Rick Perry – at the time a Republican presidential hopeful – declared that "19-year-old kids make stupid mistakes," arguing that to characterize the act as criminal was "over the top."[101] Moreover, blogs and forums saw numerous supporters of the Marines. For example, anti-Muslim blogger Pam Geller declared "I love these Marines" in response to the scandal.[102] Also, a writer in the blog "RebelPundit," which is self-identified as "citizen journalism from the belly of the beast," declared, "you pee for us all, Marine," calling the act justified, and arguing that he wished "men like those urinating Marines were running this operation [sic]."[103]

It is difficult to measure the overall public response to this incident; however, it once again raised questions as to the negative

99 "Staff NCO to Lose Rank in Urination Video," *Marine Corps Times*, accessed May 15, 2014, http://www.marinecorpstimes.com/article/20121220/NEWS/212200321/Staff-NCO-lose-rank-urination-video.

100 Lee Ferran, "Marine Who Urinated on Dead Taliban Says He'd Do It Again," ABC News, July 17, 2013, http://abcnews.go.com/Blotter/marine-urinated-taliban-dead-hed/story?id=19687916.

101 http://www.nydailynews.com/news/politics/rick-perry-defends-marines-urinated-taliban-corpses-calls-government-reaction-top-article-1.1006404

102 http://www.motherjones.com/mojo/2012/01/anti-muslim-blogger-pam-geller-alleged-corpse-desecration-i-love-these-marines

103 http://rebelpundit.com/2012/01/you-pee-for-us-all-marine/

potential of the band of brothers. The band of brothers myth links the unique bond between male soldiers to positive qualities such as bravery and honor. Moreover, the myth presumes that the bond between the men is special and essential for protecting the nation. Such generalized ideals of units as altruistic and driven by honor were undermined by questions of the negative potential of groupthink and uncritically following orders.

The combat exclusion has always been used to shape and define military identity. Examining the decision to remove the combat exclusion in this context opens the possibility for rethinking the rationale for the decision as well as the claim that it presents a groundbreaking change for women. From a publicity perspective, the announcement does more for the image of the military than it does for the individual women who are serving within it. The announcement signals a new era for women in the force and expresses solidary with women in spite of the growing and largely unaddressed sexual violence crisis. Furthermore, the announcement serves to rewrite history in a way. Characterizing the change as groundbreaking implies that it is a marked shift in previous operations. This perpetuates the misconception that women did not contribute to combat in the decades and years leading up to the announcement, writing women out of the history of the Iraq and Afghanistan wars in particular.

CONCLUSION

The nature of the wars in Iraq and Afghanistan made it impossible to exclude women from combat. Further, the reorganization of units and the creation of Lioness and Female Engagement Teams explicitly assigned women to work alongside combat units. By the time the DOD announced the "removal" of the combat exclusion in 2013, it was almost impossible to find what remained of the exclusion in order to remove it. At the same time that the application of the combat exclusion was disappearing, there were political efforts to defend the exclusion, particularly in the case of the Hunter Amendment, and in the legal resistance to the court cases raised against the DOD and Pentagon by women in the military. This chapter illustrates the tension between women's presence in combat operations in the wars in Iraq and Afghanistan, and the impression that they were absent or serving only in support roles during these missions.

3   It just doesn't *feel* right: emotion and the combat exclusion policy

"I just can't get over this feeling of old men ordering young women into combat . . . I have a gut-based hang-up there. And it doesn't make a lot of sense in every way. I apologize for it."

Gen. Merrill A. McPeak, former Air Force Chief of Staff

The combat exclusion, like other domestic and foreign policies, tends to be presented as a product of rational decision making based on evidence, experience, and public welfare. This perception leaves little space for thinking about the role of emotion in the making of military policy.[1] This chapter addresses this "emotional gap," by focusing on the role of emotion within debates on women in combat. I argue that much of the logic used to resist or oppose women in combat has been based either partially or completely on emotion. For example, in the quotation that leads this chapter, General McPeak acknowledges his "gut-based hang-up" regarding women in combat and the possible irrationality of his position. Such reactions raise several questions, including the following: What impact does such visceral, emotional opposition have on military culture, on the debates surrounding women in combat, and eventually, on the process of further integrating women into the US military? What role does the band of brothers myth play in inspiring inherent, inexplicable, or visceral emotional reactions to women in combat? This chapter addresses these questions by exploring the relationship between emotional responses and policies directed toward women in combat.

---

[1] For an excellent discussion on the role of emotion in international relations see the forum "Emotion and the Feminist IR Researcher," edited by Christine Sylvester (*International Studies Review*, Volume 13, Issue 4, 687–708).

The chapter does not treat emotion as a problem with regard to policy. Rather, it is argued that overlooking the role of emotion in policy debates obscures a large part of how policies are made, and why they are supported. Emotion matters in the discussion on women in combat for several reasons. First, emotional reactions are common and consistent elements of the debates both leading up to the removal of the combat exclusion and in the aftermath of the policy change. Such positions were expressed by those in positions of power, often as "legitimate" rationale for their support or opposition to women in combat. In other words, emotional reactions are part of the official policy dialogue related to women in combat, whether we pay attention to them or not. Second, emotional positions are expressed as inherent or deeply personal and are treated as natural and beyond critique. They are therefore difficult to counter and affect. As a result, emotional positions are barriers to those trying to change military culture or alter the process of integrating women into combat roles. Third, emotional positions are often woven through seemingly objective statements regarding women in combat. This linking and weaving muddies the debates, making it difficult to discern whether policies are based on evidence, or driven by emotional positions, or, conversely, if emotion and "rational" arguments can be separated at all.

This chapter has three central objectives. First is to identify the consistent emotional themes within discussions on women and combat and the combat exclusion. The emotional reactions to women in combat tend to be united by the underlying belief and visceral conviction that women "just do not belong" in combat for various, often nonquantifiable, reasons. These positions do not draw on data or evidence from the battlefield. They do not focus on evidence, but often make reference to the nature of men or women, or the potential threats women could pose to military culture and thereby national security, as proof of the need to exclude women from combat.

Second, this chapter links these emotional arguments to foundational assumptions associated with the nature of men and women, and the band of brothers myth. I argue that emotional reactions to women in combat draw on, and reaffirm, the types of identities and stereotypes associated with the band of brothers myth. This myth is so powerful, and so deeply embedded in Western narratives, that it shapes "gut" reactions to women in combat. In particular, inherent in the band of brothers myth are assumptions regarding the nature of men and women, which are in turn evident throughout these emotional positions. This includes the presumption that men, as a result of their physical qualities, are the natural protectors of society, inherently brave, innately aggressive, and willing to use violence. By contrast, women's bodies, and their capacity to bear children, are depicted as rendering them weaker, more likely to be concerned with protecting life, more nurturing, and prone to peaceful conduct. This chapter is essential for setting up subsequent chapters, which demonstrate how these emotional views continue to influence specific, seemingly objective arguments related to the combat exclusion, including those related to physical standards and combat cohesion.

Third, this chapter explores the relationship between emotional arguments and so-called objective positions. The purpose of this chapter is not to argue that emotion "matters more" than so-called hard data or evidence, nor does it seek to establish a cause-and-effect relationship between emotions and policy. Rather, I argue that emotional and rational arguments related to women in combat cannot be separated; there is no clear division between emotional and so-called evidence-based positions on the combat exclusion. The emotional arguments used to oppose or resist the combat exclusion are often woven through discussions of objective evidence related to the exclusion. Rarely are the two streams of argument – the emotional and rational – discussed as mutually reinforcing and constitutive. This chapter argues that the emotional positions in relation to women and combat have been essential in legitimizing, filtering, inspiring, and discounting research and "facts" related to women in combat. In other words, emotional positions are inseparable from the available data on women in combat.

Through a discourse analysis of opinion pieces, news and journal articles, and blog posts and responses, this chapter identifies the arguments that arise consistently within academic and nonacademic literature related to women and combat. The chapter begins with what I call the surface-level, "gut reaction" response, which characterizes women in combat as something that just "feels wrong" and leads individuals to conclude that "they just don't belong" regardless of evidence, politics, or rights. I show how some of these positions draw inspiration from religious faith and beliefs about the natural order of humanity. This is followed by an exploration of more specific emotions associated with women in combat, including fear, anxiety, and loss. I argue here that the majority of the emotional responses related to women in combat are broadly concerned with identity and image. In particular, these fears and anxieties center on military and soldier identity, as well as the public image and status of the military both at home and abroad.

While this chapter draws from a range of sources, Brian Mitchell's book *Women in the Military: Flirting With Disaster* plays a central role through much of it, as it has provided one of the most extensive summaries of the emotional positions against women in combat. It should also be noted that there are several prominent voices, including Martin van Creveld, who are of the opinion that women should not be in the military at all, let alone in combat units. I have included some of these more general reactions against women in the military because they are relevant to understanding the resistance faced by women in the military. Along with the more specific reactions to women in combat, this contributes to the overall argument of the chapter, which links myth and emotion to American military policy.

GUT REACTIONS, DIVINE CONCERNS, AND THREATS TO NATURE

Trusting one's gut

The first category of emotional reactions to women in combat are expressed simply as "gut reactions." The gut reaction argument is an articulation of an inherent, personal opposition to women in combat. It sends the message that women in combat defy a set of intimate beliefs, ideals, and commitments not necessarily substantiated by evidence. This position is often articulated in the form of discomfort, inability to accept, or impassioned aversion. The statement by Gen. Merrill A. McPeak at the introduction of the chapter exemplifies this position.[2] Here, General McPeak seems to acknowledge that his position may not be reasonable; however, it is such a core belief that he does not feel he can "get over" it. His point is representative of other military experts and scholars who have declared no amount of evidence or data could address their deep-rooted aversion to women in combat.

In some cases, gut reaction arguments have been explicitly made in the face of data or evidence indicating that women are capable of filling combat roles. For example, in her book, Stephanie Gutmann declared, "[a]fter all the logical arguments about women in infantry have been made...the government will still have to deal with another objection, an instinctive 'no'; the recoil of the heart, of the nerves, and of the gut."[3] This line of argument places value on nonquantifiable beliefs, indicating that research and data may not be effective in altering these beliefs. Given the vast amount of research, data, and experience to draw from in making a decision about women in combat, it is interesting to note the value and legitimacy placed on personal, emotional reactions.

---

[2] Quoted in Gutmann, *The Kinder, Gentler Military*, 272–73.   [3] Ibid., 272.

God's will

Related to the gut reaction argument is the position that women in combat defy a set of divine ideals – or what I call the "divine will" argument. Simply put, this is the belief that God would not have wanted women in combat. Like the gut reaction argument, this position draws on faith and ideals, but in this case, a more explicit link is made between these arguments and Christianity. For example, in an opinion piece, psychiatrist and Fox News contributor Keith Ablow claimed, "I can't deny my core feeling that women – by virtue of their anatomy and physiology and whatever God-given ability to nurture they possess – would be impacted more negatively by mortal combat than men."[4] Within this comment, Ablow makes two interesting points. First, he emphasizes his "core" opposition to women in combat. Second, he links this feeling to women's apparent "God-given" nature. By linking his gut feelings to divine creation, he adds further legitimacy to his position. Moreover, the explicitly religious nature of the position renders it difficult to respond to or critique with research, because it is impossible to prove what is or is not "God-given."

Later in the same opinion piece, Ablow reiterates his point by saying, "By my very nature as a man, someplace deep in my soul, somewhere connected to God and truth, I want to protect women from violent death – even in war."[5] Again, by linking his feelings to "God and truth," Ablow connects his ideological position on women in war to divine will. He also attributes it to his "very nature as a man" with his apparent drive to protect women, making it seem natural, static, and beyond debate and reason. Both the gut reaction and divine will arguments legitimize the role of faith and feeling in policy debates. They also stunt debate because they present these feelings as natural and beyond critique, rationality, or logic. In turn, such expressions are conversation stoppers when it comes to women

---

4 Dr. Keith Ablow, "Why I Don't Ever Want to See Women in Combat, on the Front Lines," *Fox News* (May 19, 2012), http://www.foxnews.com/opinion/2012/05/19/why-dont-ever-want-to-see-women-in-combat-on-front-lines/.
5 Ibid.

in combat. They indicate that the person expressing the emotion is attached to his or her position "at their core," and that no amount of debate or evidence could change this position.

Harnessing

Generalized feelings that women serving in combat "is just wrong" or "feels wrong" are consistently harnessed to seemingly more objective or quantifiable justifications. This section explores harnessing, my term for the association of apparent facts to emotional arguments and moral beliefs – for example, about the nature of women and men and their "proper" roles in society. American Civil Rights Union fellow Robert Knight's reaction to women in combat provides an excellent example with which to begin this analysis. In a *Washington Times* opinion piece, Knight declared, "The military has kept women out of direct ground combat for a moral reason: Deliberately putting women in harm's way is not right; and for practical reasons [sic]: Women are not as physically strong, and they have an impact on the men around them."[6] Knight goes on to argue, "[i]n a civilized society, men are raised to protect women. Now some of America's elite warrior units train men to be indifferent to women's screams. That's what passes for 'progress' in a 'progressive' military."[7]

Knight begins by referencing "practical reasons" and claiming that women are physically weaker than men. He also connects his judgment that "putting women in harm's way is not right" to the claim that there is objective evidence about women's physical weaknesses. Knight does not focus on these substantive points. Instead he begins making more general claims about the impact women have on men, and the uncivilized nature of women in combat. Knight links seemingly objective comments about physical standards to emotional and ideological claims. The claim that in a "civilized society" men

---

[6] Robert Knight, "Deceitful Debate over Women in Combat," *Washington Times* (November 30, 2012), http://theacru.org/acru/deceitful_debate_over_women_in_combat/.

[7] Ibid.

should protect women is an emotional belief, based on ideals, images, and myths; it has absolutely nothing to do with physical standards, or anything that could be identified as "practical." Interestingly, in a *Washington Post* article, Sally Quinn similarly concluded, "If we can't win a war without our mothers, what kind of a sorry fighting force are we? Even the evil Saddam Hussein doesn't send mothers to fight his war."[8] Grounding this emotional position in remarks about physical qualities and "practical" reasons serves to legitimize the argument. It places the emotional position on par with debates on physical standards and seemingly objective obstacles to women in combat. In this sense, the reference to "practical reasons" and the physical qualities of women stands as a sort of nodal point, from which more emotional and subjective beliefs can be harnessed and justified.

Natural order

The ideal of men as natural protectors of both women and society is prevalent in emotional arguments against women in combat. For example, in an opinion piece on women in combat, Bill Muehlenberg argued that "one of the strongest male instincts is to protect females," and that "the male role of protector is under attack by the feminist movement."[9] Neither element of Muehlenberg's position can be verified. It is not possible to detect, measure, and rank the inherent instincts of all men, and moreover, the idea that the inclusion of women within the military necessarily attacks the role of men is equally difficult to substantiate. In turn, Muehlenberg's argument should be seen as expressing two emotions, a belief about male instincts, and a fear or concern that the role of men is under attack as a result of feminist efforts to open combat roles to women.

This line of argument is not concerned with measuring the capacity of women as soldiers, or their potential role within the

---

8 "Mothers at War: What Are We Doing to Our Kids?," *Washington Post* (February 23, 1991), http://www.highbeam.com/doc/1P2-1050933.html.

9 Bill Muehlenberg, "Women in Combat," CultureWatch, accessed June 12, 2014, http://billmuehlenberg.com/2011/04/12/women-in-combat/.

institution. Instead, the inclusion of women is presented as a challenge to the nature of men and their privileged role in society. Some have explicitly identified the protective instinct of men as an inherently chivalrous characteristic that requires fostering and protection. For example, Ablow claims that including women in combat would "bleed out some wonderful chivalrous quality in men."[10] There is an emotional expression here, not only of a fear of change, but of a potential loss of precious and essential qualities in men. In other words, women might take away from men's natural roles and could alter or erode the "natural" and honorable qualities of the male protector. In turn, "honorable" men should both protect the nation and resist women taking this role from them. General Westmoreland summarizes this position, saying, "No man with gumption wants a woman to fight his Nation's battles. I do not believe the American public wants to see a woman . . . do a man's job and that is to fight."[11] Here you have assumptions made about how men should feel about women in combat, a sweeping presumption about how the American public should feel, and a reaffirmation that war is the "business of men."

Another "natural order" argument found within these discussions focuses on the capacity of women as mothers, and their presumed inherent, peaceful, and weak qualities. Perhaps the clearest articulation of this can be found in David Robertson's claim that "a woman's duty is to give life, not to take it."[12] In a blog post on women in combat, Bill Muehlenberg also offers some of the strongest arguments made in relation to mothers and combat. In his opinion piece he quotes an unnamed female soldier who served in Iraq as stating: "[i]t's like this: I'm a woman and a mother before I am a soldier. Out here I think more about my family than my job, and, yes, that could

---

[10] Ablow, "Why I Don't Ever Want to See Women in Combat."

[11] Quoted in Judith Wagner Decew, "The Combat Exclusion and the Role of Women in the Military," *Hypatia* 10, no. 1 (1995): 56–73.

[12] Gerard J. DeGroot, "A Few Good Women: Gender Stereotypes, the Military and Peacekeeping," *International Peacekeeping* 8, no. 2 (2001): 23–38.

affect my performance if things get intense here."[13] In his assessment of the statement Muehlenberg concludes: "Thankfully this soldier could not renounce her *deep-down* maternal instincts. No woman should be forced to do so. But her *proper* concern for her family meant she was far less effective as a soldier, and could potentially put her on-field comrades at real risk."[14]

Muehlenberg makes two central claims in his assessment. First, that the female soldier's comments are gender specific. That is, it is assumed that it is the woman's "deep-down maternal instincts" that motivate her to think about her family. The implication is that men would not have similar feelings or priorities. Second, there is a belief that prioritizing one's family necessarily negatively impacts the ability to do one's job as a soldier. The woman quoted admits that this "could" affect her performance, but this would be nearly impossible to prove. Yet, Muehlenberg extends this possibility and makes a general claim that the woman not only was less effective, but could also have put her fellow soldiers at risk. As a result, a potentially offhand remark about valuing family has been turned into the foundation for asserting that women are less effective soldiers who put their comrades at risk.

The view that women, being preservers of life, are naturally more peaceful has resulted in judgments about those women who choose roles in the military. Some emotional reactions against female soldiers include characterizing them as exceptions, or worse. As Laura Sjoberg and Caron Gentry noted, women who take on these "exceptional roles," particularly those who take part in violence, are often characterized as morally corrupt.[15] Brian Mitchell highlights the stereotypes associated with women who volunteer, saying, "Many Americans could believe only that the kind of women who would join the Army were not the kind to take home to mother."[16] Speaking more specifically about women in defense academies, he

---

[13] Muehlenberg, "Women in Combat."   [14] Ibid. Emphasis added.

[15] Laura Sjoberg and Caron E. Gentry, *Mothers, Monsters, Whores: Women's Violence in Global Politics* (Zed Books, 2007).

[16] Mitchell, *Women in the Military*, 5.

goes on to note, "As the first few women wandered in, rumors arose impugning the honor of the recruits. Tales of rampant promiscuity and lesbianism were met with indignant denials from the services. Official investigations found little to substantiate the rumors, but the damage was done nonetheless."[17] In many ways, it is unclear what Mitchell's point is in reiterating "rumors" that were found to be untrue. Thus, Mitchell's comments in fact revive and give life to such characterizations of women as exceptional, unsavory, and potentially immoral.

The belief that women are "natural" peacemakers and that men are "natural" protectors of society seem to go hand in hand. Women's "violation" of their natural role is treated as an affront to men's privileged role as protectors. Moreover, women's participation in violence is sometimes treated as a sign of a natural imbalance, or of men's inability or failure to sustain their duties to society. Dr. Keith Ablow summarizes the belief that women should be protected rather than protectors, saying, "In my opinion, I do not believe women should serve as combat soldiers. I know they are fully able to do so. I know they would acquit themselves spectacularly well. But I can't deny that I value the special place of women in society as a protected gender."[18] This is a conflicted position because it presents women as a special "protected" gender at the same time that it acknowledges women might be able to fulfill combat roles. This serves to reify a notion of the natural place of men as the protectors and women as the protected. Again, here we have an example where emotions and beliefs are given greater value and legitimacy than evidence, practice, or research.

MILITARY AND SOLDIER IDENTITY

Fear

In addition to gut reactions, divine concerns, and threats to nature, there is another category of emotional reactions centered around

---

[17] Ibid.   [18] Ablow, "Why I Don't Ever Want to See Women in Combat."

military and soldier identity. In particular, fear is a prominent emotion expressed in relation to women in combat. Although fear is not an emotion that is necessarily grounded in "rational" evidence, fears associated with almost any aspect of the military tend to be taken seriously. Specifically, fears surrounding a soldier's ability to do his or her job, a unit's capacity to fulfill a mission, or the military's ability to win a war are translated into fears of decreased security. Because no one wants to risk or threaten national security, fears about the potential of such risks carry significant weight.

There are five discernable fears associated with women in combat. First is the fear that women will feminize the military. The main idea here is that including more women, and in particular, allowing women to "infiltrate" male-only units and take on traditionally male-only roles, will alter the character of the military. It is thought that women threaten the masculine nature of the military, or feminize the institution. This position is perhaps most clearly articulated by Anita Blair, the former Chairman of the Congressional Commission on Military Training and Gender-Related Issues. Blair concluded, "the objective for many who advocate greater female influence in the armed services is not so much to conquer the military as conquer manhood: They aim to make the most quintessentially masculine of our institutions more feminine."[19] Military historian Martin van Creveld has also consistently argued that the increase in women in militaries across the world has coincided with the decline of the institutions.[20] The logic here is that the military thrives on a masculine culture that is central to operational effectiveness. Women necessarily detract and weaken this essential character and thereby the effectiveness of the forces. This links back overtly to the band of brothers myth, which treats war as the business of men, and women as outsiders or even a threat to this natural configuration.

---

[19] Quoted in Helena Carreiras and Gerhard Kümmel, *Women in the Military and in Armed Conflict* (Springer Science & Business Media, 2008), 25.

[20] Martin van Creveld, "The Great Illusion Women in the Military," *Journal of International Studies* 29, no. 2 (2000): 429–42.

A second, related fear is that women will somehow castrate the military, or make it androgynous. Throughout the literature and debates on women in the military, individuals express an explicit fear that threats to masculine practices and a reduction in the number of men would create an "androgynous" military. In an opinion piece on women in combat, Bill Muehlenberg accuses feminists of threatening the gender identity of the military, claiming that "feminists have long argued for not just the right but the necessity of having women in combat roles. This is part of their vain attempt to push for androgyny and a gender-neutral society."[21] In his description of gender integration within military academies, Brian Mitchell contends that the "sharing of experience by men and women in order to mold androgynous warriors would necessarily have made the women more masculine and the men more feminine, had not the men resisted this imposition on their inner most self."[22] Interestingly, androgyny has also been talked about as a characteristic that military women may embody if they take on too many masculine traits. Antifeminist author Carolyn Graglia blames feminist advocates for pushing women into masculine roles. She concludes that these efforts represent the "goal of defeminizing women so as to make them androgynous male equivalents."[23]

Explicit references to the castration of the military as a result of women in combat are largely found in more informal blogs and opinion pieces. A *New York Times* article on the removal of the combat exclusion noted some of the negative responses to the announcement found within online discussions, including the comment "the castration of the U.S. Army continues."[24] In a blog post on diversity in the military, Johnny Cirucci laments the devolution of an institution that is the "linchpin for all society." He specifically argues that the inclusion of openly serving gays and lesbians and women has eroded

---

[21] Quoted in Muehlenberg, "Women in Combat."

[22] Mitchell, *Women in the Military*, 44.   [23] Quoted in "Women in Combat."

[24] "Women in the Battlefield," *New York Times* (January 24, 2013), sec. Opinion, http://www.nytimes.com/2013/01/25/opinion/women-in-the-battlefield.html.

the essential nature of the military. Pointing to the follies of "the left" and the Pentagon, he worries that "they won't stop until every real, God-fearing man of courage and integrity is turned into a castrated metrosexual pansy."[25] The website "Leatherneck.com" hosts more than 100,000 members who participate in forums on various US military issues. A 2004 post by one of the moderators was entitled "The Castration of the U.S. Military." It criticized the recent decision to change the Uniform Code of Military Justice, making paying for sex a punishable offense. The moderator links this decision to broader signs of the "feminization" of the military: "The people who introduced the world to the Tailhook Kangaroo Court, sensitivity training for combat troops, stress cards, coed basic training, grandmothers in combat zones – and my personal favorite, the "maternity battle dress uniform" – have now decided that prostitution is to be a military crime."[26]

There are two important conclusions to draw from this position that link back to the band of brothers story. First, metaphor and imagery, here in the image of castration, are explicitly used to express a fear. Using an emotional argument, based on a metaphor, to oppose a "real" policy brings home the significance of emotion, belief, myth, and ideas to politics and identity. Second, the imagery of castration implies that women remove some essential element of the military and thereby are a threat to military culture and identity. In turn, there is a tendency not only to explicitly identify military culture and identity as male, but also to treat the military as if it is the phallus of the nation, and combat units as if they were the "tip of the spear" of this phallic member. In this sense the size, nature, and capabilities of the military are positively associated with national identity. This

[25] Johnny Cirucci, "GENDERCIDE: How Women And Gays Are Destroying the U.S. Military," Before It's News, June 27, 2013, http://beforeitsnews.com/blogging-citizen-journalism/2013/06/gendercide-how-women-and-gays-are-destroying-the-u-s-military-2448232.html.

[26] "The Castration of the U.S. Military," Forum, Leatherneck.com (June 2002), http://www.leatherneck.com/forums/showthread.php?16930-The-Castration-of-the-U-S-Military.

casts the military as both protector of the nation and an institution in need of preservation and protection. To put it more crudely, the "phallus" of the nation, by nature, cannot include women, and combat units, the most important and yet vulnerable part of the military, most assuredly cannot include women.

The third related fear associated with women in the military generally, and women in combat more specifically, is that women will diminish essential military culture. Terms such as "weakening," "diluting," and "softening" have all been associated with transitions that have taken place as women are integrated into the military. Brian Mitchell posits that "life in the services had softened considerably" as a result of the changes following the transition to an all-volunteer force in the US military.[27] Mitchell sarcastically quips that occupants of dormitories "were allowed to decorate as they please" [while] "[m]ess halls became 'dining facilities.'"[28] He quotes Lieutenant General Albert P. Clark, who concluded that gender integration risked "water[ing] down the entire program."[29] Again, this position treats the military as an inherently masculine institution and characterizes women as a threat that erodes its essential qualities.

The fourth fear linked to the increase of women in the military is that women will cause a recruitment problem. This is a fear that men, or the "right" kind of men, will no longer want to join the US forces as the number of women increases. Mitchell argues that one problem with the move to an all-volunteer force that includes women is that it has "sought to decrease the need for men by taking greater use of civilians and women, never considering that an all-male military might attract more men than a thoroughly feminized one."[30] Van Creveld expresses a similar fear that "as women enter them, the armed forces in question will become both less willing to fight and less capable of doing so."[31] Mitchell concluded that within

---

[27] Lieut. Gen. Clark quoted in Mitchell, *Women in the Military*, 24.
[28] Ibid., 24.   [29] Ibid.   [30] Mitchell, *Women in the Military*.
[31] Martin van Creveld, *Men, Women & War: Do Women Belong in the Front Line?* (London: Cassell, 2002).

the first year of the all-volunteer force, "it had already become apparent that the services were not attracting enough of the right kind of men."[32] Echoing elements of the band of brothers myth again, these quotes indicate a firm belief that the "right" kind of man does not want to work alongside women. Conversely, it would follow that men, naturally, "should" prefer all-male units.

The fifth fear associated with the inclusion of women is that women threaten the essential masculine atmosphere of training academies and operational units. In his discussion of the changes to military academies as a result of gender integration, Mitchell laments that, as a result of gender integration, "the academies were converted from 'bastions of male chauvinism' to institutions officially dedicated to the feminist principles of equality and androgyny."[33] Here, Mitchell is describing what he sees as an unfortunate attack on the masculine traditions and practices within military academies for the sake of integration and improved gender relations. He argues that the move to integrated military academies has resulted in a threat to the "Spartan atmosphere – which is so important to producing the final product."[34] This fear that women threaten the atmosphere of training academies depicts women as a threat to the sacred masculine space that the military requires. Once again, this reflects key elements of the band of brothers myth in that it treats the all-male space and units as revered and necessary for the preservation and progression of society.

Loss

Related to this fear of altering the essential training atmosphere is the emotion of loss. The characterization of the military as masculine classifies the institution as a "natural home" for men, and a place where they can fully articulate their gender identity. According to this perspective, women's integration in the military not only threatens

---

[32] Mitchell, *Women in the Military*, 24.   [33] Ibid., 55.
[34] Lieut. Gen. Clark, cited in Mitchell, *Women in the Military*, 29.

the masculine character of the military, it also jeopardizes what is seen as a sacred space for men. In his Afghanistan war memoir, US Army Infantry Officer Andrew Exum emphatically described the infantry as "one of the last places where that most endangered of species, the alpha male, can feel at home."[35] In turn, women's inclusion evokes a sense of loss for men, as well as feelings of nostalgia for an earlier time. Reflecting elements of the band of brothers myth, masculine men are depicted as a threatened or diminishing class that requires a sort of protected physical space within institutions such as the military. The implication is that integrating women inevitably reduces these spaces and harms the ability of particular ideal types of men to thrive.

Embarrassment and shame

A related emotional argument is that the inclusion of women somehow embarrasses military men and reduces their ability feel proud as soldiers. When describing how the first integrated basic training (BT) class of the Air Force in 1980 was treated, Mitchell reports that the men in the class were frequently identified as "Eighty's Ladies" and accused of going through an easier BT than previous cohorts.[36] Similarly, all-male Marine units have been cast as superior and training better soldiers than integrated units in other services – for example, "The Marines self-consciously trained warriors, and compared to the new, more motherly Army, the Marines are indeed extreme."[37] These fears that women's presence somehow taints the natural and sacred environment of the alpha male and reduces the masculine character of men is not only reflective of band of brothers narratives, but also reminiscent of children's schoolyard games where boys and girls protect imaginary boundaries and scream with terror that they are infected with boy or girl cooties by their mere presence or touch.

There are four assumptions behind both the "feminizing the military" and the "androgynous military" fears. First, that the

---

[35] Exum, *This Man's Army.*   [36] Ibid.
[37] Mitchell, *Women in the Military*, 42–43.

military has a gender, and that the gender is masculine. Second, that the military attains some of its positive image and reputation from its masculine character/image. Third, that associating women or feminine qualities with the military will corrupt this character. And finally, that the masculine character or image of the military comes from male bodies and warrior culture, and the qualities of bravery and chivalry are connected to male bodies.

This simplistic view holds that fewer male bodies would equal less masculine qualities for the military. It also assumes that all men are able to fulfill the masculine expectations of the military equally. That men are naturally, inherently, and eagerly masculine in the way that the military expects them to be. It treats masculinity as singular and men as unified, ignoring the potential for any variation of qualities, personalities, or desires among men or women. The thinking is that in order for the military to be effective, it must be a masculine institution, assuming that all men within the institution exhibit or can exhibit particular masculine traits. There seems to be a presumption that masculinity is inherent and necessary. This is a remarkable position in that it identifies warfare as an expression of masculinity and not a political response or a foreign policy tactic.

Body bags and emotions

A final emotional argument to discuss centers around the image of the female body bag. One of the most common concerns associated with women in combat is summarized in the title of a 1991 *Boston Globe* article: "Women in harm's way: Is America really ready to see female soldiers die?"[38] It is interesting to note that discussions of female casualties are consistently framed around the image of women in body bags. As indicated earlier, Brian Mitchell has argued that women, because of their ability to give birth, should be protected in society. He laments feminist calls for women to go into battle alongside their male counterparts, despite this biological difference. Mitchell

---

[38] Ibid., xii.

declares, "society must concede, say feminists, that the potentiality of motherhood is no reason for viewing a young woman's remains in a body bag with any more horror than a young man's."[39]

The body bag image and description has become a fixation that signals a variety of anxieties, fears, and concerns related to women in combat. A 2013 news article summarized the overarching claim: "Traditional attitudes make many people both uncomfortable with the idea of women fighting and unable to handle the image of mothers coming home in body bags."[40] In her personal blog, pediatrician Meg Meeker pushes the argument further, contending, "Mothers should not come home in body bags... *When a woman becomes a mother, she signs off the right to deliberately put herself in life-threatening situations.*"[41] There are three sets of emotional claims tied to the "body bag" image: first, that the American public will react differently to the death of women in war – specifically, that female casualties will negatively impact support for a war; second, that the difference between male and female casualties lies, at least in part, in women's capacity to give birth; and third, that the death of American female soldiers represents a weakness of the military as an institution in its inability to protect its most vulnerable.

The first emotional claim associated with the body bag image – that the American public will react differently to female casualties and there will be less support for war as female deaths increase – is somewhat more quantifiable compared to some of the emotional reactions discussed earlier in this chapter. Interestingly, although it is treated as common sense that the general public has difficulty seeing women, especially mothers, go to war and struggles with the prospect of having them come home in body bags, available evidence

---

[39] Otile McManus, "Women in Harm's Way: Is America Really Ready to See Female Soldiers Die?," *Boston Globe* (January 24, 1991), online edition, sec. Special sections.

[40] Muehlenberg, "Women in Combat."

[41] Emily Sohn, "Why Can't Women Serve at the Front?," DNews, November 28, 2012, http://news.discovery.com/human/psychology/women-military-front-120213.htm.

does not support this. An ABC News report on the Gulf War found that although the Pentagon may have "fretted about a public opinion backlash" regarding female deaths, according to research, "it was a fear that largely proved unfounded."[42]

Similarly, while the media tends to treat instances of female death and injury as unique (the attention given to Jessica Lynch is a good example), there is little indication that the death of female service members evokes a unique public reaction. In an extensive study on casualties and public opinion, Scott Sigmund Gartner concluded that the gender of a casualty has "little role" in public opinion except when "casualty uncertainty" (or the inability of individuals to predict casualty patterns) is high.[43] Moreover, in a more general study, Christopher Gelpi noted that there is little relationship at all between *any* casualty rates, male or female, and public support for war. Gelpi argues that the public tends to be supportive of wars, even those with high casualty rates, so long as the war is deemed to be winnable and achieving legitimate objectives.[44] The body bag argument, therefore, should be seen as a set of anecdotal claims centered around the presumption that public support for the war depends on all-male units and the protection of women.

The third element of the body bag argument is that female casualties negatively impact the image or reputation of a military in a way that male casualties do not. Ablow summarizes this position by saying, "I just don't think it is some vestige of a prejudiced, Neanderthal perspective I harbor that I believe our nation could be doubly demoralized by women coming back from war in body bags in

---

[42] Meg Meeker, "Moms, Body Bags, and Combat," Meg Meeker, M.D, January 28, 2013, http://www.megmeekermd.com/2013/01/moms-body-bags-and-combat/. Emphasis in original.

[43] Leela Jacinto, "Girl Power: Women Join the Boys in Combat, But Not Without a Fight," ABC News, January 14, 2011, online edition, sec. Original Report, http://www.realnews247.com/girl_power.htm.

[44] Scott Sigmund Gartner, "Secondary Casualty Information: Casualty Uncertainty, Female Casualties, and Wartime Support," *Conflict Management and Peace Science* 25, no. 2 (April 1, 2008): 106.

equal numbers to men."[45] Unfortunately, this broad position is also difficult to quantify, as it refers to subjective value judgments external actors may hold regarding a national military. The fear expressed in this argument depicts a generalization that militaries should only have to rely on women in emergency situations, and that militaries that use women are less noble and masculine.

There is no doubt that the image of women in body bags holds significant emotional purchase. Interestingly, it is the verbal or written reference to the female body bag, and not any specific image, that is evoked by media and military experts. This image is used to instill fear and anxiety about women's vulnerability in war, and to warn them of a publicity crisis that might arise as a result of women's deaths. Yet the available research tells us that these concerns are largely unfounded. Rather than reflecting evidence regarding public perceptions of female casualties, the image of a woman being brought home in a body bag has come to symbolize specific fears associated with increasing the role of women in the forces. These fears reaffirm key elements of the band of brothers myth. In particular, they are based on the presumption that all-male units instill confidence in the public and are the rightful protectors of the nation. The body bags argument, therefore, perpetuates perceptions that female casualties enfeeble a military and taint its reputation in a way that male casualties do not.

CONCLUSION

One of the key objectives of this chapter was to demonstrate how influential the band of brothers myth has been in shaping emotional reactions to women in combat. Although one certainly cannot establish a "cause and effect" relationship when it comes to emotion, it is possible to show trends. In the case of women in combat, emotional reactions are consistently shaped by ideals associated with natural

---

[45] Thomas J. Leeper, "Fallen Soldiers, Declining Support for War," *Psychology Today* (May 25, 2012), accessed June 12, 2014, http://www.psychologytoday.com/blog/polarized/201205/fallen-soldiers-declining-support-war.

order, divine will, the inherent nature of men and women, and the rightful place of men and women in a civilized society. These ideals have been shaped and influenced by band of brothers myths, which depict men as inherently violent, brave, and heroic – the natural protectors of society – and the all-male unit as essential to order and social progress. Conversely, women are treated as essential in reproducing the nation by maintaining a role as mothers in the home. When one places the emotional reactions against women in combat within this context, it is possible to trace each of the emotions, whether it is fear, aversion, or faith, to messages and ideals established by the band of brothers myth.

More specifically, the fear that women in combat goes against the will of God assumes as a certainty that violence and protectiveness are natural to men, while women are inherently peaceful. It determines that a public, politically active, potentially violent female violates these divine qualities. The fear that women dilute or weaken the military requires an ideal of a masculine, male-dominated military structure and a weaker, feminized subject that cannot contribute to the institution in the same manner as men. Third, the fear that women in combat dilute the image of the military presumes that progress, honor, and civility are dependent on an all-male military and that women's contribution or sacrifice for the national military sends a message that the men of the military are not able to do the job and are not able to sufficiently protect "their" women.

Discussions and debates about women and combat are emotional. Politicians, scholars, and the public readily express strong reactions, feelings, and beliefs about women's natural and appropriate place during war. This chapter has attempted to place emotion at the center of the analysis on women in combat. I argue that it is very difficult to study the combat exclusion without first mapping out the main emotional reactions to women in combat. This chapter provides such an overview. Moreover, the chapter makes the case that these emotional positions are not "separate" or disconnected from seemingly more objective positions on the subject. Rather, emotional arguments are often attached, interwoven, or harnessed to apparently fact-based positions, including statements about physical standards, troop dynamics, and women's capabilities. In other words, the position "it is just wrong" or "it feels wrong" is linked to seemingly more objective or quantifiable reasons as to why this feeling is justified. In turn, understanding the core emotional reactions and responses to this issue is essential to providing a complete picture of the debates and policy changes regarding women in combat. This chapter is essential for setting up the analysis because, through the rest of the book, I demonstrate how these core emotional arguments often underpin and inform so-called objective debates related to women in combat.

4 Faster, stronger, more male: women and the failure of physical standards

"Have men these days 'gone soft?' Is our generation less manly than past generations? Are we less tough than our grandfathers?"[1]

The argument that women simply cannot "make the cut" and compete physically with men has consistently been the most prominent argument for keeping them out of combat units. Stephanie Gutmann summarizes this position: "When butts drop onto seats, and feet grope for foot pedals, and girls of five feet one (not an uncommon height in the ranks) put on great bowl-like Kevlar helmets over a full head of long hair done up in a French braid, there are problems of fit – and those picayune fit problems ripple outward, eventually affecting performance, morale, and readiness." This chapter argues that these physical arguments are not as objective and straightforward as they appear. Physical capabilities seem to be easy to measure and evaluate – particularly in comparison to subjective qualities such as bravery, or complex concepts such as cohesion. Moreover, the main argument associated with women and physical standards appears to be quite simple – women are described as weaker than men, and therefore less able to do the types of activities required by infantry soldiers. Assessing the validity of this physical argument should also be relatively straightforward. Evidence indicates that there are clear differences in physical qualities between men and women and that, on average, women are indeed weaker than men.

---

[1] Brett McKay and Kate McKay, "Are You as Fit as a World War II GI?" (September 12, 2011). The Art of Manliness, accessed June 13, 2014, http://www.artofmanliness.com/2011/09/12/are-you-as-fit-as-a-world-war-ii-gi/.

However, if we go beyond this initial position, the arguments associated with physical standards are more complex. It is quite a large leap from the assertion that women are weaker than men, to the argument that this weakness necessarily renders women incapable of fulfilling combat roles. There are two key assumptions inherent in this argument. The first is that the physical difference between men and women is insurmountable. In other words, biology is destiny, even with training or adapting tasks. The second assumption is that combat requires unique physical skills not needed for other military roles, and that women lack these particular physical skills. These assumptions treat combat as exceptionally physically demanding and an activity that necessarily requires male bodies.

This chapter endeavors to unravel the physical standards argument. Although the combat exclusion has been lifted, debates about the physical capabilities of women ensue within both the public and the armed forces as the military leadership makes decisions about the physical standards for men and women. There continues to be a widespread understanding that women are a physical liability when it comes to combat, and that it is only exceptional women who are able to match their male comrades physically. The point of this chapter is not to argue that there are no physical differences between women and men, but rather, to demonstrate the subjective nature of the physical capabilities debate. Although physical standards appear unbiased, these discussions are often woven together with emotions, ideals, and the band of brothers myth. In particular, the belief that male bodies are essential components of fighting units, and that all-male units are capable of achievements that mixed-gender units are not, shapes much of this debate. This chapter builds on Carol Cohn's work on physical standards, which concluded that "standards discourse cannot be understood on its own terms ... it also stands in for, and ventriloloquates, a series of *feelings* and meanings that are not acceptable for men to say directly in public, or sometimes, even to themselves. For some men, these include not only anger about having to compete with women, but also feelings of rage and loss about the ways *their* institution has changed."[2]

This chapter begins with an analysis of physical standards, which are presented as gender-neutral mechanisms for ensuring physical fitness, readiness, and capacity to serve within the military. I review current physical requirements in order to evaluate the argument that women not only are weaker, but are held to a lower standard than men in the forces. Next, I focus on the widely held belief that there are specific standards and requirements for infantry within the Army. This assumption has been the linchpin of the arguments for the combat exclusion and has been perpetuated not only by the media, but also by military experts who consistently refer to women not making the cut when it comes to combat. Three specific emotional positions related to physical standards are explored in this analysis. The first is fear that women will dilute or weaken physical standards. The second is frustration or anger that women are privy to double standards when it comes to physical requirements. And the third is pride in the exceptional physical capabilities of infantry forces, and a desire to protect the exclusivity of this group.

A recent *USA Today* article on the subject summarized the question dominating discussions of women in combat: "The debate about whether women should serve in the infantry and other direct ground combat roles has come to this: Are they physically strong enough?"[3] This question implies that there are in fact specific physical standards for combat roles, and that women are not readily able to meet them. This argument is summarized within Lieutenant

[2] Carol Cohn, "'How Can She Claim Equal Rights When She Doesn't Have to Do as Many Push-Ups as I Do?' The Framing of Men's Opposition to Women's Equality in the Military," *Men and Masculinities* 3, no. 2 (October 1, 2000): 147 Emphasis added.

[3] Jim Michaels, "Strength Key in Women-in-Combat Debate; Services Look at Physical Demands of Certain Jobs," *USA Today*, February 4, 2013.

General Jerry Boykin's opinion piece, released shortly after the combat exclusion was lifted. Boykin claims:

> [The removal of the combat exclusion] is the wrong policy because
> it ignores fundamental biological differences between the sexes,
> and the natural implications of those differences. While so much
> is made of new "high-tech" forms of warfare, we have seen in Iraq
> and Afghanistan that ground combat still requires levels of sheer
> physical strength, speed and endurance that are relatively rare
> among women. If current physical standards are maintained, few
> women will be able to meet them, and there will be demands that
> they are lowered. If those standards are lowered, the effectiveness
> of the fighting force will be directly compromised.[4]

Seven key questions must be addressed in order to unpack the arguments surrounding the physical capabilities of women in combat. These include:

i. Are women weaker than men?
ii. Is physical difference insurmountable?
iii. What are the physical standards for men and women in the military, and are there double standards for women?
iv. Are there combat-specific physical requirements?
v. Do combat roles require enhanced, or different, physical capabilities than other roles within the military?
vi. Do physical standards discriminate against women?
vii. Is the physical argument only about standards?

The structure of this chapter reflects these seven questions. Given the vast amount of research related to this topic, some of which is conflicting, I have tried to simplify the discussion as well as I can while still presenting a thorough overview of the data related to each of these questions.

---

[4] Jerry Boykin, "New Policy Ignores Biological Realities," *USA Today*, January 25, 2013.

I. ARE WOMEN WEAKER THAN MEN?

One of the arguments used to justify the exclusion of women from combat has been that women are weaker than men, which renders them unable to meet the physical requirements of combat. Kingsley Brown summarized the first element of this position by saying, "the sexes differ not only in strength...but in a host of other attributes, such as speed, aerobic and anaerobic capacity, endurance, throwing speed and accuracy, height, weight, bone mass, and amount of oxygen-carrying hemoglobin to their blood."[5] The second element of this argument is that the physical difference between men and women translates into poor job performance in the military. For example, Brian Mitchell claims that "the lack of physical strength among women will directly degrade the ability of units to fight and survive on the modern battlefield, inevitably resulting in a greater loss of life and a greater risk of defeat."[6] The following sections explore elements of this "weaker than" argument and consider whether physical difference is necessarily a liability for the ability of women to serve.

There is no denying that that on average there are physical differences between men and women, particularly in terms of strength. In her research report "Physical Fitness and Occupational Performance of Women in the U.S. Army," Marilyn Sharp describes some of these key differences: "The average female soldier weights 20% less than the average male soldier, has 10% more body fat, and has 30% less muscle mass... As women have more body fat and less fat-free mass, they are more likely to have slower run times and lower strength levels."[7] Researchers have also noted that, compared to men, women need to use a greater percentage of their strength to lift a similar load, and that women are less able to withstand pain.[8] In

---

[5] Browne, *Co-Ed Combat*, 22.   [6] Mitchell, *Women in the Military*, 147.

[7] Marilyn Sharp, "Physical Fitness and Occupational Performance of Women in the U.S. Army" (Occupational Physiology Division, U.S. Army Research Institute of Environmental Medicine, October 2, 1994), http://www.dtic.mil/cgi-bin/GetTRDoc?AD=ADA285676.

[8] "Women Feel Pain More than Men," BBC, July 4, 2005, sec. Health, http://news.bbc.co.uk/2/hi/health/4641567.stm.

formulating his argument against women in combat, Brian Mitchell also cites a comprehensive study on male and female athletes. It found significant differences in physical capacities, even among extremely fit individuals.[9] Mitchell uses this study to conclude that the "likelihood that a randomly selected man would be stronger than a randomly selected woman is over 99 percent."[10] Again comparing combat to sports, Browne laments the inclusion of women in the military when physical differences are so apparent, saying, "One must question a system that rigorously segregates the sexes in sports but is willing to integrate them in the military where the stakes are so much higher – with lives and not just trophies on the line."[11]

II. IS PHYSICAL DIFFERENCE INSURMOUNTABLE?

The "weaker than" argument treats physical differences between men and women as an indication that women cannot complete all of the same tasks as men. Although it has been acknowledged that men and women are, on average, physically different, evidence suggests that this does not necessarily mean that women are unable to complete the same physical tasks as male soldiers. In other words, biology might not be operational destiny.

Research from militaries around the world has shown that with proper training and necessary adaptations, women can complete the same physical tasks as men. For example, the Canadian military initiated the Service Women in Non-Traditional Environments and Roles (SWINTER) trials in the late 1970s to test women's physical, psychological, and social capacity for all military roles.[12] These trials were replaced with the Combat Related Employment of Women (CREW) trials, which focused more specifically on women in combat roles.

---

[9] P. Bishop, K. Cureton, and M. Collins, "Sex Difference in Muscular Strength in Equally-Trained Men and Women," *Ergonomics* 30, no. 4 (April 1987): 675–87, cited in Mitchell, *Women in the Military*, 24.

[10] Mitchell, *Women in the Military*, 24.   [11] Browne, *Co-Ed Combat*, 19.

[12] Laurie Lee Weinstein and Christie C. White, *Wives and Warriors: Women and the Military in the United States and Canada* (Westport, CT: Greenwood Publishing Group, 1997).

The trials were largely seen as a success[13], and evidence from the results informed the final Canadian Human Rights Tribunal decision to remove their combat exclusion. In its ruling, the tribunal declared, "Women are, with training, capable of combat roles... Performance was not an issue as a result of SWINTER trials. Cohesion and the physical and environmental elements are susceptible to management."[14] Denmark lifted their combat exclusion[15] after conducting similar fitness trials in the late 1980s. The Danish trials concluded that women performed as well as men in land combat roles.[16] Research by the US military, from as early as 1994, has similarly concluded that "if the task does not require a maximal effort, or if she is allowed to self-pace, a woman can perform many tasks and meet the male standard of performance."[17] This same study noted that in many cases, physical tasks designed for male bodies could be redesigned or replaced with alternatives that better suited women's capabilities.

More recently, the Israeli Defense Forces sought to determine "whether gender differences in certain anthropometric and physical fitness parameters that are relevant to military task performance can be lessened after a 4-month gender integrated basic training (BT) period."[18] They found that while there was still a gap between male and female physical fitness after BT, there were several strategies for reducing this gap, including making more of an effort to recruit physically fit women, developing a pre–basic training course for women,

[13] Ibid.

[14] Canadian Human Rights Commission, "Annual Report" (Minister of Supply and Services Canada, Ottawa, 1994).

[15] Countries that allow women to serve in combat roles (in varying capacities) include Canada, Denmark, New Zealand, Poland, Romania, Eritrea, South Korea, Australia, Norway, Germany, Israel, Finland, Italy, Norway, Serbia, Sweden, and Switzerland.

[16] Paul Cawkill et al., "Women in Ground Close Combat Roles: The Experience of Other Nations and a Review of the Academic Literature" (Defence Science and Technology Laboratory UK, September 29, 2009), 21.

[17] Sharp, "Physical Fitness and Occupational Performance of Women in the U.S. Army."

[18] Ran Yanovich et al., "Differences in Physical Fitness of Male and Female Recruits in Gender-Integrated Army Basic Training," *Medicine and Science in Sports and Exercise* 40, no. 11 Suppl (November 2008): S654–59.

and employing an "assignment dependent basic selection regime, independent of gender, in order to decrease physical fitness differences between the battalion's soldiers."[19] Although the study acknowledged physical differences between men and women, it also identified mechanisms to reduce the impact of differences on operational capacities.

The physical capabilities argument also tends to ignore both the overlap in the physical capabilities of men and women, and the areas of physical fitness in which women consistently excel. For example, physical standards tests tend to focus on upper body strength, an area in which women on average are confirmed to be weaker. They tend to neglect the aspects of physical fitness in which women seem to consistently surpass men. For example, flexibility, endurance, and tolerating heat and humidity are all areas in which women tend to perform well.[20]

The physical capabilities argument is also weakened when one considers the problems inherent in comparing "average" male and female bodies.[21] Maia Goodell contends that the comparison of abstract averages ignores evidence about the types of women and men who actually join the military. Goodell points out that the military attracts individuals who are above average in terms of physical fitness and that physical training often minimizes differences between so-called average men and women. Goodell concluded that "while it is clear that the average man is stronger than the average woman, some women are stronger than some men." There is, in fact, an overlap in terms of strength capabilities.[22] Research from a position paper on the Canadian military written three years before it lifted the

---

[19] Ibid.

[20] "Five Myths about Women in Combat," *Washington Post* (May 25, 2011). Accessed June 13, 2014, http://www.washingtonpost.com/opinions/five-myths-about-women-in-combat/2011/05/25/AGAsavCH_story.html.

[21] Maia Goodell, "Physical-Strength Rationales for De Jure Exclusion of Women from Military Combat Positions," *Seattle University Law Review* 34, no. 1 (August 31, 2010): 17.

[22] Sharp, "Physical Fitness and Occupational Performance of Women in the US Army," 82.

combat exclusion supports the "overlap" claim: "physical conditioning increases the capabilities of women . . . while average differences between the genders persist after conditioning, the gender distributions tend to overlap. Thus, where these abilities are relevant to particular military trades, it is rational to screen for the ability rather than for gender, thereby selecting the most qualified individuals."[23]

In sum, biology is not destiny when it comes to women's ability to serve as soldiers. Women might "on average" be weaker than men, but the attention to averages has tended to privilege the male body and ignore the unique physical capabilities and positive physical attributes of women.

III. WHAT ARE THE PHYSICAL STANDARDS FOR MEN AND WOMEN IN THE MILITARY, AND ARE THERE DOUBLE STANDARDS FOR WOMEN?

Before considering questions of double standards, it is necessary to understand physical standards within the US military. The US military started trying to find ways to assess the fitness of its members as early as the 1920s. One of the first fitness tests included a 100-yard run, running jump, wall climb, hand grenade throw, and obstacle course. A more formalized assessment, called the Army Ground Forces Test, was introduced in 1942, to help ensure that new recruits would be physically ready to serve in World War II. Four years later, in 1946, a Physical Training School was created at Fort Bragg, where a training program and fitness test were codified in the Army's physical training manual. Physical standards have been revised multiple times since the 1940s, with the Army moving toward testing general fitness and not soldiers' capacity to complete operational tasks.[24]

[23] Donna Winslow and Jason Dunn, "Women in the Canadian Forces: Between Legal and Social Integration," *Current Sociology* 50, no. 5 (September 1, 2002): 653.

[24] Joseph J. Knapik and Whitfield B. East, "History of United States Army Physical Fitness and Physical Readiness Training," *U.S. Army Medical Department Journal*, June 2014, 5–19.

The contemporary Army Physical Readiness Test (APRT) was established in 1984. Although efforts are currently underway to revise it, the APRT remains the test that all recruits are subjected to when they enlist, and then twice yearly while serving. The test is composed of sit-ups, push-ups, and a timed run.[25] Despite the common perception that performance in the APRT directly correlates to job capacity, the General Accounting Office acknowledges that physical standards tests are not necessarily an indicator of operational effectiveness: "The physical fitness program is actually intended only to maintain the general fitness and health of military members and fitness testing is not aimed at assessing the capability to perform specific missions or military jobs."[26] In fact, there is some debate about the utility of generalized fitness tests for a military that requires varied skills and operational capabilities. One researcher found "no conclusive evidence that all military members, regardless of occupational specialty, unit assignment, age or gender, should acquire the same level of physical fitness."[27]

Military efforts to measure fitness are guided by federal laws related to affirmative action. In 1993, a federal law instructed the military to avoid double standards, gender quotas, or modified physical standards as a means of proactive recruiting. This has not always been interpreted by the military to mean that men and women are required to meet the exact same physical standards. In fact, in 1998, the General Accounting Office concluded that "a single fitness standard applicable to both men and women would be unfair to women

---

[25] In order to graduate from basic training, soldiers must attain 60 points for each of the three events. If soldiers fail, they retake the test within 3 months. Those who fail the Army Physical Fitness Test (APFT) are not eligible for promotion, reenlistment, or enlistment extension.

[26] US General Accounting Office, "Gender Issues: Information to Assess Servicemembers' Perceptions of Gender Inequities Is Complete. Report to Congressional Committees" (US General Accounting Office, November 1998).

[27] Helena Carreiras and Gerhard Kümmel, "Off Limits: The Cults of the Body and Social Homogeneity as Discursive Weapons Targeting Gender Integration in the Military," in Women in the Military and in Armed Conflict, edited by Carreiras and Kümmel, 29–47, http://www.springerlink.com/content/n437m33q28q88gk3/abstract/.

Table 1 *Physical requirements for service personnel*

Requirements for a maximum score	Army		Navy		Air Force		Marine	
	Male [17–21]	Female	Male [20–24]	Female [20–24]	Male [18–30]	Female	Male	Female
Push-ups	70	42	87	48	33	18		
Sit-ups	78	78	105	105				
Pull-ups							20	8
Run time [miles/minutes]	2/13	2/15:36	1.5/8:30	1.5/9:47	1.5/13:36	1.5/16:22	3/18	3/21
Crunches							100	100

because meeting that standard would require a much higher level of effort from a woman than it would from a man." In recognition of this, the services developed their own mechanisms for ensuring "equivalent training."[28] This meant developing mechanisms that required men and women to "exert the same amount of energy in a particular task, regardless of the work that is actually accomplished by either." As a result of what the military came to call "gender norming," specific physical requirements, such as running times or number of push-ups, differ between men and women in each of the services. It is interesting to note how this plays out in practical terms for each of the services. Table 1 clarifies the different requirements for each of the services.[29]

Establishing separate standards was meant to achieve the objective of standards, which is to measure the physical fitness of men and women. However, the creation of *dual* standards for men and women soon became seen as evidence that women were privy to *double* standards, or preferential treatment. Drawing on interviews with military officers, Carol Cohn concluded that "having different physical training standards for men and women is seen as special treatment for women, lowering standards for women, and/or evidence that women cannot cut it in the military."[30] There has been considerable debate regarding the necessity and impact of establishing separate physical standards for men and women within the military. For example, in her analysis of women in the military, Melissa Herbert questions the very rationale for separate standards. She argues "[t]he primary reason for ending sex-integrated training [in a 1983 trial] was the perceived problem of fraternization between female and male soldiers." However,

---

[28] Amanda Datnow, *Gender in Policy and Practice* (New York: Routledge, 2002), 173.
[29] Chief of Naval Operations, OPNAV Instruction 6110.1J: Physical Readiness Program (Washington, DC, July 11, 2011), http://www.navy-prt.com/files/6110.1J-_Physical_Readiness_program.pdf Commandant of the Marine Corps, Marine Corps Order 6100.13 W/CH 1: Marine Corps Physical Fitness Program (Washington, DC, August 1, 2008), http://www.marines.mil/Portals/59/Publications/MCO%206100.13%20W_CH%201.pdf.
[30] Cohn, "How Can She Claim Equal Rights?"

the "public" story focused on the belief that the presence of women lowered the standards, thereby making the men's training easier, in reality a secondary concern at best.[31] Regardless of why dual standards exist for men and women, the effects have been clear: perceptions of double standards and the overall weaker physical qualities of women dominate discussions of women and physical standards – both within the military and among the general public. In other words, dual standards became code for double standards.

The conflation of dual and double standards is often part of the rationale for arguing that women are weaker than men. In other words, the creation of dual standards is taken as indication of the military "softening" or "lowering" standards in order to include women. For example, Brian Mitchell has argued "the very presence of women in the ranks was made possible only by lowering or eliminating physical standards."[32] Mitchell claimed that "[a]bandoning the double standard would have drastic consequences for women in commissioning programs: 80 percent would not qualify for an Army commission."[33] This position treats the separate physical standards as a symbol of women's weakness, ignoring calls to measure effort or to recognize difference. Linda Bird Francke has countered this position, claiming double standards were "a tired complaint," arguing, "many women [in the US military] performed at male standards, and the alleged lowering of physical criteria was a myth created by men."[34]

In her book *Women in the Line of Fire: What You Should Know about Women in the Military*, Erin Solaro comes to a similar conclusion regarding standards: "The double standards of the APFT are widely understood by men and women alike to be an indicator of profound physical weakness in women. Women must do only 50–60% of the pushups men must and they have 19–29% more time than

---

[31] Herbert, *Camouflage Isn't Only for Combat*, 16.

[32] Mitchell, *Women in the Military*, 142.   [33] Ibid., 222.

[34] Linda Bird Francke, *Ground Zero: The Gender Wars in the Military* (New York: Simon & Schuster, 1997).

men to complete their run."[35] Solaro points out that both men and women may disparage the separate standards. The separate physical standards establish male fitness as superior and can cause women to feel pressured to prove they are capable of doing their job. Melissa Herbert explains, "Demonstration of physical strength, whether through physical development or task accomplishment, is apparently one mechanism by which women try to be perceived as masculine and therefore, as fitting in...a number of women mentioned not allowing coworkers to help them with physical tasks."[36] Herbert found that women were resistant to asking for help when lifting, and lifted excessive weight or improvised a task in an effort to avoid seeming weak or needing to ask for help.[37]

The two essential points to be made here are that physical standards were meant to provide clear, objective guidelines as to how to measure physical fitness in the military, and different standards were created in recognition of the physical differences between men and women. Despite the seemingly clear-cut nature of standards, there remains a great deal of disagreement, debate, and competing perceptions associated with physical requirements: tests designed to measure fitness are sometimes treated as indicative of job capacity; "gender norming" and "equivalent training" are treated as symbolic of the military weakening or diluting its standards; and the separate standard seems to codify and formalize male physical fitness as superior.

IV. ARE THERE COMBAT-SPECIFIC PHYSICAL REQUIREMENTS?

In her article "What Women Bring to the Fight," Ellen Haring answers this question about combat standards succinctly: "the combat arms branches have never established a single set of occupational physical standards required of all combat arms soldiers."[38] There are no

---

[35] Solaro, *Women in the Line of Fire*, 250.
[36] Herbert, *Camouflage Isn't Only for Combat*, 96.   [37] Ibid.
[38] Ellen L. Haring, "What Women Bring to the Fight," *Parameters* 43 no. 2 (2013): 27–32.

current fitness requirements for serving in combat positions in the Army beyond the Army's standard physical fitness test for all soldiers, which, as indicated earlier, includes push-ups, sit-ups, and a two-mile run and grades men and women on different scales.[39] It has been made explicit that "the intent of the Army physical fitness test is not to determine qualifications for combat."[40] This means that soldiers who enter the infantry go through the same BT, and are required to meet the same physical requirements, as all Army soldiers. The Marines, which has different physical requirements than the Army, established a Combat Fitness Test (CFT) in 2009. The CFT includes a 880-yard run while wearing boots and a uniform; lifting a 30 lb ammunition can over the head; and an obstacle course called "maneuver under fire," which includes dragging a casualty, carrying ammunition cans, tossing an imitation grenade, and push-ups.[41] In October 2014, 93 men and 7 women began the Marine's infantry training. Of these, 3 women and 67 men passed the "grueling" CFT, "paving the way for the first woman to potentially graduate from the program."[42]

V. DO COMBAT ROLES REQUIRE ENHANCED, OR DIFFERENT, PHYSICAL CAPABILITIES THAN OTHER ROLES WITHIN THE MILITARY?

Although there are no combat-specific physical tests, there is still a perception that women are not physically capable of performing combat operations. Combat is understood to be physically demanding and, in many cases, is described as more physically demanding than other military roles. Kathleen Parker argues, "ground combat

---

[39] "'Half My Body Weight': Women Get Taste of Combat Tasks in Army Study," CBS News. Accessed June 13, 2014, http://www.cbsnews.com/news/half-my-body-weight-army-study-gives-women-taste-of-combat-tasks/.

[40] Rosemarie Skaine, *Women at War: Gender Issues of Americans in Combat* (Jefferson, NC: McFarland & Co., 1999), 183.

[41] http://usmilitary.about.com/od/marines/a/cft.htm

[42] http://www.washingtonpost.com/news/checkpoint/wp/2014/10/03/three-women-pass-marine-corps-endurance-test-paving-way-for-possible-first-female-graduates-of-infantry-school/

is one area in which women, through quirks of biology and human nature, are not equal to men – a difference that should be celebrated rather than rationalized as incorrect."[43] Women, therefore, are perceived to be disadvantaged in combat because of their different, and seemingly less rigorous, physical capabilities. This claim is difficult to substantiate because there are no clear and established guidelines as to what physical tasks combat soldiers might typically engage in, or how these physical requirements differ from those for support roles.

One argument used to support the claim that women are not physically fit for combat is that BT tasks, such as pull-ups and scaling walls, are relevant to combat roles. The fact that women do not tend to perform as well as men, or have separate standards, is taken as an indicator that they are at a disadvantage in combat. Focusing on the Marines, one official summarized this argument, saying:

> [P]ull-ups have been used to test Marines' upper body strength for over 40 years. The ability to pull-up one's own body weight over a bar shows the upper body strength that, in combat, is needed to lift fallen comrades, pull one's self over a wall, and carry heavy munitions. Combat Marines also carry a pack that weighs around 90 pounds, with gunners carrying an additional 50 or 60 pounds.[44]

Another Marine official noted that separate standards for women "[does not] set them up for success and actually puts them at risk for injury...A lot of the tasks on that course require students to lift their own body weight plus their equipment."[45]

[43] Kathleen Parker, "Parker: Military Is Putting Women at Unique Risk," *Washington Post* (January 28, 2013), http://www.washingtonpost.com/opinions/parker-military-is-putting-women-at-unique-risk/2013/01/25/33d9eca6-6723-11e2-9e1b-07db1d2ccd5b_story.html.

[44] Barbara Boland, "Female Marines Not Required To Do 1 Pull-Up," CNS News, August 20, 2013, http://cnsnews.com/news/article/barbara-boland/female-marines-not-required-do-1-pull.

[45] Heather Sweeney, "PT Standards in Question for Women in Combat," Text, Military.com, accessed June 13, 2014, http://www.military.com/daily-news/2013/11/14/pt-standards-in-question-for-women-in-combat.html.

This argument treats equivalent standards as proof of women's inability to complete operational tasks. Moreover, the position conflates physical standards with the capacity to complete operational tasks – despite evidence that standards are not linked with operational tasks. This perpetuates the impression that combat indeed requires soldiers to have exceptional physical qualities. Moreover, this position implies that separate standards for women do not prepare them for the physical challenges that might await them in combat roles. The argument that dual standards equal double standards, therefore, creates a self-perpetuating perception of women's inadequacy. The military established dual standards to recognize physical difference, yet it used those dual standards as justification for the exclusion of women from combat roles. Several questions remain unanswered in this regard, including, are there women who meet the male physical standards and, if so, would the US military have allowed them into combat roles? What specific physical tasks are combat relevant, and why doesn't the military use tests and measurements linked to these tasks? Are there other military roles whose physical demands are equal to, or greater than, those of combat? Is the perception that combat roles are the most physically demanding accurate?

In an opinion piece in the *Wall Street Journal*, Michael O'Hanlon, a senior fellow at the Brookings Institute, identifies two physical capacities he sees as "essential to combat." This includes lifting oneself over a wall wearing body armor pack, and being able to drag a heavy weight a distance, which mimics moving a wounded soldier or hauling dismantled mortar.[46] For O'Hanlon, the existing physical tests ensure that Marines have the strength to accomplish these tasks, and should therefore not be altered. Major Scott Cuomo, the director of the Infantry Officer Course, reiterates the physically demanding nature of combat. He reminds readers that modern warfare might

---

[46] Michael O'Hanlon, "A Challenge for Female Marines: The Grueling Infantry Officer Course Was Too Much for Women Who Volunteered," *Wall Street Journal* (November 13, 2012), https://global-factiva-com.ezproxy2.library.usyd.edu.au/aa/?ref=WSJO000020121113e8bd0002u&pp=1&fcpil=en&napc=S&sa_from=.

involve brutal face-to-face physical fighting, saying, "sometimes we forget that even in Iraq and Afghanistan there have been many situations where Marines are fighting with their bare hands against the enemy."[47]

However, not everyone agrees as to the exceptional physical demands of combat roles. In response to O'Hanlon, David S. Holland, a US veteran of the Vietnam War, questioned the emphasis on upper body strength in physical testing.[48] He argued that in his experience in Vietnam, endurance was more relevant to combat service. This is an interesting conclusion, given evidence that women – in fact – tend to surpass men when it comes to endurance.[49] Holland also characterizes tests of upper body strength as "contrived and subjective."[50] Holland questions O'Hanlon's assertion that being able to lift oneself over a wall in full body armor and a pack is essential for combat. He asks, "How high are the walls? Four feet? Six feet? Ten feet? What is the combat load? Is there any research as to what and how often walls of various sizes are encountered? Or is the standard a seat-of-the-pants estimate by someone who happens to be blessed with superior upper-body strength?" Holland recalls that during his service, he "encountered zero walls in need of climbing." Finally, Holland questions the presumption that a Marine must be able to move a wounded soldier across a battlefield – pointing out the variety of body types and means to move the wounded available to soldiers.[51]

There is no definitive answer to the question of physical skills required for combat. One certainty is that there is a perception that combat is more challenging than other military roles and that women

---

[47] Jim Michaels, "Marines Experiment Puts Women on Infantry Course for First Time; Rigorous Program Tests Officers' Mental, Physical Endurance," *USA Today* (October 3, 2012).

[48] David S. Holland, "Women Marines Need Endurance More Than Strength," *Wall Street Journal*, November 20, 2012.

[49] Jane Blair, "Five Myths about Women in Combat," *Washington Post* (May 27, 2011), http://www.washingtonpost.com/opinions/five-myths-about-women-in-combat/2011/05/25/AGAsavCH_story.html.

[50] Holland, "Women Marines Need Endurance More Than Strength." [51] Ibid.

are less equipped to deal with these challenges. It should be noted that two of the physical tasks most associated with combat, scaling a wall and dragging a body to safety, perpetuate an unrealistic image of what combat looks like. Linking these physical tasks to combat reiterates the ideal of combat as heroic and exceptional, requiring men to rescue comrades and perform impressive physical feats. There is, however, no evidence to suggest that combat soldiers climb more walls while on duty, or drag more weight across battlefields.

VI. DO PHYSICAL STANDARDS DISCRIMINATE AGAINST WOMEN?

Although much of the physical standards debate focuses on women's limitations, there are indications that existing physical standards and training methods might limit and disadvantage women. Some experts have noted that physical requirements for women do not go far enough in recognizing the physical differences between men and women. Erin Solaro noted that the weight restrictions for women do not take into account the fact that they naturally carry more body fat than men. As a result, existing restrictions do not allow women to develop sufficient muscle mass "while maintaining a realistic level of body fat."[52] Solaro concludes that "any discussion of female physical abilities, then, must start with the unrealistically low weight expectations female soldiers are expected to meet."[53]

Colonel Gillian Boice, a graduate of West Point, also noted that men and women tend to develop different physical capabilities through their adolescent years. "Traditional" men's sports, including football or weight lifting, tend to emphasize and develop more upper body strength. The result is that women are naturally and socially at a disadvantage at the start of BT. However, Boice found "great success in developing fitness in our female cadets, and once women become fit in our program, I believe it is easier for females to achieve a 300 (maximum score) on APFT than it is for males."[54]

[52] Solaro, *Women in the Line of Fire*, 246.   [53] Ibid.   [54] Ibid., 261.

Equipment is another way in which women are at a disadvantage. Just as "most combat tasks were designed with the average male body in mind,"[55] so too is the equipment for soldiers. This can significantly disadvantage women who are attempting to carry weights, scale walls, and run, wearing equipment that is not designed for their bodies. Campbell elaborates on this problem, saying, "To put it bluntly, the problem boiled down to hips and breasts. Over the past decade, as female U.S. troops were placed in de facto front-line roles in Iraq and Afghanistan, they were often encumbered by the weight and shape of body armor designed for men."[56] Sargent Bobbie Crawford describes her experience using ill-fitting equipment when she served in Afghanistan as part of the 1st Brigade Combat Team, Airborne Division: "It rubbed on my hips and limited my mobility... You definitely had to find a lot of workarounds, you had to learn to become creative."[57] Creating physical tests and equipment with a male body in mind is a form of discrimination by design. These standards do not ensure excellence; rather, they ensure that men can succeed more easily than women and systematically ignore women's bodies and potential.

VII. IS THE PHYSICAL ARGUMENT ONLY ABOUT STANDARDS?

Although much of the debate about women's physical capability and combat focuses on standards, there are several other elements to the physical argument regarding capability in combat. In particular, within debates, commentary, policy discussions, and media responses to women in combat, three aspects of women's bodies are consistently identified as proof of their inability to succeed as combat soldiers – menstruation and hormones; pregnancy and motherhood;

---

[55] Ernesto Londoño, "A Decade into War, Body Armor Gets Curves; Female Troops Have Often Been Encumbered by Body Armor Designed for Men. This Fall, a New Generation of Body Armor for Women Will Be Tested," *Washington Post* (September 21, 2012).

[56] Ibid.   [57] Ibid.

and PTSD. Through these arguments, women's bodies become established as external, different, and a potential threat to "normal" operations. This raises questions about whether the issue is women's ability to meet physical standards, or whether there are more general concerns about women being physically different from men. These subarguments are explored in the following sections.

Hormones and menstruation... the real security threat?
Menstruation is consistently identified as a potential threat to women's capacity to work within the military. According to this position, hormone fluctuation, combined with the sanitary conditions associated with menstruation, makes it more difficult, if not impossible, for women to serve as soldiers. There are two elements to this argument. The first relates to the impact of fluctuating hormones and menstruation on judgment, and the second relates to sanitary conditions.

The first element of this position is that menstruation and premenstrual syndrome (PMS) cause hormone fluctuations that impede female soldiers' job capabilities. Jude Eden, a female Marine and Iraq War veteran, summarizes this aspect of the argument:

> [U]ntil women stop menstruating, there will always be an uphill battle for staying level and strong at all times. No one wants to talk about the fact that in the days before a woman's cycle, she loses half her strength, to say nothing of the emotional ups and downs that affect judgment. And how would you like fighting through PMS symptoms while clearing a town or going through a firefight?[58]

It is important to note the use of terms that suggest instability, fluctuation, and unpredictability as a result of menstruation. Eden

---

[58] Jude Eden, "The Problems of Women in Combat – From a Female Combat Vet," Western Journalism, January 26, 2013, http://www.westernjournalism.com/the-problems-of-women-in-combat-from-a-female-combat-vet/.

defines menstruation itself, a regular, monthly occurrence for most women, as an "uphill battle" and questions whether women can remain "level" and "strong" as a result. There is also the general, unsubstantiated statement that women lose half their strength and necessarily face emotional instability as a result of menstruation.

The characterization of menstruation as volatile is reiterated in several resources on women in combat. For example, Brian Mitchell declares, "Though many military women deny or downplay the effects of premenstrual syndrome on the behavior of women, medical experts estimate that 5% to 10% of all premenopausal women[59] experience severe PMS-related symptoms, including incapacitating depression, suicidal thoughts, extreme mood swings, self-abuse, and violence . . . the impact of PMS on unit effectiveness is compounded by the natural, involuntary tendency of women living in close quarters to synchronize menstrual cycles."[60] Kingsley Browne similarly associates fluctuating hormones with fluctuating capabilities, or instability in terms of women's ability to perform their job, arguing, "women's risk-taking activities vary over the course of the menstrual cycle, declining during the ovulatory phase of the cycle, when estrogen levels are especially high."[61] These are important positions to take note of, as they attach a physical condition, menstruation, to subjective judgments about women's capabilities. The presumed effects of menstruation are presented as medical realities. This is ludicrous considering the reality that women across the world and across professions are able to manage themselves and their jobs month in and month out.

In her article "Women Can Never 'Belong' in Combat," Anna Simons furthers the argument that menstruation can make women a security "liability" to their units and mission. She quotes an unnamed retired admiral who "laughed at the preposterousness of women on

---

[59] It should be noted that Mitchell does not clarify if this is all women, all American women, or all military women, nor does he provide a citation for the statistic.

[60] Mitchell, *Women in the Military*, 149.   [61] Browne, *Co-Ed Combat*, 2007, 46.

SEAL teams operating in shark-infested waters," and asked, "What group of SEALs would launch an ocean mission with a menstruating woman in their midst?" Simons then concludes that "one might also wonder what woman would put herself in this kind of danger."[62] This position is a more explicit attempt to associate women's bodies with risk and instability. Despite no recorded evidence – ever in history – of sharks being attracted to women's bodies while carrying out military duties in water, this retired admiral makes the case that including women would necessarily put troops at risk due to the *possibility* of such a scenario. Rather than evaluate this likelihood, or considering whether there is evidence of sharks or menstruation posing a risk to existing troops, Simons shares this emotional hypothetical to support her position. Again, this is evidence of emotional arguments and stories overshadowing, and even taking the place of, evidence or research.

A second element of the menstruation and combat argument relates to sanitary conditions. Several authors have suggested that the close confines, lack of showers, and grueling and intimate conditions associated with combat are particularly challenging for menstruating women. Browne summarizes, "Many women experience changes in their periods, and water is not always available to clean with . . . one woman commented that if she had been in combat with the menstrual periods she has now, she would not have been able to cope."[63] Browne adds, "The impairment of performance associated with the menstrual cycle can be serious, especially because many women are reluctant to admit problems."[64] One can see in both quotes that there is a mysteriousness and taboo attached to menstruation. It is spoken about as if it is a problem women hide, or are not willing to address. Moreover, cycles are described as unpredictable and requiring discreet and almost secret hygienic practices. Such arguments fail to acknowledge that menstruation is something that happens to most women every

---

[62] Anna Simons, "Women Can Never 'Belong' in Combat," *Orbis* 44, no. 3 (June 22, 2000), https://global-factiva-com.ezproxy2.library.usyd.edu.au/aa/?ref=orbs000020010809dw6m0000x&pp=1&fcpil=en&napc=S&sa_from=.

[63] Browne, *Co-Ed Combat*, 259.   [64] Ibid.

month, for many years of their lives. Women in other physical or high-stress environments presumably menstruate. Yet, the cycles of female soldiers are depicted as something exceptional that stops women in their tracks, catches them off guard, requires exceptional attention, and depletes their physical capabilities. Jude Eden claims that "in the field," a unit would have to "sto[p] the convoy" if a woman's cycle was starting, implying that menstruation disrupts a woman's physical capabilities as well as military operations.[65]

Research is somewhat divided on the issue. A large study sought to determine the impact of menstruation and pre-menstruation on female trainees.[66] It found several negative impacts for women in training, including "a significant perceived impact of menstrual and premenstrual symptoms on academic, physical, and military activities; and difficulties in obtaining, changing, and disposing of menstrual materials in a military setting."[67] In contrast, a study of US Air Force and US Army rated women found only 9 percent reporting any form of menstrual distress.[68] In other research reports, women pointed to the practical problem of the disposal of menstrual products, hygiene concerns, including "feeling dirty," and embarrassment as potential issues. This same study found that women were able to create solutions to the disposal problem, including packaging and burying.[69] A third study identified several contraceptive options that US women can and do take in order to suppress menstruation.[70] The

[65] Eden, "The Problems of Women in Combat."

[66] Marcie B. Schneider et al., "Menstrual and Premenstrual Issues in Female Military Cadets: A Unique Population with Significant Concerns," *Journal of Pediatric and Adolescent Gynecology* 12, no. 4 (November 1999): 195–201.

[67] Ibid.

[68] Lorry Fenner and Marie deYoung, *Women in Combat: Civic Duty or Military Liability?* (Washington DC: Georgetown University Press, 2001), 138.

[69] Diane Wind Wardell and Barbara Czerwinski, "A Military Challenge to Managing Feminine and Personal Hygiene," *Journal of the American Academy of Nurse Practitioners* 13, no. 4 (April 2001): 187.

[70] Leslie A. Christopher and Leslie Miller, "Women in War: Operational Issues of Menstruation and Unintended Pregnancy," *Military Medicine* 172, no. 1 (January 2007): 9–16.

study concluded, "The ability to support menstrual cycle suppression, to prevent pregnancy, and to provide short and long-term health benefits to women already exists."[71]

Pregnancy and motherhood

Another set of arguments about women's physical capacities relates to pregnancy and motherhood. There are two specific subarguments here. First, leave associated with pregnancy is depicted as a tactical and financial liability to the military. It is said to render women "nondeployable," forcing them to leave their unit and a war zone, disrupting unit cohesion and the overall mission, and costing the military money. Second, when women become mothers, an argument is made that their commitments change (or should change), making them less dedicated and less capable soldiers. These two arguments directly relate to women in combat debates because they treat pregnancy as a risk to unit cohesion, something that has been established as essential to combat operations.[72] Moreover, it calls into question the commitment and dedication of women, something that, if uncertain, could put troops and the nation at risk, particularly in combat zones.

There is no doubt that some women in the US military get pregnant. Moreover, women do not always get pregnant at a time that is best suited to military operations. In fact, research shows that women in the military are 50 percent more likely to become pregnant unexpectedly.[73] In 2008, nearly 11 percent of more than 7000 active-duty women surveyed by the DOD reported an unplanned pregnancy.[74] These pregnancies do have a potential negative impact on military operations and budgets. Unwanted or ill-timed pregnancies can be a significant contributor to healthcare expenditures.

[71] Ibid.   [72] See Chapter 5 for more on combat cohesion.

[73] Wilson, "Unplanned Pregnancies May Be on Rise in Military." Citing a yet unpublished study by Daniel Grossman and Kate D. Grindlay (forthcoming in *Obstetrics & Gynecology* 2014).

[74] "Unplanned Pregnancies May Be on Rise in Military," CNN, accessed June 13, 2014, http://www.cnn.com/2013/01/23/health/unplanned-pregnancies-military/index.html.

Indeed, according to the April 2012 issue of *Medical Surveillance Monthly Report* among all US service members, more than 13 percent of total bed days, and about 5 percent of total lost work days, were related to pregnancy and delivery.[75]

Pregnancy also contributes to service interruption or even dropout. This is because women who become pregnant while at home cannot be deployed, and women who become pregnant while overseas are often sent home.[76] By far, the largest reason for female attrition is pregnancy, accounting for 25 percent to 50 percent of women who fail to complete enlistment contracts.[77] According to research, the number one reason for women leaving their positions within the US armed services has been pregnancy for at least the past three decades.[78] Women's decision to leave the military due to pregnancy, combined with the challenge of either sending women home or being unable to deploy them, is considered to be a major readiness problem.[79] The unpredictability of women's pregnancies, combined with the financial and deployability impacts, contribute to an overall perception that pregnancy is a significant risk and liability for the military.

In addition to considerations of risk, pregnancy is depicted as something that is the result of irresponsible behavior. Discussions of "ill timed" pregnancy contribute to the idea that women are reckless or irresponsible in terms of family planning. There is also a perception that women may use pregnancy strategically to avoid duty, or to escape of difficult or long deployments. In an article for *The New Republic*, journalist Stephanie Gutmann reports that "soldiers say [pregnancy is] sometimes used to get out of 'hell tours' like Bosnia,

---

[75] Artin Terhakopian, "Time to Curb Unintended Military Pregnancies," *Time Magazine*, January 31, 2013, http://nation.time.com/2013/01/31/time-to-curb-unintended-military-pregnancies/.

[76] Servicewomen who become pregnant while overseas must be sent home, which can cost the military around $10,000.

[77] Mitchell, *Women in the Military*, 152.

[78] Terhakopian, "Time to Curb Unintended Military Pregnancies."

[79] Mitchell, *Women in the Military*, 220.

to go home."[80] She quotes Specialist Carrie Lambertus, who agrees that strategic pregnancy, designed to shirk on military duty, "happens all the time."[81] Women's ability to "get out" of difficult tours or assignments as a result of pregnancy has been identified as something that clearly differentiates female soldiers from male soldiers. Reporter Cort Kirkwood described pregnancy as a sort of "get out of jail free" card that was not available to men, stating, "If men want to get out of their combat tour, it is nigh unto impossible unless they complete their tour or get injured. Women need only to become pregnant."[82]

These perceptions weaken confidence in women's ability to serve as soldiers: they might get pregnant unexpectedly, they may not be able or willing to avoid pregnancy, and they might use pregnancy strategically to shirk their duties. Former soldier Bethany Saros has written about her firsthand experience facing judgment with regard to pregnancy. She reports that pregnancy places a stigma on women, with other soldiers assuming that "she did it on purpose." Saros continues:

> It's whispered about any time the word "pregnancy" comes up right before and during a combat tour. The unspoken code is that a good soldier will have an abortion, continue the mission, and get some sympathy because she chose duty over motherhood. But for the woman who chooses motherhood over duty, well, she must have been trying to get out of deployment.[83]

Saros laments that becoming a parent is seen as a problem only for women, not men. She goes on to state that a mother may be seen as "a faker, a soldier who couldn't take the pressure and went to extreme lengths to get out."[84]

[80] Stephanie Gutmann, "Sex and the Soldier," *The New Republic*, February 24, 1997.
[81] Ibid.
[82] R. Cort Kirkwood, "Women in Combat: War for and against Women," April 12, 2013, https://www.thenewamerican.com/culture/item/15012-women-in-combat-war-for-and-against-women.
[83] Bethany Saros, "My Shameful Military Pregnancy," November 14, 2011, http://www.salon.com/2011/11/13/my_shameful_military_pregnancy/.
[84] Ibid.

Such perceptions of shirking or using pregnancy to avoid service contribute to a "profound sense of resentment" directed at women who choose to become parents.[85] There are multiple gender biases at play here. Parenthood is treated as a problem, a sign of shirking, and a symbol of weakness for women in ways that do not apply to men. Moreover, similar to menstruation arguments, this associates an objective biological regularity with subjective judgments about women's abilities and morals.

An additional argument related to pregnancy and combat is that motherhood does or should change the priorities of women. As a result, they will or should be less able and less willing to fight the nations wars. Brian Mitchell summarized this logic, claiming, "Not surprisingly, children also increase dissatisfaction with military life among women . . . generally the families of female graduates had fewer children than the families of male graduates, but even one child is enough to alter a woman's desires for the future radically. Many resign. Others accept less demanding assignments."[86] Mitchell draws on research from Harvard pediatrician T. Berry Brazelton, who found that "for the very young child, the absence of a parent is like the death of a parent. You create an orphan if you send the main caretaker away."[87] Mitchel also suggests there will be a negative public reaction, noting that there is "widespread opposition to sending mothers to war."[88]

Arguments associated with pregnancy and motherhood are perfect examples of how objective facts can bleed into ideological claims related to women in combat. It is a fact that women in the military get pregnant. However, related arguments about a woman's commitment to her job after motherhood, pregnancy destroying unit cohesion,

---

[85] Thomas E. Ricks, "Knocked up and Deployed: An Army Captain's View," Foreign Policy Blogs, December 22, 2009, http://ricks.foreignpolicy.com/posts/2009/12/22/knocked_up_and_deployed_an_army_captains_view.

[86] Mitchell, *Women in the Military*, 74.

[87] Testimony before the subcommittee on military personnel and compensation, committee on armed services, House of Representatives, February 19, 1991. Cited in ibid., 200.

[88] Ibid., 233.

women choosing to get pregnant strategically, and women becoming "soft" as a result of motherhood are based in part on gendered ideals and myths and are nearly impossible to substantiate. In turn, blanket claims about mothers and soldiering are often entirely moral judgments that link the objective physical condition of pregnancy to subjective moralistic claims about the ability of women to do their job. Perhaps one of the best examples of subjective judgments bleeding into objective data is the claim that motherhood impacts women's commitment or drive to serve their country. There is almost no conclusive evidence to support this claim. Moreover, it is unclear whether children of service members are impacted differently by their mother serving as opposed to their father.[89]

There is some available research through which we can evaluate the claims regarding women and pregnancy in the military. Available evidence does not support the claim that pregnancy presents an exceptional cost to the military, either financially or in terms of disrupting cohesion. In her book *Ground Zero: The Gender Wars in the Military*, Linda Bird Francke notes that "[l]ost time off the job became a military mantra against pregnant women."[90] At the time that this mantra became dominant in the late 1980s and early 1990s, available data indicated that, for the Navy, the total time lost for all women due to pregnancy was one hour a month.[91] Francke compares this to an earlier study that found men lost 190,000 days to drug rehabilitation and another 196,000 days to alcohol rehabilitation – almost twice the amount of time "lost" to pregnancy during the same period.[92] James Hogg, a retired admiral, highlighted the other reasons for "lost time," saying, "We have a much higher disciplinary problem with the men, unauthorized absenteeism, absence in the brig for more serious offences. Pregnancy is a wash."[93] Despite pregnancy being one of

[89] Fenner and deYoung, *Women in Combat*, 183.
[90] Francke, *Ground Zero: The Gender Wars in the Military*, 108–109.
[91] http://dacowits.defense.gov/ReportsMeetings/1991Fall.aspx
[92] Francke, *Ground Zero: The Gender Wars in the Military*, 108–109.
[93] Ibid., 251.

many possible reasons why service members might need to take leave, it continues to be presented as an exceptional risk. Furthermore, there is rarely a discussion about how parenthood impacts men's service. In a brief on sex discrimination and pregnancy, American Supreme Court Justice Ruth Bader Ginsburg noted that Air Force regulations provided male officers with a three-month deferment from overseas duty when their wives became pregnant, at the same time that it depicted women's leave as a "problem."[94]

Although unexpected pregnancies may pose logistical challenges for the military, there has been little research into why the numbers of unexpected pregnancies are so high for women serving in the US military as compared to civilians. One possible answer could be the lack of access to medical abortions. Until 2013, women serving in the US military were not allowed to use their government-issued health care to attain an abortion, even if they were raped.[95] This distinguishes military women from all other federal employees and Medicaid recipients, including prisoners.[96]

Although it is impossible to demonstrate a correlation, it is certainly worth noting that women in the military are significantly more likely than civilians to face rape while serving. The full extent of the US military's sexual violence epidemic is not addressed in this book; however, it is clear that the incidence of rape within the military is alarmingly high, with one study finding that 37 percent of female veterans reported being raped at least twice while

---

[94] Neil S. Siegel and Reva B. Siegel, "Struck by Stereotype: Ruth Bader Ginsburg on Pregnancy Discrimination as Sex Discrimination," *Duke Law Journal* 59 (2010): 771–98.

[95] In 1988, military hospitals and clinics worldwide were banned by DOD from providing abortions, except when the woman's life was in danger, or when the woman had been raped – and in cases of rape, women had to pay for it. Further restrictions, including forcing women to report a rape within a short time period, and eventually banning all abortions except in cases where a woman's life was threatened, meant that almost no female service women had access to abortions.

[96] "Military Women Get (Slightly) More Access to Abortion," *Mother Jones*, accessed June 13, 2014, http://www.motherjones.com/mojo/2012/12/military-women-get-slightly-more-access-abortion.

serving.[97] Despite the sexual violence epidemic, the military implemented increasing restrictions on access to abortion over the past four decades. In the 1970s, approximately 26,000 female service members and wives of service members obtained abortions within military hospitals,[98] but in 2012, only four abortions were performed within military hospitals.[99] Again, it is difficult to prove a correlation; however, if we are to assess the physical impacts of pregnancy in any meaningful way, access to safe abortion in an environment with a high incidence of rape is an important consideration.

The pregnancy and menstruation arguments are united by the underlying belief that women's physical differences render them inherently unpredictable, and these differences are both insurmountable and threatening. Menstruation and pregnancy are considered indicators of the threat women's bodies represent to operational and mission stability. A woman's monthly cycle is characterized as unpredictably fluctuating and always impacting a female soldier's ability to make decisions and fulfill her duty. The looming threat of pregnancy adds another element of unpredictability to the ability of women to serve. By contrast, the male body is represented as the standard, and more predictable, stable, and reliable. This characterization reflects a key aspect of the band of brothers myth, which is the idea that male bodies are inherently more capable of protecting society. The emphasis on unpredictability also perpetuates the idea that biology is destiny. There is little discussion of the mechanisms and strategies women use to manage and plan when it comes to pregnancy and menstruation. Instead, the unpredictability of pregnancy and menstruation are treated as unavoidable, unmanageable, and inevitable risks associated with women serving.

---

[97] Anne G. Sadler et al., "Factors Associated with Women's Risk of Rape in the Military Environment," *American Journal of Industrial Medicine* 43, no. 3 (March 1, 2003): 262–73.

[98] "Will Abortion Law Change Help Female Troops?" *Stars and Stripes*, accessed June 13, 2014, http://www.stripes.com/news/will-abortion-law-change-help-female-troops-1.209513.

[99] Ibid.

Medical differences

The third, catch-all category of physical arguments related to women in combat is the tendency to focus on the specific medical needs of women. This ranges from concerns about bone fractures to emphasis on women's susceptibility to PTSD. Underpinning these is the argument that women require more medical attention than men, and therefore will be less dependable soldiers. Perhaps most relevant for current debates is the attention given to PTSD. Fortunately, there has been more attention given to the symptoms, effects, and treatment of PTSD over the past twenty years. Perceptions about the disorder are changing, but it is often still represented as a sign of weakness or emotional vulnerability.

The US military has made significant efforts to raise awareness about PTSD. In its section on PTSD, Military.com reports that 7.8 percent of Americans will experience the disorder. They note that in the general population, women are twice as likely as men to develop PTSD, at a rate of 10.4 percent versus 5 percent.[100] A study by the University of California, San Francisco and the Northern California Institute for Research and Education noted that "women in the study were more likely than men to develop a stronger fear response" and were therefore "more likely to have stronger responses to fear-inducing stimuli."[101] The headlines from the research were that "women exposed to trauma may be at greater risk of developing post-traumatic stress disorder" as a result of this heightened fear response.[102] It was also reported by the 2011 American Psychiatric Association that women deployed in the wars in Iraq

---

[100] Military.com "PTSD Frequently Asked Questions," Text, Military.com, accessed June 13, 2014, http://www.military.com/benefits/veterans-health-care/ptsd-frequently-asked-questions.html.

[101] Jeffrey Norris, "Gender Differences in PTSD Risk May Be due to Heightened Fear Conditioning in Women," UCSF, November 19, 2012, http://www.ucsf.edu/news/2012/11/13155/gender-differences-ptsd-risk-may-be-due-heightened-fear-conditioning-women.

[102] Ibid.

and Afghanistan are particularly vulnerable to PTSD.[103] The study, focusing on 922 National Guard members deployed to Iraq in 2008, showed that women were far more likely to meet the criteria for PTSD (18.7 percent) than were men (8.7 percent). The study also concluded that there were no significant differences, in terms of combat exposure, between men and women.

This research stands in contrast with the results of several other investigations into PTSD. For example, a 2007 study of more than 100,000 US veterans returning from Iraq and Afghanistan found "minimal absolute differences between men and women, racial and ethnic subgroups, and component types regarding risk for receiving mental health and PTSD diagnoses."[104] Similarly, the authors of "Gender Differences in Rates of Depression, PTSD, Pain, Obesity and Military Sexual Trauma among Connecticut War Veterans in Iraq and Afghanistan" concluded that women who served in Iraq were less likely to face PTSD than were men.[105] They reached this conclusion by screening veterans for depression, PTSD, pain, and MST. Their findings also indicated "female veterans were more likely to screen positive for depression . . . but less likely to screen positive for PTSD."[106] A study focused on UK soldiers deployed in the Gulf and Iraq Wars found no difference in psychological symptoms between men and women.[107] Commentary on the study concluded that "the high intensity and persistent level of threat, acts as a great equalizer

---

[103] Shari Roan, "Women on War Front More Likely to Get Post-Traumatic Stress Disorder than Men, Study Finds," *Los Angeles Times*, May 19, 2011, http://articles.latimes.com/2011/may/19/news/la-heb-ptsd-women-military-20110519.

[104] Seal KH et al., "Bringing the War Back Home: Mental Health Disorders among 103,788 US Veterans Returning from Iraq and Afghanistan Seen at Department of Veterans Affairs Facilities," *Archives of Internal Medicine* 167, no. 5 (March 12, 2007): 476–82.

[105] Sally G. Haskell et al., "Gender Differences in Rates of Depression, PTSD, Pain, Obesity, and Military Sexual Trauma Among Connecticut War Veterans of Iraq and Afghanistan," *Journal of Women's Health* 19, no. 2 (February 2010): 267–71.

[106] Ibid.

[107] Roberto J Rona et al., "Women in Novel Occupational Roles: Mental Health Trends in the UK Armed Forces," *International Journal of Epidemiology* 36, no. 2 (April 2007): 319–26.

of risk, resulting in similar rates of PTSD and depression for men and women."[108] There is clearly a need for more research on this topic, as existing evidence is varied and at times conflicting.

Another interesting aspect of the PTSD debates is that the military used the combat exclusion as justification for withholding treatment for PTSD from women. This decision was doubly ignorant as it assumed that only front line combat soldiers experience PTSD, and it also assumed that women were not exposed to combat. Women were not able to receive treatment with their government-issued medical benefits until 2010 because access to treatment was restricted to those with combat experience. By this point, more than 250,000 women had served in Iraq and Afghanistan, and there was widespread recognition that these women had faced violent and hostile situations. However, the formal combat exclusion prevented women from claiming any combat-related trauma, based on the idea that women should not be near the so-called front lines.

While the dismantling of the combat exclusion will alter women's access to these services, it does not address MST, which is the primary cause of PTSD for women. Military sexual trauma is defined by the Department of Veterans Affairs as "sexual assault or repeated, threatening sexual harassment that occurred while the veteran was in the military."[109] MST is an epidemic within the forces affecting both women and men, with 40 percent of claims being made by men. Claims and requests for resources for MST are consistently denied because soldiers are expected to prove an "initial stressor." For MST this means proving an initial sexual harassment, assault, or rape, something that is difficult and complicated within the current military structure.[110] There clearly is a need for further research on MST

[108] Charles W. Hoge, Julie C. Clark, and Carl A. Castro, "Commentary: Women in Combat and the Risk of Post-Traumatic Stress Disorder and Depression," *International Journal of Epidemiology* 36, no. 2 (April 1, 2007): 327–29.

[109] http://www.mentalhealth.va.gov/msthome.asp.

[110] "Should More Veterans Get P.T.S.D. Benefits?," Room for Debate, accessed June 13, 2014, http://roomfordebate.blogs.nytimes.com/2010/07/08/should-more-veterans-get-p-t-s-d-benefits/.

and women's vulnerability to PTSD. Although there is no conclusive evidence about women's vulnerability to PTSD, it continues to be perceived as something women are particularly susceptible to. This perception is largely based on assumptions about women's emotional vulnerability, and not on evidence from available studies.

CONCLUSION

This chapter has addressed several major questions related to the physical arguments associated with women in combat. In particular, it has directly unpacked claims related to physical standards and female soldiers. There was an attempt to provide clarity on issues related to the physical standards used in each of the services as well as the separate standards established for women. Most importantly, it was shown that there is no singular physical standard for combat roles. This point undermines consistent and prominent arguments that women do not have what it takes to serve in front line combat roles.

In addition, this chapter demonstrated that many of the arguments related to women and physical fitness actually extend beyond standards. Positions related to menstruation, pregnancy, and PTSD are evidence that physical arguments are fueled by emotional assumptions and fears about the supposedly inherent unpredictability of women's bodies. Although it seems that physical standards concerns are motivated by, and draw from, objective evidence, this chapter shows that there is a great deal of emotion, stories, and myth influencing the physical debate. Fears of sharks potentially attacking menstruating women, and narratives depicting weak women, unable to drag their comrades to safety on the battlefield, are memorable and influential within these discussions. By contrast, growing evidence that women are able to meet military physical requirements remains overshadowed by these hypothetical and incredibly emotional narratives.

The point of this chapter is not to prove or disprove the validity of physical standards, or to introduce new and better means of measuring men and women's bodies. It is to show that the perception of physical standards as objective, clear, and fixed is misleading. Physical standards have changed over time, have been developed in relation to men's bodies, and do not reflect one's ability to complete military tasks. Within broader discussions of women's ability to make the cut, physical standards play a small role. Overshadowing the relatively simple set of military physical standards are a vast array of stories and perceptions about the physical nature of war and men and women's bodies. These stories used to sustain perceptions that men are elite and combat is exceptional.

5   Sex, cohesion, and national security

One of the most common arguments used to justify the combat exclusion in the US and elsewhere has been that women undermine the types of bonding necessary for combat troops to operate effectively. This 'cohesion hypothesis' presumes a positive relationship between group cohesion and soldier performance,[1] and a negative relationship between the inclusion of women and the rates of bonding and trust necessary for such cohesion. In other words, all-male combat units are more cohesive, and therefore more effective, than mixed-gender units. This became the dominant rationale for excluding women from US combat operations in the two decades leading up to the policy change, and it remains the primary justification for sustaining combat exclusions in several militaries across the world.[2] Erin Solaro summarizes the significance of the cohesion hypothesis: "The single biggest issue in integrating women into the military, much less into the combat arms, has been held to be cohesion: the emotional bonds between members of a unit...In the military mind, cohesion had become more than just a contributor to combat effectiveness. It was now synonymous with it."[3]

The link between cohesion and troop performance was perhaps most clearly articulated in policy terms in the 1992 Presidential Commission on the Assignment of Women, which was established to review the combat exclusion. The commission recommended that

---

[1] Leora N. Rosen et al., "Cohesion and Readiness in Gender-Integrated Combat Service Support Units: The Impact of Acceptance of Women and Gender Ratio," *Armed Forces & Society* 22, no. 4 (July 1, 1996): 537–53.

[2] For critical reflections on gender, cohesion, and the UK military, see Anthony King, "Women in Combat," *The RUSI Journal* 158, no. 1 (2013): 4–11.

[3] Erin Solaro, *Women in the Line of Fire: What You Should Know about Women in the Military* (Berkeley, CA: Seal Press, 2006).

the combat exclusion be sustained, citing that although "[t]here are no military studies concerning mixed-gender combat unit cohesion... some research indicates that unit cohesion could be affected by the introduction of women."[4] The commission identified several factors that could impact cohesion, including the "real or perceived inability of women to carry their weight without male assistance, a 'zero privacy' environment on the battlefield, interference with male bonding, cultural values, the desire of men to protect women, inappropriate male/female relationships, and pregnancy – particularly when perceived as a way to escape from combat duty."[5] This quotation summarizes the cohesion hypothesis and illustrates how it is tied to broader gender assumptions – in this case, assumptions that male bonding is something requiring preservation, that men naturally desire to protect women, and that pregnancy is used as a means to escape combat duty.

There is research on cohesion and mixed-gender non-combat units; however, the combat exclusion has only recently been lifted in the US military. As a result, there is an absence of data on mixed-gender combat units that could conclusively confirm or weaken the cohesion hypothesis. As the 1992 Presidential Commission looking at women in military summarized, "[t]here are no authoritative military studies of mixed-gender ground combat cohesion, since available cohesion research has been conducted among male-only ground combat units."[6] Despite the lack of research on mixed-gender combat units and cohesion, there are a variety of avenues available to explore the cohesion hypothesis. This chapter unpacks the cohesion hypothesis. It highlights the relationship between the hypothesis and gender stereotypes and identifies the cohesion hypothesis as a key element of the band of brothers myth. It demonstrates that the evidence used to

---

[4] The Presidential Commission on the Assignment of Women in the Armed Forces: Report to the President, November 15, 1992 (Washington, DC: 1992), http://hdl .handle.net/2027/umn.31951d00277676f.

[5] Ibid.

[6] M. McSally, "Women in Combat: Is the Current Policy Obsolete?" *Duke Journal of Gender Law & Policy* 14, no. 2 (2007): 1011–59, p. 1035.

establish the relationship between cohesion and troop performance is conflicting, drawing on disparate and confusing definitions of cohesion.

Cohesion arguments are framed as objective concerns related to military bonding and task effectiveness; however, I argue that the cohesion hypothesis largely refers to male bonding and is an emotional position, which reifies the ideal that the US military is a band of brothers who are loyal, masculine, and honorable men protecting both their country and their female comrades. Cohesion arguments presume not only that troops must "like" each other, in that they should trust one another and have established bonds, but they should *be* like each other, in that they should have shared identities and values. The cohesion hypothesis is therefore less about troop effectiveness, trust, or enhancing national security, than it is about sustaining myths about ideal soldiers and "real" warfare that require women to be subordinate outsiders in need of protection. In order to support this position, the first section includes a discussion of the varying, and often contradictory, definitions of cohesion through history. Following this are the three main premises of the cohesion hypothesis: first, that women weaken group cohesion; second, that social cohesion leads to troop effectiveness; and third, that cohesion is necessarily a positive aspect of troop dynamics. The final section illustrates the gendered nature of cohesion and the relationship of narrative and mythology to the cohesion hypothesis.

DEFINING COHESION

Although there is some evidence that unit cohesiveness is "the critical factor"[7] in successful troop dynamics, there exists neither a clear definition of cohesion nor a common approach to measuring cohesion and its impacts. Definitions of cohesion range from "trust,"

---

[7] Jeremy J. J. Phipps, *Forward, Unit Cohesion: A Prerequisite for Combat Effectiveness*, National Security Affairs Issue Paper (National Defense University, 1982), i–vii.

and "'camaraderie' or the 'buddy–system,'"[8] to more elaborate descriptions of vertical and horizontal cohesion between peers and leadership structures.[9] Others have described cohesion as a multifaceted concept containing elements including commitment, communication, cooperation, and command.[10] Still another, somewhat confusing, approach places heavy emphasis on cohesion as both a mechanism and an outcome, claiming that it is "in part, both the facilitator and an outcome of the coordination of joint lines of action but is not itself such coordination."[11] Such variable and wide-ranging definitions of cohesion make assessing the cohesion hypothesis nearly impossible.

What is more frustrating is that despite the varying and sometimes vague definitions given, cohesion remains linked to multiple positive outcomes for troop dynamics.[12] In their well-known study, "Why They Fight: Combat Motivation in the Iraq War," Leonard Wong et al. identify cohesion as "critical" and conclude that "US soldiers continue to fight because of the bonds of trust between soldiers."[13] Major Brendan McBreen reaffirms these positions, stating that "improving infantry cohesion is more important than any combination of doctrinal, organizational, training, or equipment

[8] Stephan Maninger, "Women in Combat: Reconsidering the Case against the Deployment of Women in Combat-Support and Combat Units," in *Women in the Military and in Armed Conflict*, edited by Helena Carreiras and Gerhard Kümmel (VS Verlag für Sozialwissenschaften, 2008), 9–27, http://www.springerlink.com/content/l883735108x76p2r/abstract/, p. 23.

[9] See for example, Guy L. Siebold, "The Essence of Military Group Cohesion," *Armed Forces & Society* 33, no. 2 (January 1, 2007): 286–95, and James Griffith, "Further Considerations Concerning the Cohesion-Performance Relation in Military Settings," *Armed Forces & Society* 34, no. 1 (October 1, 2007): 138–47.

[10] Robert L. Grice and Lawrence C. Katz, *Cohesion in Military and Aviation Psychology: An Annotated Bibliography and Suggestions for US Army Aviation* (Arlington, VA: United States Army Research Institute for the Behavioral and Social Sciences, 2005; http://hqda.army.mil/ari/pdf/TR1166.pdf), 3.

[11] Siebold, "The Essence of Military Group Cohesion."

[12] James Griffith, "Multilevel Analysis of Cohesion's Relation to Stress, Well-Being, Identification, Disintegration, and Perceived Combat Readiness," *Military Psychology* 14, no. 3 (2002): 217–39; Laurel W. Oliver et al., "A Quantitative Integration of the Military Cohesion Literature," *Military Psychology* 11, no. 1 (1999): 57–83.

[13] Wong et al., *Why They Fight*.

improvements."[14] Put simply, this amounts to the claim that we do not know exactly what cohesion is, but we know it is "good" and necessary.

The way cohesion is defined by the US military has changed over time. Before World War II, little attention was given to cohesion in research or discussions related to the US military. References to cohesion at this stage primarily linked cohesion to "authoritarian leadership, training together, living together, and functioning in an uncertain environment that was believed to promote bonding among members in order to survive."[15] In other words, cohesion was historically associated with institutional practices and leadership, rather than bonding or a shared identity.

Efforts to link cohesion to troop effectiveness largely began with the end of the Vietnam War. At this time there was a general recognition, both internally and externally, that the image of the US military had suffered as a result of the disastrous war. Military image and morale issues in the US military were portrayed as a product of declining "traditional" military norms. As a result, greater cohesiveness was identified as a solution for the institution:

> National will during the Vietnam era was sharply divided. There has since been an erosion of traditional military values. Soldiers, some say, look upon the military as a job, hardly a profession and certainly not a calling. Unless the military creates a better environment that gives rise to loyalty, trust, and commitment of families as well as soldiers, service people will resign midway in their careers to seek a more satisfying environment for their families.[16]

Cohesion came to be associated not only with a unified force, but also with "sameness" and "traditional" values. This

---

[14] McBreen, "The Strength of the Wolf Is the Pack."

[15] Griffith, "Multilevel Analysis of Cohesion's Relation to Stress"; Oliver et al., "A Quantitative Integration of the Military Cohesion Literature."

[16] Phipps, *Forward, Unit Cohesion*, 3.

understanding drew on the now-iconic military text "Cohesion and Disintegration in the Wehrmacht in World War II," which was an effort to understand the unique bonds and loyalty among German troops. Shils and Janowitz argued that homogeneity, in terms of age, ethnicity, and cultural background, was essential to group dynamics, warning of the "disintegrating influences of heterogeneity" among troops.[17] Decades later, the Walter Reed Army Institute of Research (WRAIR) echoed Shils and Janowitz's anxiety in a study that linked cohesion to positive interaction, shared values, and common experiences.[18] Another more recent research report on cohesion in the military also identified diversity as a potential threat to troop dynamics.[19] Thus, over time, cohesion evolved from a concept linked to leadership and institutional practices to one inextricably tied to a particular white-male-heterosexual ideal of social uniformity. This logic has been employed to make the case for excluding other social minority groups from the military, including African Americans and openly serving homosexual and queer soldiers.[20]

The removal of past exclusionary policies should shed some light on the repercussions of repealing the combat exclusion. Despite claims that racially integrated units would be ineffective, and concerns that African American service members could not be trusted, research indicates that integration did not disrupt cohesion. Similarly, any concerns about the risk that homosexual troops might pose in terms of moral or sexual distraction have proved moot since the repeal of the "Don't Ask, Don't Tell" policy. In the cases of both African American and openly gay and lesbian service members, it became clear that the underlying fear associated with integration was

---

[17] Edward A. Shils and Morris Janowitz, "Cohesion and Disintegration in the Wehrmacht in World War II," *Public Opinion Quarterly* 12, no. 2 (1948): 287.

[18] Frederick J. Manning, *An Investigation into the Value of Unit Cohesion in Peacetime* (U.S. Army Medical Research and Development Command, 1983).

[19] Grice and Katz, "Cohesion in Military and Aviation Psychology," 9.

[20] See for example Aaron Belkin, "Don't Ask, Don't Tell: Is the Gay Ban Based on Military Necessity?" Center for the Study of Sexual Minorities in the Military, July 1, 2003, http://escholarship.org/uc/item/0bb4j7ss.

not group cohesion and effectiveness, but rather fears about what integration might mean for the dominant hetero-white hypermasculine military identity. Although race relations within the military are certainly not ideal today,[21] and gay and lesbian soldiers still face various forms of discrimination and insecurity, speculation about the inherent weaknesses of African American soldiers and concerns that gay soldiers would threaten the comfort levels of straight soldiers now largely seem antiquated and unreasonable. However, not very long ago, these ideas served as the basis for policy.

Perhaps also in an effort to recover military identity, military leaders and researchers began describing a lack of social cohesion as one of the major causes for defeat in Vietnam. At the same time they described unified norms and practices and strong social bonds as essential elements of hypothetical future battles. For example, in the early 1980s, Lieutenant Colonel Jeremy J. J. Phipps of the British Army declared that unit cohesion in US army combat units was the single most important factor for winning the "next major war."[22] Several years later, military researchers Guy Siebold and Dennis Kelly agreed that "the future battlefield is expected to demand higher levels of [leadership, cohesion, and commitment to squads, platoons and companies] for combat success than in the past."[23]

The shift in emphasis from leadership and institutional strategy to small group bonding and culture has had a significant impact on military identity. This narrative recast the defeat in Vietnam as a product of a lack of social cohesion, instead of a failure in strategy.[24]

---

[21] For further discussion of racial discrimination and the intersection of race and gender in the US military, please see Brenda L. Moore, "A Time to Reassess: The Intersection of Race and Class," *Critical Studies on Security* 1, no. 2 (August 1, 2013): 246–48; Brenda L. Moore, *To Serve My Country, to Serve My Race: The Story of the Only African-American WACS Stationed Overseas during World War II* (NYU Press, 1997); David J. Armor, "Race and Gender in the U.S. Military," *Armed Forces & Society* 23, no. 1 (October 1, 1996): 7–27.

[22] Phipps, *Forward, Unit Cohesion*.

[23] Guy L. Siebold and Dennis R. Kelly, *Development of the Combat Platoon Cohesion Questionnaire*, October 1988, p. vii.

[24] William Darryl Henderson summarizes: "a combination of very strong cohesion and of sometimes skimpy but overall adequate logistical support allowed the NVA

It also shifted the emphasis of military identity to small groups at the platoon level. Band of brothers narratives revived enthusiasm for participation in, and support of, the military. Shifting the attention away from broader discussions of the ethics of specific wars and military strategy to the group level also made support for the military more attractive to the general public. This is reflected in recent responses to the wars in Iraq and Afghanistan, where there was a significant emphasis on "supporting the troops," which seemed separate from political debates on the wars. That is, one was, and is, expected to support the troops irrespective of the logic or justness of the wars.

DISMANTLING THE FOUNDATIONS OF THE SEX AND COHESION HYPOTHESIS

The claim that women are a threat to cohesion gained widespread credence despite the disparate and evolving use of cohesion within the military vernacular, and the lack of consensus in research related to women and cohesion. This section explores three premises of the cohesion hypothesis with regard to women in combat: first, that women negatively impact cohesion; second, that cohesion leads to troop effectiveness; and, third, that enhancing cohesion will necessarily have positive impacts on troop dynamics. Using available research to evaluate each of these assumptions demonstrates that none of them can be substantiated with any confidence.

i. Women and cohesion

There are certainly some indications that women impact cohesion. For example, an extensive study on women and cohesion found that "for junior enlisted males . . . gender ratio correlated negatively with horizontal cohesion, vertical cohesion, combat readiness, and acceptance of women."[25] However, this same study found that *acceptance* of women positively correlated with horizontal cohesion and combat

---

to endure." William Darryl Henderson, *Cohesion: The Human Element in Combat* (Honolulu, HI: University Press of the Pacific, 2002).

[25] Rosen et al., "Cohesion and Readiness in Gender-Integrated Combat Service Support Units," 547.

readiness. This means that acceptance of women, not women themselves, might be the key factor in determining whether troops feel women negatively impact cohesion. Another study found that units with higher numbers of women may report lower levels of cohesion because women tend to report lower perceptions of cohesion, combat readiness, and general well-being than men.[26] In sum, although these two studies identify a negative relationship between the integration of women and cohesion, there are indications that the relationship is not a simple "cause and effect" one. Instead, low female morale, combined with gender bias and negative attitudes toward women, may account for differences in cohesion between mixed-gender and all-male units.

Arguments linking women to lower levels of cohesion are further weakened by research that finds no association between the integration of women and diminished cohesion. For example, studies conducted internally by the US military have found little correlation between numbers of women and diminished cohesion. As early as 1977, the US military conducted the "Women Content in Units Force Development Test," which determined that women did not have a significant effect on operational capabilities.[27] These conclusions are supported by a subsequent General Accounting Office report from 1993, which found that gender homogeneity was not listed by focus participants as a requirement for effective unit cohesion during the deployment. Similarly, a 1997 study by RAND examining the effects of increased numbers of women in the US forces on readiness, cohesion, and morale within units found that women's integration has had a limited impact. However, they found that the "real" cohesion story is one of leadership: "leadership, training and unit workload are perceived as having a far more profound influence [on readiness, cohesion, and morale within units]."[28] In turn, there is little

---

[26] Ibid., 550.
[27] *Women Content in Units Force Development Test: (MAX WAC)*. (U.S. Army Research Institute for the Behavioral and Social Sciences, 1977).
[28] Margaret C. Harrell et al., *National Defense Research Institute* (RAND Corporation, 2002).

conclusive evidence that women negatively impact cohesion and troop effectiveness. Moreover, research supports the position that leadership, training, and efforts at improving attitudes and perceptions of women within the forces could mitigate any negative impact gender integration may have on cohesion.

ii. Conflation of task and social cohesion

The second premise of the cohesion hypothesis is that group trust and bonding necessarily leads to increased troop performance. This position links together two separate understandings of cohesion, both social and task, and presumes that more of the former leads to more of the latter. Social cohesion refers to the emotional bonds between members of a group, particularly the feelings of trust and camaraderie. Military sociologist Anthony King explained, "military sociology has generally explained social cohesion in the Armed Forces by reference to the intimate personal bonds produced in informal rituals."[29] By contrast, task cohesion typically refers to the commitment of a group toward a shared mission or set of objectives. Again, King clarifies task cohesion as "a function of how successfully a group is able to coordinate the activities of its members toward a unifying end."[30] Similarly, task cohesion has been defined as "the shared commitment among members to achieving a goal that requires the collective efforts of the group."[31] The distinction between task and social cohesion is simplified in the following quote: "[s]ocial cohesion... refers to whether group members like each other, while *task cohesion* refers to whether they share the same goals."[32]

---

[29] Anthony King, "The Word of Command Communication and Cohesion in the Military," *Armed Forces & Society* 32, no. 4 (July 1, 2006): 493–512.

[30] Anthony King, "The Existence of Group Cohesion in the Armed Forces A Response to Guy Siebold," *Armed Forces & Society* 33, no. 4 (July 1, 2007): 638–45, p. 640.

[31] Piet Van den Bossche et al., "Social and Cognitive Factors Driving Teamwork in Collaborative Learning Environments Team Learning Beliefs and Behaviors," *Small Group Research* 37, no. 5 (2006): 490–521, p. 499.

[32] MacCoun, Kier, and Belkin, "Does Social Cohesion Determine Motivation in Combat?," 2006, p. 647.

It is necessary to reflect on various articulations of the cohesion hypothesis in order to highlight the emphasis placed on social cohesion, or whether troops "like" and trust each other. Earlier in the chapter, Erin Solero was quoted as saying the "single biggest issue in integrating women into the military, much less into the combat arms, has been held to be cohesion: *the emotional bonds* between members of a unit."[33] Here, women's effect on social cohesion is clearly emphasized as problematic. Similarly, Wong depicts women as a threat to a man's primary motivation for fighting, which he identifies as "the bonds of trust between soldiers."[34] It is clear that the anxieties about women and cohesion have typically been in relation to social cohesion, not task cohesion.

Despite the important distinctions between social and task cohesion, researchers often either ignore or conflate the differences. For example, Carron et al. defined cohesion as "a dynamic process which is reflected in the tendency for a group to stick together *and* remain united in the pursuit of its goals and objectives."[35] Similarly, in a literature review on military cohesion, the primary dimensions of cohesion are described as "1. Commitment, the degree of loyalty a member holds for the team and team goals; 2. Communication, the exchange of information; 3. Cooperation, the motivation of members to work together in the accomplishment of team goals; and 4. Command, the administrative and managerial role of directing and sustaining teams."[36] Definitions or explanations of cohesion that tie social and task cohesion together treat the two concepts as if they were part of a single, measurable understanding of cohesion. Researchers using these multifaceted definitions of cohesion are at a disadvantage. If they cannot disaggregate the two concepts and control their

---

[33] Solaro, *Women in the Line of Fire*, 297–298. Emphasis added.

[34] Wong et al., *Why They Fight*, 25.

[35] Mark A. Eys and Albert V. Carron, "Role Ambiguity, Task Cohesion, and Task Self-Efficacy," *Small Group Research* 32, no. 3 (June 1, 2001): 356–73, p. 359. Emphasis added.

[36] Grice and Katz, "Cohesion in Military and Aviation Psychology," vii.

analysis, they cannot determine if one aspect of cohesion is as important as another. This conflation is especially relevant to discussions of women in combat. The cohesion hypothesis conflates social and task cohesion in that it presumes that women disrupt the trust and camaraderie of men (social cohesion), and therefore disrupt troop effectiveness (task cohesion).

Much of the research that distinguishes social cohesion and task cohesion concludes that task cohesion is more strongly linked to group cohesion and mission effectiveness.[37] In a seminal study conducted by the US Army Research Institute for the Behavioral and Social Sciences, Mullen and Copper found "the relation between cohesiveness and performance is due primarily to the 'commitment to the task' component of cohesiveness, and not the 'interpersonal attraction' or 'group pride' components of cohesiveness."[38] Similarly, MacCoun et al. decisively concluded, "all of the evidence indicates that military performance depends on whether service members are committed to the same professional goals, not on whether they like one another."[39] In their research on the Israeli Defense Forces, Ben-Shalom et al. also found that cohesion can be inspired through shared commitment to a mission or objective irrespective of previous social or personal interactions.[40] This research demonstrates that uniting toward a shared mission or task is a greater indicator of group effectiveness than social cohesion. In turn, research that conflates social and task cohesion may erroneously emphasize social cohesion as a causal factor with regard to military effectiveness.

[37] Stephen J. Zaccaro and Charles A. Lowe, "Cohesiveness and Performance on an Additive Task: Evidence for Multidimensionality," *Journal of Social Psychology* 128, no. 4 (1988): 547–58.

[38] Brian Mullen and Carolyn Copper, "The Relationship between Group Cohesiveness and Performance: An Integration" (US Army Research Institute for the Behavioral and Social Sciences, February 1995).

[39] Robert J. MacCoun, Elizabeth Kier, and Aaron Belkin, "Does Social Cohesion Determine Motivation in Combat? An Old Question with an Old Answer," *Armed Forces & Society* 32, no. 4 (July 1, 2006): 646–54, p. 652.

[40] Uzi Ben-Shalom, Zeev Lehrer, and Eyal Ben-Ari, "Cohesion during Military Operations A Field Study on Combat Units in the Al-Aqsa Intifada," *Armed Forces & Society* 32, no. 1 (October 1, 2005): 63–79.

This is not to say that social cohesion is irrelevant. Rather, that the presumed cause-and-effect links between women and social cohesion may be misunderstood or misrepresented. Furthermore, when social cohesion is correlated with readiness, it tends to be because of strong leadership rather than whether troops trust each other or get along. In fact, in many military studies it is nearly impossible to disaggregate the impacts of social cohesion from leadership. For example, Griffith determined that perceptions of combat readiness, as well as task and emotional cohesion, increased when it was combined with quality leadership.[41] A Canadian report on gender and diversity determined that the cohesion of mixed-gender combat units was primarily a leadership challenge.[42] Finally, one of the largest studies of cohesion in the US military concluded that the relevance and effectiveness of training, including strong leadership, had the "greatest effect" in terms of operational outcomes.[43] In other words, social cohesion might matter to troop dynamics, but leadership is the strongest factor determining social cohesion, not "sameness," trust, or gender segregation.

In sum, the hypothesis that social cohesion leads to military effectiveness is weak. Although there may be a weak link between task cohesion and military effectiveness, there is no causal link between social cohesion and military effectiveness, with Elizabeth Kier concluding that "only a modest positive correlation has been identified and, even in this case, analysts seem to be more confident that successful performance leads to cohesion than the contrary."[44] The weakness in this supposed causal link was perhaps best exposed by those examining "Don't Ask, Don't Tell," the former policy preventing openly gay and lesbian individuals from serving. For

[41] Griffith, "Multilevel Analysis of Cohesion's Relation to Stress."

[42] Franklin C. Pinch et al., editors, *Challenge and Change in the Military: Gender and Diversity Issues* (Canadian Defence Academy Press, 2006).

[43] Harrell and Miller, "New Opportunities for Military Women."

[44] Elizabeth Kier, "Homosexuals in the U.S. Military: Open Integration and Combat Effectiveness," *International Security* 23, no. 2 (October 1, 1998): 5–39, p. 40.

example, Kier concluded that "the results from more than five decades of research in group dynamics, organizational behavior, small-group research, sports psychology, social psychology, military history, and military sociology challenge the proposition that primary group unit cohesion enhances military performance."[45] Research from various disciplines, including from military experts, consistently undermines key elements of the cohesion hypothesis, calling into question the causal link between bonding and job performance. If the link between social and task cohesion is called into question, a key foundation for the cohesion hypothesis collapses.

iii. Negative impacts of cohesion

There are further consequences for conflating social and task cohesion. While evidence suggests that increasing task cohesion can enhance performance, research is conflicted about the impact of increasing social cohesion. For example, in her analysis of gender integration, Erin Solaro concluded that "[c]ohesion is not the same as combat effectiveness, and indeed can undercut it. Supposedly 'cohesive' units can also kill their officers, mutiny, evade combat, and surrender as groups."[46] Conversely, researchers note the benefits of heterogeneous groups: "[They] can enhance the quality of group problem-solving and decision-making, and...[broaden] the group's collective array of skills and knowledge."[47] In their article on the role of social cohesion in combat, MacCoun et al. emphatically argue that years of research indicates that "(1) task cohesion has a modest but reliable correlation with group performance, whereas (2) social cohesion has no reliable correlation with performance and, at high levels ('clubbiness'), can even undermine task performance."[48] This research undermines the third premise of the cohesion hypothesis, that enhancing cohesion will necessarily be advantageous for troop dynamics and performance.

---

[45] Ibid., 12. [46] Solaro, *Women in the Line of Fire*, p. 20.
[47] MacCoun et al., "Does Social Cohesion Determine Motivation in Combat?"
[48] Ibid., 2–3.

In addition to the destructive potential of troop cohesion, the mechanisms for generating it throughout history have often been negative. A large study on discipline within the Wehrmacht found that allowing "troops to go unpunished for unauthorized acts of brutality, indiscriminate shootings of prisoners of war and civilians, looting, and wanton destruction" were found to enhance military cohesion as it provided an "outlet" for soldiers faced with "the grim realities of an extraordinarily brutal and costly war on the one hand, and with the prospects of harsh punishment for any attempt to evade it on the other."[49] The Shils and Janowitz contribution mentioned earlier has become iconic and is typically considered evidence of the need for strong social connections between troops; however, competing research demands a reexamination of the article. Key aspects of the contribution are often ignored; in particular, the authors note that the Wehrmacht encouraged unity and respect for authority by allowing troops to commit minor crimes. It is worth quoting the authors at length here:

> Not only was the position of German officers strengthened by
> their mixture of severe domination and benevolence, but
> additional support for their authority came from the provision for
> the blameless gratification of primitive impulses and from the
> sanctioning of all types of aggressive social behaviour outside the
> army group. Private personal transgressions of "civil" ethics were
> regarded as of slight importance, since they were outside the
> limits of the "manly comradeship" of the military primary group.
> Drunkenness and having women in the barracks were crimes
> which the officers overlooked... Provision was made for official
> houses of prostitution in which soldiers could reassure themselves
> about their manliness without disrupting the disciplinary
> structure of the Wehrmacht.[50]

---

[49] Omer Bartov, "The Conduct of War: Soldiers and the Barbarization of Warfare," *Journal of Modern History* 64 (December 1, 1992): S32–S45, p. S35.

[50] Shils and Janowitz, "Cohesion and Disintegration in the Wehrmacht in World War II," 298.

In sum, illegal activity, including crimes of war, was seen as means for soldiers to "let off steam" while at the same time fostering group unity. It is noteworthy that this iconic article has become essential reading within military academies, yet it endorses criminal behavior and the use of prostitutes in the name of "manly comradeship." This often-overlooked section of the article demonstrates the dark underbelly of troop cohesion. It does not treat cohesion as a romantic bond between honorable troops; instead, it reveals that bonding can be built on misogyny, misconduct, and the abuse of women.

COHESION AS GENDERED: THE BONDING OF BROTHERS

As the previous section demonstrated, the key assumptions of the cohesion hypothesis not only are unsupported, but, in some cases, are completely undermined by current research. The effort made to cling to cohesion arguments, despite the lack of evidence, raises questions about the underlying motivations or biases of those promoting this position. I argue that gender bias and infatuation with the band of brothers myth underpin the cohesion arguments. This section presents evidence of flagrant sex discrimination within the cohesion hypothesis. There are two main indicators of gender bias in the way cohesion is conceptualized. First, it is often referred to, both implicitly and explicitly, as male bonding, or as the expression and development of masculinity. Second, evidence indicates that the main impediment to cohesion is men's attitudes toward women, not women themselves or their ability to perform.

Cohesion as male bonding

Discussions on women's potential impact on social cohesion is often code for fears that women will spoil male dynamics and male bonding. This position presents the all-male unit as central to military identity, and a requirement for troop motivation and morale. Hypermasculinity is described as an essential characteristic of troops, and the exclusivity of the male-only unit as a key motivation for soldiers.

In turn, women are seen as a threat to cohesion, not because they cannot perform their professional tasks, but because they are considered unable to replicate the bonds between men.

The first element of this position assumes that unit cohesiveness requires sex segregation – that it is the masculine nature of the bonding, not the bonding or trust itself, that is essential. Anthony King acknowledges that "sociologists have generally preferred to emphasize the role of informal masculine rituals in sustaining cohesion."[51] Defining military cohesion and troop effectiveness by masculine rituals and male bonding places women as outsiders and threats by their very nature, regardless of their performance as soldiers. Military researchers Savage and Gabriel claim that women are a threat regardless of their skills: "the expanded role for women in the military is based on the false assumption that technical skills are the major contributing factor to the combat effectiveness of military units. The fallacy resides here. The fact is that combat effectiveness is only partially, and probably only a small part, the results of well applied technical skills. Most skills in the military, especially combat skills, are learnable by anyone within 6 to 8 weeks. But military unit effectiveness and cohesion are far more the result of sociopsychological bonding – anthropologically, male bonding – among soldiers within, groups."[52] According to this position, even if women meet the physical requirements and complete the same tasks as men, in fact, even if they exceed men, it is still justifiable to exclude them from combat based on their sex. Therefore, the cohesion hypothesis is not an argument to enhance the effectiveness of troops. Rather, it is a position to protect the masculine nature of the military. It prioritizes male bonding over combat effectiveness and defends the need for the all-male unit regardless of female performance.

---

[51] King, "The Existence of Group Cohesion in the Armed Forces," 638.
[52] Rosen et al., "Cohesion and Readiness in Gender-Integrated Combat Service Support Units," 538.

Erin Solero, a researcher and journalist embedded with combat troops in Iraq and Afghanistan, described how such interpretations of cohesion not only emphasize masculinity, but seem to require the exclusion of women. She concludes that "cohesion [among US combat troops] was understood to be male bonding, and the exclusion, and often the denigration, of women was thought to be central to male bonding... some opponents to women in the service propose that men and women cannot bond because male bonding is essentially sexual – that it entails establishing a sexual polarity between men and women."[53]

Male bonding and soldier motivation

The second element of cohesion-as-gendered position focuses on the role of the all-male unit in soldier motivation. Kingsley Browne, the former US Supreme Court clerk and staunch opponent of mixed-gender troops, summarized the links between male bonding and motivation as follows: "Men fight for many reasons, but probably the most powerful one is the bonding – 'male bonding' – with their comrades... Perhaps for very fundamental reasons women do not evoke in men the same feelings of comradeship and 'followership' that men do."[54] Here, Browne is arguing that men want to fight because they want to be around other men, and women ruin this. In an editorial on the subject of women in combat, Robert Scales reiterates this position: "[Men] fight and often die not for country or mission but for each other. We borrow a phrase from Shakespeare's 'Henry V' and term this phenomenon the 'band of brothers effect.' This is the essential glue in military culture that causes a young man to sacrifice his life willingly so that his buddies might survive... The precious and indefinable band of brothers effect so essential to winning in close combat would be irreparably compromised within mixed-gender infantry squads."[55]

[53] Solaro, *Women in the Line of Fire*, 297.   [54] Browne, *Co-Ed Combat*, 7.

[55] Robert H. Scales, "Can a Band of Brothers Include Women?" *Wichita Eagle*, accessed March 26, 2014, http://www.kansas.com/2012/12/10/2595960_robert-h-scales-can-a-band-of.html.

Here male bonding, rather than factors such as training, leadership, or mission objectives, is determined as key to the motivation and success of a military unit.

Cohesion and attitudes

Another indication of gender bias with regard to cohesion arguments stems from attitudes. As indicated earlier, evidence suggests that the main impediment to cohesion is men's attitudes toward female soldiers, not women's performance. Rachel Martin, who wrote a series for National Public Radio on the changing nature of women in the military, concludes, "A big part of this debate isn't about whether or not women can do this work, it's whether or not they should, that there is somehow a general disconcertedness or uncomfortableness with the idea of idea of women, potentially mothers, wives, serving in combat."[56] It seems that irrespective of women's performance, negative attitudes about their place in the military persist. In reference to a pilot program focused on gender integration, an officer acknowledged that "about one third of the male trainees who arrive resenting the notion of integrated training leave with their views unchanged. That lowers the sense of group cohesion."[57] The same source found that regardless of performance or group dynamics, mixed-gender training units "always scored lower on cohesion surveys" compared to male-only infantry and armor positions.

There is also evidence that when attitudes change, combat effectiveness and perceived levels of cohesion increase. Specifically, research on mixed-gender units found that *acceptance* of women positively correlated with horizontal cohesion and combat readiness.[58] Similarly, a study focused on US military exercises in Honduras found

---

[56] Rachel Martin and Kayla Williams, "Female Troops: Combat Ban out of Step with Reality," NPR.org, accessed March 21, 2013, http://www.npr.org/2011/03/01/134168091/Female-Troops-Combat-Ban-Out-Of-Step-With-Reality.

[57] Bradley Graham, "Coed Training, Army Revisiting Basic Strategy," *Washington Post* (November 21, 1994).

[58] Rosen et al., "Cohesion and Readiness in Gender-Integrated Combat Service Support Units."

that "over time, the women came to be regarded and evaluated as individuals rather than as a sexual category. This individuation contributed more than anything else to the successful incorporation of women into non-traditional assignments."[59] These conclusions are supported by the General Accounting Office's 1993 report, which positively correlated the integration of women with group cohesion and effectiveness: "members of gender-integrated units develop brother-sister bonds rather than sexual ones...Experience has shown that actual integration diminishes prejudice and fosters group cohesiveness more effectively than any other factor."[60]

CONCLUSION

This chapter has demonstrated that combat cohesion is not a gender-neutral concept. Rather, it signals a commitment to male bonding and camaraderie at the exclusion of women. Despite the gendered conceptualization of cohesion, and confusing and varying definitions of the concept, the cohesion hypothesis continues to dominate debates on women in the military, even after the removal of the US combat exclusion in 2013. An essential element of the band of brothers myth is the "unexplainable" or "indescribable" bonds of the all-male group. Cohesion is a formal concept that is largely based on such myths. The term is ill defined, and the premises of the cohesion hypothesis are not clearly supported by research. Despite this, there has been consistent and widespread acceptance of the position that male bonding is essential to troop effectiveness. Romantic ideals of the connection and faith between male troops are all too often treated as "fact," rather than narrative. Moreover, the unsavory and negative aspects of group bonding and groupthink are often overlooked or represented as exceptional. In other words, while the incredible ties between the

---

[59] Charles C. Moskos in Helena Carreiras and Gerhard Kümmel, "Off Limits: The Cults of the Body and Social Homogeneity as Discoursive Weapons Targeting Gender Integration in the Military," in *Women in the Military and in Armed Conflict*, edited by Helena Carreiras and Gerhard Kümmel (Verlag für Sozialwissenschaften, 2008), 29–47, p. 38.

[60] Ibid., 39.

Wehrmacht troops are remembered, the illegal activity, including the violation of women, in the name of bonding is forgotten.

Not only is the cohesion hypothesis based on weak foundations, but it leaves several important questions unanswered: Do women only hinder cohesion for combat troops? Do combat troops require a different type of cohesion from other units? And are training initiatives within the military ineffective in fostering task and social cohesion? The "mysterious" and "indescribable" characterization of cohesion has made it a moving target for those trying to integrate women into the military. With no clear definition or means of measuring cohesion, it has become difficult to counter ideological arguments that women will spoil the atmosphere of trust and camaraderie necessary to fight the nation's wars. And the truth is, maybe women will change or undermine particular aspects of masculine culture within the military. However, there is no reason to treat this as a negative outcome, and there is no evidence that such a cultural shift would decrease the effectiveness of troops. Women might make the military less misogynist, and less about proving one's masculinity, and that might not be a bad thing.

6 Using online debates to map public reaction to the combat exclusion

One key objective of this book is to understand how myths and stereotypes shape debates on the combat exclusion. The previous chapters have largely relied on media articles, opinion pieces, public opinion polls, and public policy debates. Although these resources are useful, they provide a limited window into wider public opinions on the combat exclusion. Polls merely assess individual responses to set questions, leaving no room for the public to frame the issue in their own terms. For example, although a poll might indicate that 60 percent of Americans were in favor of removing the combat exclusion, it tells us little about what reasons they have for supporting or opposing the policy change. As a result, it is worthwhile to draw from more diverse sources of public discourse for a richer understanding of public opinions on women and combat.

This chapter provides an analysis of online comments written in response to three online articles on the combat exclusion for women. It addresses three central questions. How can we analyze online discussions and use them as a source of discourse? What are the dominant reasons users commenting in these discussions offer with regard to their support or opposition to the combat exclusion? Do these reasons reflect the themes in the literature, and do they relate to the band of brothers myth? In answering these questions, this chapter has three objectives. The first is to present a methodology for analyzing a vast quantity of online comments. The second is to determine the main arguments online contributors offered in support or opposition to the combat exclusion and assess whether these reasons reflect official political discourse on the topic. The third is to consider whether tropes, messages, and narratives linked to the band of brothers myth are evident in online discussions related to women in combat.

Online mediums are often perceived as attracting unrepresentative contributors and exchanges and therefore are treated as if they do not provide an accurate picture of political discourse. Online comments are all too often placed in the same category as anecdotes. However, online discussions matter politically and should "count" in an analysis of political discourse. Considering that over 80 percent of Americans have an online presence,[1] 66 percent of American adults have engaged in civil or political activities[2] on social media, and about half of those who visit discussion groups have contributed, these mediums should be treated as legitimate sites of political engagement and an important source of political discourse.

My interest in online discourse stems from my role as a regular blogger and my experience engaging in debates that ensue online. In addition, through my research and by reading forums and online comments, I have become aware of several very active online communities that were extensively debating the issue of women in combat. This includes forums on military.com and defencetalk.com, and Facebook groups such as "Grunts 11 Bravo, U.S. Infantry Soldiers," and "Smoking hot and sexi navy chicks!" Arguably, open and equal access to the internet by the majority of the public in America, combined with the ability to choose anonymity,[3] results in frank, uncensored opinions and comments that individuals would perhaps be less willing to express in more formal venues such as surveys or interviews.

This chapter does not consider online comments as "real" or more authentic representations of public opinion. Instead, it treats these engagements as one of many resources that can shed light on public opinion. In addition to the opportunities associated with

---

[1] "Internet World Stats," *Internet World Stats*, August 11, 2014, http://www .internetworldstats.com/stats.htm.

[2] Pew Research, "Politics Fact Sheet," *Pew Research Center's Internet & American Life Project*, November 14, 2012, http://www.pewinternet.org/fact-sheets/ politics-fact-sheet/.

[3] It should be noted that different online forums allow for various degrees of anonymity, depending on the requirement for registration, offering an email address, or signing in through Facebook.

studying online discourse, there are several obstacles and drawbacks. Foremost is that online discussions pose significant challenges in terms of methodology. Drawing on existing work on discourse and online sources, in the following section I offer a methodology for conducting a content and discourse analysis of online comments. The next section applies this method to the more than 700 comments posted to three articles on women in combat. The final section analyzes the results and makes some broader conclusions.

METHODS FOR ONLINE CONTENT

As already indicated, there are several challenges and opportunities associated with studying online content. This section maps out the unique nature of online content and how this influences the types of strategies necessary for a discourse analysis. In addition, the section aims to provide the guidelines I used for conducing a combined content and discourse analysis of online content. The section is organized around the following questions:

i. What makes online discourse different?
ii. How can you establish parameters when analyzing online content?
iii. How do you organize and analyze vast quantities of online material?

i. What makes online discourse different?

Multiple modes of expression Online material uses multiple modes of expression, including emoticons, hyperlinks, images, video, moving images (gifs), graphic design, avatars, and color. This multimodality adds complexity and, I argue, richness to a discourse analysis. However, the researcher must pay attention to, and be aware of, how particular signals are used, what the signals refer to, and how the signals relate to wider debates.[4]

---

[4] Jannis Androutsopoulos, *From Variation to Heteroglossia in Computer-Mediated Discourse*, in *Digital Discourse: Language in the New Media*, edited by C. Thurlow and K. Mroczek (New York: Oxford University Press, 2011), 277–298, p. 281.

Unstable, instant, and edited Online content is unstable, instant, and edited in ways unavailable to printed text. Articles, conversations, and posts can be published, responded to, retweeted, then retracted or edited all within a few hours. Moreover, striking through a comment is a common tool, or stylistic marker, used to indicate alternative, previous, or contradictory expressions. Online content can also be moderated and/or deleted by website or conversation editors with little or no acknowledgment. Tamara Witschge has pointed out that such editing is a signal of the power relations involved in online discussions.[5] Readers are not always aware of the self-editing process, or of the editing that may be conducted by website moderators. This leaves the context and history of a particular publication or post unknown to the reader. Greg Myers calls this "defeasibility" and argues that it limits one's ability to conduct a fixed, stable discourse analysis.[6] In sum, online content is not static; as a result, an analysis of such content must acknowledge that the content represents an unstable, edited, and potentially altered discourse.

ii. How can you establish parameters when analyzing online content?

Choosing what to include Although the method for conducting a discourse analysis is detailed and complex, most analyses follow a broad, common pattern. Researchers choose resources to consider, identify themes within the content, and conduct an analysis, using representative examples to help illustrate the findings. One of the greatest challenges to conducting an analysis of online material is choosing which resources to include, or establishing

---

[5] Tamara Witschge, "Examining Online Public Discourse: A Mixed Method Approach," *Javnost – The Public* 15, no. 2 (2008): 75–92.

[6] Greg Myers, *The Discourse of Blogs and Wikis* (Chippenham, UK: Continuum International, 2010), 125.

parameters. There are few established guidelines for categorizing and selecting online content. This is largely because the internet does not have "readymade sampling frames, such as indexes, catalogues or directories."[7] As a result, researchers have to make choices about appropriate sources with few guidelines or established rules.

A variety of options are available for selecting the parameters of online comments or contributions. For example, one might limit the analysis by choosing comments to well-known, respected, popular, or frequently shared articles on a particular topic. It is also possible to center an analysis on an "iconic" article or post and the discussion it inspired. Hotly debated articles, such as Foreign Policy's feature "Why Do They Hate Us," provide a great potential example. Researchers might also focus on posts or comments within a particular time frame. As with any discourse analysis, the key is to be clear and consistent in establishing the sources.

For this analysis, I chose to focus on the comments and discussion provoked by the following three articles, which were written on the combat exclusion on the online news site *The Daily Beast*: "Overdue: Why It's Time to End the U.S. Military's Female Combat Ban" by Megan MacKenzie, October 2012; "The Truth about Women in Combat," by David Frum, March 2013; and, "End of Combat Ban Means Women Finally Fully Integrated into Military," by Gayle Tzemach Lemmon, January 24, 2013. I chose to analyze all the comments written from the time of publication to March 2014.

The people who chose to read one of these articles and write a comment in the comments section may not necessarily be representative of the broader public. Contributors are distinct because they are more likely to have an interest in women in combat, to be savvy about the internet and online forums, and to have access to the internet and the ability to express their opinions on a political debate.

---

[7] Maria Grazia Sindoni, *Spoken and Written Discourse in Online Interactions: A Multimodal Approach* (New York: Routledge, 2013), 131.

Although statistics range, we know that a very small percentage of online readers comment on articles they read; there is often a small number (approximately 6 percent) of readers who "always" comment, and a silent majority (37 percent) who "never" comment.[8] Moreover, online comments sections can be "hijacked" or "trolled" by one or a few individuals who seek to influence the discussion. Although these comments represent one particular picture of the broader debates on women and combat, the discussions are rich and worthy of analysis, even in light of these restrictions.

These three articles were chosen for several reasons. I was initially surprised, intrigued, and baffled by the wave of responses to the article I wrote for the *Daily Beast*. The candor of the comments and the intensely emotional reactions and fierce debate begged for analysis and engagement. In addition to my curiosity about reactions to my article, the three articles were chosen because the *Daily Beast* is one of the most popular news websites in North America.[9] *The Daily Beast* featured an ongoing series on women and war in 2012, and articles posted on this topic garnered significant discussion. Articles from before and after the combat exclusion was removed were included to consider if the main arguments for and against women in combat changed significantly as a result of the policy change. The first article was published two months before the combat exclusion was removed. The article calls for a change in the policy, and it provoked a heated debate on the topic. Of the two articles published after the policy change, one endorses the policy, and one condemns it.[10]

---

[8] http://betabeat.com/2011/08/6-of-online-news-readers-always-comment-on-stories-compared-to-37-who-never-do/

[9] *The Daily Beast* and the Newsweek merged in 2010. In June 2014, Capital New York published a memo stating that *The Daily Beast's* average unique monthly visitors was approximately 17 million.

[10] It is not clear whether an article will necessarily evoke like-minded comments. As a result, both a "pro" and an "anti" combat article were included to avoid the possible bias involved in simply including one perspective.

Choosing what to exclude: or, how to deal with trolling   Conducting a discourse analysis of online content involves sifting through verbal insults, links to pornography, advertising, and a host of unrelated comments. It is widely acknowledged that the analysis of online content increasingly must consider trolling, flaming, spamming, and flooding as behaviors designed to influence, "hijack," or disrupt the democratic and equal discussion space that the internet creates for the public. Claire Hardaker argues that "'trolling' has become a catch-all term for any number of negatively marked online behaviors," including rants, deceptive comments, offering "poor advice," and provoking.[11] Given some of the ambiguities in terms of defining and controlling for "trolls," researchers need to make common-sense decisions about what should be omitted from the analysis, while still acknowledging that this constitutes a form of editing.

Comments that were excluded from this analysis fell into four categories: insults, irrelevant, utterance, and repeats.[12] Insults included personal attacks on other contributors or the author of the article, as well as crass comments directed at those involved in the discussion, and not the discussion itself. Irrelevant comments include tangential comments or interventions that did not contribute to the debate regarding women in combat. There were two dominant categories of irrelevant comments. The first was random and sometimes confusing posts such as, "Girls will be boys and boys will be girls, it's a mixed up muddled up shook up world except for Lola Lo-lo-lo-lo Lola." A second was side debates, or discussions that became

---

[11] Claire Hardaker, "Trolling in asynchronous computer-mediated communication: From user discussions to academic definitions, *Journal of Politeness Research* 6 (2010), 215–242, p. 224. Accessed http://clok.uclan.ac.uk/4980/2/Hardaker,%20C. %202010.%20Trolling%20in%20ACMC.pdf.

[12] It should be noted that scholars such as Ashley Anderson et al. categorize these comments together under the umbrella of "incivility"; however, I felt it was worth distinguishing particular subthemes and being as specific as possible. http://onlinelibrary.wiley.com/store/10.1111/jcc4.12009/asset/jcc412009.pdf; jsessionid=4C6CCD40CF7743676E08E1E6A10A7EFE.f01t03?v=1&t=hz3my3xg&s =7f7469df3ac02eef53585960b4b862936e4c53ce

disconnected from the topic of women in combat. These included discussions about the morality of the war in Afghanistan, or the apparent fitness of modern soldiers compared to World War II soldiers. If the comments did not relate back to women in combat in any way, they were not included. In the comments section of the second article by David Frum, this omitted a substantial portion of the comments, as there were several side debates between contributors on a variety of unrelated topics.

A third category of comments that were removed was utterances. Utterances included single comments, or comments in a conversation thread, that were not substantial enough to be attributed to a particular argument, such as "oh" "are you kidding me?" or "whatever." Finally, repeat posts, or posts that were directly copied and pasted and reentered into the debate, were excluded. The original comment was included in the analysis, but subsequent copies were excluded. Repeating their comments multiple times is one of the strategies trolls use to dominate or influence discussions. As will be explained later, this was a particular problem for the David Frum article. A final note on representing comments: in order to effectively represent the informal and conversational style and tone of the conversation, comments are quoted exactly as they were printed, without changing the format or including [sic] every time there is a spelling or grammatical error. Given the casual and unedited nature of forums, this means that many of the comments are littered with such errors, as well as including some vulgar language.

iii. How do you organize and analyze vast quantities of online material?

Themes Discourse analysis is typically distinguished from content analysis for its attention to qualitative content and meaning, as opposed to a more quantitative analysis of word use. Given the volume of online material, there is value in using both approaches in an analysis of online content. Gruber and others have used critical discourse analysis of computer-mediated content (CMC) with content analysis, including software tools. Although such tools were not used in this analysis, both qualitative and quantitative methods have been employed to organize and represent the themes found within the comments. In practical terms, this includes a chart for each of the articles with a breakdown of the number of comments that mention each of the major themes. This is followed by a more qualitative analysis of representative examples of comments within each of the themes.

Once the parameters of the online discourse analysis have been established, the sheer volume of online material can be daunting. Gruber recommends organizing online material into themes and identifying sample texts that are representative of the themes. Gruber argues that distinct methods are needed for identifying "successful" or representative comments within online comment. Gruber recommends considering factors such as "(1) the communicative activity of single contributors and (2) the perceived relevance of their contributions."[13] Some comments, for example, might garner numerous responses, or be requoted or shared throughout a conversation thread, whereas other contributions may be "dead ends," never getting a response or reaction. Gruber argues that although the latter cannot be completely disregarded, the former type of contribution is of interest for a discourse analysis because they are the ones influencing and shaping a great deal of the debate.

In this analysis, comments to the three articles were categorized into themes based on the dominant focus of each comment. This can be a blunt tool for categorization, because many comments focus on multiple issues. However, in order to be consistent, each comment was only "counted" for one theme, based on the primary focus. Early in the analysis, dominant themes began to emerge,

[13] Helmut Gruber, "Analyzing Communication in the New Media," in *Qualitative Discourse Analysis in the Social Sciences*, edited by Ruth Krzyzanowski and Michael Krzyzanowski (Houndmills, UK: Palgrave Macmillan, 2008), 65.

including physical standards, references to women and men's "nature," and concerns about rape and sexual assault. In addition to sorting comments into themes according to topic, comments that provoked a discussion thread of more than four exchanges were separated. The initial comment that provoked the thread, or the lead comment, was analyzed further to consider why it may have provoked debate or discussion. Where possible, lead comments were included as examples when analyzing themes, given their significance within the debate. In cases where a comment generated exceptional debate, the comment is identified in the analysis. Finally, comments were divided into those that were generally supportive of women in combat and those that generally argued against including women in combat roles. Although most contributions expressed a clear opinion in this regard, there were some comments that seemed to use sarcasm, or expressed support with hesitation, making it difficult to know for certain if they supported or opposed women in combat. Again, this mechanism for categorization is somewhat blunt; however, there were very few comments that fell into the ambivalent or unclear category.

Stylistic markers   In addition to analyzing the topics covered within the online conversations, it is necessary to analyze stylistic markers and mechanisms of conveying meaning that are particular to online contributions. The first type of stylistic marker involves marking one's place. Greg Myer has noted that contributors may use references to personal location, experience, or background, with the objective of "claiming an identity, making a contrast, giving a perspective on the topic, telling a story."[14] Myer notes that marking one's place might give a contributor more authority or legitimacy in terms of their contribution; examples of this include, "after 16+ years of service I'd like to think I know a thing or two from personal experience"[15] and "I am an Army veteran – a staff sergeant with 7 years'

---

[14]   Myers, *The Discourse of Blogs and Wikis*, 57.
[15]   "AlanWeinraub" January 29, 2013, comment on Gayle Tzemach Lemmon, "End of Combat Means Women Fully Integrated Into Military," Daily Beast- Women in the World, January 24, 2013.

experience."[16] These identifiers distinguish the contributor from civilians and convey experience and authority on the issue.

Nicknames can also be a means of marking a commenter's place. According to Sindoni, the names people use to represent their "virtual identity" can serve as an "authentic self-representation, performance and fiction."[17] A contributor's nickname might signal their location, or their ideological position. For example, one of the contributors to the discussion on Article 1 used the name "Real_Black_Men_R_Heterosexual," which sends a very explicit set of messages along with his or her individual contributions. It should be noted that commenters are referred to by their chosen online nicknames – in quotation marks – throughout the chapter.

ANALYSIS OF THREE ARTICLES

The comments to all three of these articles were dominated by debates on women's physical fitness. As indicated by the tables that follow, both supporters and opponents of women in combat centered their comments on women's physical capabilities or inadequacies. The following sections explore the subthemes to the physical arguments, including comparisons of combat to professional sport and concerns about double standards. The sections also include an analysis of other prominent themes within the comments section, using representative quotations, where possible, to highlight the arguments.

"OVERDUE: WHY IT'S TIME TO END THE U.S. MILITARY'S FEMALE COMBAT BAN" BY MEGAN MACKENZIE, OCTOBER 2012

This article makes the case that women should be allowed to formally serve in combat roles. It provides a general survey of some of the main arguments for allowing women into combat. This includes the lack of clear front lines in modern warfare, the lack of evidence supporting claims that women spoil unit cohesion, and questions surrounding

---

[16] "EPENN", January 24, 2013, comment on ibid.

[17] Sindoni, *Spoken and Written Discourse in Online Interactions*, 171.

Table 2 *MacKenzie Article Comments*

Supporting Comment Themes[18]	Comment Count
Physical	18
Rape	5
Women already on front lines	3
Other	2
Total	28
Opposing Comment Themes	**Comment Count**
Women lack physical strength	34
Rape	5
Women as poor communicators	2
Problem with author	2
Menstruation	3
Women are sexual distraction	2
Other	2
Total	50
Total Pacifist Comments[19]	5
Total Comments Overall	83

[18] Although these comments have been categorized as "positive" or in favor of women in combat, in essence they are largely making the case that rape is not a reason to keep women out of combat rather than making a clear case about why women should be allowed to serve in these roles. It should be noted that very few comments seemed ambivalent about the issue of women and combat and most did express explicit opinions about the issue; however, these responses indicate a weakness in categorizing comments within affirmative or negative themes. Such a categorization assumes that all contributors are "for" or "against" women in combat and makes it difficult to include – and devalues – ambivalent comments, questions, or comments that might weigh in on one of the subthemes without necessarily making a normative claim about whether women should be allowed to serve in combat. In this case I chose to categorize these rape comments as "affirmative" contributions, both because they critiqued claims for keeping women out of combat due to rape, and because they explicitly ("let the woman choose which part of the military she chooses to join and which risk she chooses to accept") or implicitly indicate support for women's presence and enhanced presence in the military.

[19] In the responses to all articles, there were a few comments that did not advocate or critique women's inclusion into combat. Instead, they took a pacifist stance. These contributors questioned the usefulness of war and mentioned their hesitancy in

physical standards and women. As of March 2014, the article was "shared" 787 times, was "liked" on Facebook 671 times, and was retweeted 98 times. Although there were more than 120 comments, 82 comments were included in the analysis, after eliminating insults, irrelevant comments, and utterances. The majority (50 comments, or 61 percent of the contributions) disagreed with the author and expressed the view that women should not be allowed in combat roles. Table 2 provides an overview of some of the themes found within those comments, both supportive and opposed to women in combat.

The physical

The majority of the comments to this article – both those supportive of and those opposed to women in combat – focused on physical arguments. Those opposed to the idea of women in combat reiterated most of the subarguments established in Chapter 4. The overarching point was that "[t]he average female individual" is not as physically cable of performing in combat situations as well as the average male.[20] There were four subthemes to comments focused on physicality. In the sections below, these themes are discussed and linked to broader ideals and assumptions associated with the band of brothers myth, including: the perception that all-male units are necessary for the protection of society; that all-male units are more capable of achieving military objectives than mixed-gender units; and that the male body is *different* from and *superior* to female bodies. The story or image of a weak female unable to drag her male comrade to safety is also retold or referenced in several comments. This story contrasts the band of

putting either men or women into combat. One contributor warns "ladies" that "%99.9 of the time, war is f***** stupid" and goes on to argue "Women should be in no hurry to involve themselves in unnecessary military conflicts. No offense to anyone who serves I have loved ones that do, but being a willing participant in todays theaters doesnt simply make you a hero, it makes you an enabler of an unreasonable, hostile, reactionary foreign policy."

20 "mjmdmd19," December 12, 2012, comment on Megan H. MacKenzie, "Overdue: Why It's Time to End the U.S. Military's Female Combat Ban," Daily Beast – Women in the World, October 26, 2012, http://www.thedailybeast.com/articles/2012/10/26/overdue-why-it-s-time-to-end-the-u-s-military-s-female-combat-ban.html.

brothers – a unit that is presumed to be unified, physically equal, and able to protect themselves – with the insecure potential that women represent to forces. As indicated in Chapter 4, it is fascinating how embedded this story is in the minds of those discussing women in combat; although it is a fictional story, it is consistently retold as proof of women's incapacity to fight as combat soldiers. Rather than separate those comments that were supportive of women and combat from those opposed, these sections illustrate the dialogue and contrasting views of commenters with regard to each subtheme.

Equal rights and standards Those supportive of the idea of women in combat consistently linked equality to physical standards. There are two elements to this overarching position. First, women who meet the existing requirements should be included in combat. Second, that an effort should be made to ensure existing standards were not lowered to accommodate women. "jdr9599"'s contribution summarizes these two elements: "Tell you what if a woman can do all the same things physically as a man (that means no more gender biased physical fitness test), and can mesh with the team as well as a group of guys... yes we should allow all soldiers into direct combat operations."[21] Similarly, "Superlib87" responded directly to the article and the claim that women should be allowed to fight:

> I agree with you completely, Megan... women SHOULD be
> allowed to serve in combat roles... but to qualify for combat
> service, we should have to pass exactly the same physical
> standards that men have to. Combat soldiers frequently have to
> carry heavy loads for a long time, covering long distances. That is
> a hard physical standard for many men to meet, and it will be
> even harder for women... a woman may also have to help carry
> extra gear and wounded soldiers on the return trip. And because
> physical strength and endurance is a "sine qua non" for a combat

[21] "jdr9599" October 29, 2012, comment on ibid.

soldier, that is going to disqualify a lot of women . . . many of whom will probably be real pissed off because of that. But no matter how much they might complain, that requirement should not change.[22]

It is useful to analyze this rather lengthy contribution in its entirety because it illustrates how contributors blend their comments from seemingly subjective statements about standards with stories about carrying soldiers and presumptions about women's emotional reactions to physical requirements. Such comments seem to affirm the principle of gender equality and reiterate (i) that women are usually or naturally physically weaker than men; (ii) that dual standards are double standards, constituting "gender bias"; and (iii) that combat requires exceptional physical qualities not typically attributed to women. Here, equality is linked to "do[ing] the same things physically as a man," with the contributors arguing that women must meet the same standards as men in order to be considered true equals.

Responding to negative comments about women and physical standards on the thread, "Jane Lane" calls into question the expertise and authority of some of the contributors. He/she cites personal experience and knowledge of soldiers in making the following argument: "@Medic5392 @John_7469 I have known tons of military people both current and former and not one of them has ever complained to me about the women in their unit not being able to pull their own weight. Men in the Navy, the Marines, the Army and the Air Force do not complain en mass that women can't do the job that they do. So how come it is that every time there's an article on this, there are a bunch of dudes who have probably not served complaining about how women can't do the job?"[23] In this instance "Jane Lane" is implying that some contributions are based on sexist attitudes and not experience or in-depth knowledge of the military.

[22] "Superlib87," October 29, 2012, comment on ibid.
[23] "Jane Lane," October 30, 2012, comment on ibid.

Dragging a comrade As already indicated, within the physical theme, several contributors mentioned women's inability to carry or drag a comrade across a battlefield. The comments focus on the story or ideal of a man and woman caught on the battlefield, with women unable to help their comrades or drag them to safety. This story is retold as proof of the argument that women should not be in combat. This mirrors the "comrade" story and themes established within the literature on women in combat. For example, responding to calls for equal treatment of men and women in the military, "Medic5392" accuses supporters of women in combat of being unable "think of things outside of [their] 'feelings' that this is a 'rights' issue."[24] He/she asks "What about the rights of the male troops are killed due to not being able to be dragged back to safety, who can't reach the target because the women can't keep up, can't carry the same weight or don't have the upper body strength to perform...?"[25] Similarly, "Goosen" notes that he/she is "all for equality" but adds, "[t]he physical differences are limiting to a female soldier. This article fails to mention that one of the requirements of a soldier is that he can carry a wounded soldier on his shoulders. Not many women I know can carry a 200 lb man on her shoulders."[26] In both cases, the contributors use the image of a woman unable to drag a male body – rather than specific evidence or physical standards – as evidence to support their case that women should be excluded from combat.

Sports Sports references constituted another subtheme within the physical comments. Again, as with the story of women unable to drag her male comrades, such sports references are very common in the literature on women in combat. "Mr.Wonderful_1" compares women's inferiority in professional sports to their weaknesses in military situations: "[i]t's funny at a picnic when someone throws a baseball 'like a girl', not so funny in combat when you throw a hand grenade 'like a

[24] "Medic5392," October 29, 2012, comment on ibid.
[25] "'Medic5392,'" October 29, 2012, comment on ibid.
[26] "Goosen," January 3, 2012, comment on ibid.

girl'."[27] "Jeffreygeez" also references professional sports as evidence of women's lack of competence for combat roles. Referencing gender segregation in sports such as tennis, he/she argues "women cannot compete physically with men...so cut the BS forever, please...women have more inate intelligence than men, therefore they should not be allowed to fight, only the stupid women will want to do that, stupid and physically inferior to a male enemy."[28] Here, the author uses gender segregation in sports as evidence of "innate" differences between men and women. Interestingly, the author also harnesses his/her conclusions about men and women's bodies to a broader claim about women's intellect and the types of women who would volunteer for combat. Although the move might seem flippant, it signals the tendency to link claims about women and men's so-called inherent biological differences to subjective claims about men and women's capacities or natures.

Other contributors responded critically to the comparison between combat and professional athletes. "Melissapeddy" disagreed with "Mr.Wonderful_1"'s comment, stating "@Mr. Wonderful_1 Wonder why all these men in combat didn't join the NY Yankees then, making millions of dollars and enjoying fame, instead of joining the military? People have all different physical abilities, and war today is no longer just about brawn. Women definitely have a place & should be allowed to fight."[29]

These comments demonstrate that physical requirements are a central focus within debates on women in combat. Both those opposed and those supportive of women in combat largely reaffirm the perception that men are "ideal" soldiers because of their physical nature. Women are seen as capable only through their ability to "equal" or

[27] "Mr.Wonderful_1," October 27, 2012, comment on Megan H. MacKenzie, "Overdue: Why It's Time to End the U.S. Military's Female Combat Ban," *Daily Beast – Women in the World*, October 26, 2012, http://www.thedailybeast.com/articles/2012/10/26/overdue-why-it-s-time-to-end-the-u-s-military-s-female-combat-ban.html.

[28] "Jeffreygeez," January 4, 2013, comment on ibid.

[29] "Melissapeddy," October 29, 2012, comment on ibid.

match men's physical strength. None of the contributors questioned the nature of physical testing or the consequences of holding male bodies as the standard. In turn, the debate largely reinforced the military as essentially a band of brothers that should include only those women who can perform – as brothers – physically.

Rape

After comments on physical standards, the second most common theme among the comments opposed to women in combat was rape. Contributors expressed concerns about the possibility that women could be "taken prisoner and repeatedly raped and sexually abused" as well as the threat from "the sexual advances of the other soldiers around them"[30] due to the "sexual aspect of allowing women in such close quarters with men."[31] "Mr. Wonderful_1" challenges supporters of women in combat, writing "don't be crying here when they are taken prisoner and repeatedly raped and sexually abused and just one more little thing if you can't fight off the sexual advances of the other Soldiers around them, then they really have no place on the battlefield, which is not a playground nor a Laboratory for some Leftist Social experiment, it is an ugly, brutal, and barbaric place, Welcome to the Jungle." This contribution treats the potential for soldiers to be raped by both opposing forces and comrades as rationale for excluding them. Moreover, the assertion that women are unable to stave off rape, or protect themselves from assault, is offered as evidence of women's weakness and further proof that women should be excluded from combat.

The previous comment is illustrative of comments that link sexual violence to other claims about women and combat – in that case rape and physical fitness. The following comment by "LadyEI" is another example the tendency to link several arguments and claims about women in combat together

---

[30] "Mr. Wonderful_1," October 27, 2012, comment on MacKenzie, "Overdue."
[31] "LadyEl," October 27, 2012, comment on ibid.

There is so much more to allowing women into combat officially and on the front lines particularly. The sexual aspect of allowing women in such close quarters with men alone is not even explored in this article. We already know the military has problems with rape. I agree with one of the comments below what about when our women are captured? I think women should be allowed to serve, in many many capacities but it is a much greater sign of our strength and our leadership capabilities to step back and say in this area men are much more suited to carryout the actions necessary. For physical and practical reasons, what do you do if you are on your period in a forward combat position? There is no where to attend to your needs! The majority of women are not well suited to the demands of combat. The "male bonding" issues you cite also put women in a position to be abused by their male counterparts. Not that this should be accepted or excused but it is a reality of the stress of combat situations.[32]

Here, "LadyEI" addresses a number of issues related to women in combat – rape, menstruation, physical standards, and male bonding – in one relatively short comment. The author seems to effortlessly link extremely different issues together, showing a "cluster" of concerns related to women and combat. The author also presumes that readers understand certain "truths" about women and bases her positions on these apparent truths. For example, the statements "we already know the military has problems with rape" and "the majority of women are not well suited to the demands of combat" both make vast assumptions – in the former instance that the military has a rape problem that is universally understood, and in the latter instance, that there is a general understanding of "the demands of combat" and that "the majority" of women are not suited to these demands. The richness and multiple focus of the comment make it somewhat difficult to categorize and illustrates another challenge to the quantitative

---

[32] "LadyEl," October 27, 2012, comment on ibid.

content analysis offered earlier. This contribution was "counted" as one on rape, because more of the content focused on rape than any other issue. However, such a categorization cannot account for its complexity.

Five contributors focused on rape in their affirmative comments regarding women and combat roles. These contributors question the tendency to blame women for the threat of sexual assault, and decry the presumption that men "can't keep their dicks to themselves."[33] For example, in response to this type of argument from "@Mr.Wonderful_1," "Kathy Sammons" writes "Overly emotional men who are incapable of controlling themselves and resort to raping women in their own units – fellow Americans and soldiers – should not be allowed in combat. You cannot stand by a code of morality among our soldiers and then say that it's not only expected for them to rape women, it's practically a right of passage. This thinking does a disservice to our brave men in uniform and it denigrates the military as a whole."[34] "Jane Lane" also questions the logic that rape and sexual violence rates are proof that women and men cannot work together. He/she laments, "I don't understand why, when we talk about rape, the problem is the women and not the rapists."[35] "Roadstraveled" also makes the case that "[r]ape happens to prisoners regardless of gender, it's not about sex it's about humiliation and power. Above all let the woman choose which part of the military she chooses to join and which risk she chooses to accept."[36]

"Mr. Wonderful_1" and "Kathy Sammons" had a few exchanges on this issue. After "Mr. Wonderful_1" makes the comment about women being unable to "fight off the sexual advances of the other Soldiers," "Kathy Sammons" responds in a way that seemingly defends the honor of American male troops: "@Mr. Wonderful_1 I have been in combat. I have witnessed first-hand what happens in the field of

33 "Jane Lane," October 30, 2012, comment on ibid.
34 "Kathy Sammons," October 27, 2012, comment on ibid.
35 "Jane Lane," October 30, 2012, comment on ibid.
36 "Roadstraveled," October 27, 2012, comment on ibid.

war; the bloody battles, the mourning of the dead, the unbearable heat and tedium. I think you do our men a great disservice in saying that they are merely animals incapable of controlling their base instincts. Perhaps that is how you behave in your life, but the men I fought alongside (and they were, in fact, men and not uncontrollable, hormonal little boys) would despise your cavalier, ill-informed attitude. Either you hold yourself up to the military standard or you do not. Either you are a good soldier or you are not. Either you are a man of honour or you are not. There is no justification for rape, and implying that combat takes away our humanity is repugnant. It dishonours our living as well as our dead."[37] Here, "Kathy Sammons" is simultaneously establishing expertise and authority by pointing to his/her experience, and discrediting "Mr.Wonderful_1" by accusing him/her of not being a "man of honour" based on his/her comments. Although the comment critiques the construction of women as weak and unable to stave off sexual violence, it also serves to construct and reify a particular ideal of "good" and "honorable" male soldiers.

Women "already there"

Among the comments in support of women in combat, the position that women are "already there" was the second most common theme. Contributors pointed out "the thousands of women that have spent the last ten years in Iraq or Afg experiencing combat. The official line of the government is that this is not the case."[38] The prevailing position was that changing the combat exclusion policy would merely recognize, or "put on paper," women's previous and ongoing service.[39] Similarly, referencing Iraq and Afghanistan, "John_7469" wrote "speak to anyone that has been there and you will hear a story not of 1950's army rhetoric – ie front line vs support – and instead of a combat situation that is now termed '360 degree combat' . . ." This contributor not only argues that "women are already there," but also

---

[37] "Kathy Sammons," October 27, 2012, comment on ibid.
[38] "John_7469," October 27, 2012, comment on ibid.
[39] "Jane Lane," October 30, 2012, comment on ibid.

highlights the nature of modern warfare and the disconnect between the combat exclusion and counterinsurgency warfare.

It is important to note that posts referencing women's existing contribution were regularly discredited or critiqued. For example, "StandupGuy9366," responded to such claims with the following: "IT's not the reality, it's a media hype story because women are on bases and in convoys that get hit by IEDs. That does not prove you can or should be in the Infantry or SOF. Pilots? I must have missed the last air to air dogfights we had the last 12 years. No man pads either." This contributor is casting doubt as to whether depictions of women contributing to war represent "reality."

"Other": Menstruation

Although the vast majority of comments focused on physical fitness, rape or whether women are already on the front lines, there were several comments outside of these themes that should be recognized. In particular, one subtheme of comments focused on menstruation. Although there were only a handful of online comments that mentioned menstruation, they mirror the way that menstruation is treated in the literature and this chapter and are therefore worth quoting:

- @Ohyes I can just envision it now. WWIII breaks out and we have all women on the frontline. First, we ambush the enemy with laughter once they see a bunch of pre-menstrual infantry charging them, and then when all the females get wiped out by the female-loathing, Allah-praising insurgents, the feminists go nuts on the army for putting the women up front. It'll be like something out of a Sacha Baron Cohen movie.[40]
- Just this week I was talking to a nice young lady who is very tall and athletic. She goes to college on an athletic scholarship and regularly does things that would have killed me on the best day of my life. And

---

[40] "mjmdmd19," October 27, 2012, comment on ibid.

this week her boy friend had to carry her upstairs to her bed because her monthlies hit her so hard. Physically, we are just not the same.[41]

The first comment uses humor and sarcasm to argue that menstruating women would not only be a liability for the military, they could also be a source of humiliation and embarrassment. Rather than focusing on any specific aspects of menstruation, the contributor offers a fictitious situation – the enemy laughing at pre-menstrual women, before defeating them – as a warning of the potential results of allowing women into combat. Here, "pre-menstrual" seems to be used as a descriptor, indicating weakness and vulnerability. According to the contributor, the "enemy" would somehow "see" women's pre-menstrual state, necessarily think this is funny, and use women's pre-menstrual condition to their advantage in battle. When one dissects the logic of the comment, it seems quite ridiculous, yet the values and assumptions embedded in the comment are similar to other mentions of menstruation in the literature on women in combat. Authors treat menstruation as mysterious, awkward, and an obvious disadvantage for women. The second comment uses menstruation to make the argument that even women who are physically fit become weak and vulnerable as a result of menstruation. This reiterates comments made by authors in Chapter 4, casting menstruation as a sign of women's inherent instability and unpredictability as soldiers.

"THE TRUTH ABOUT WOMEN IN COMBAT," DAVID FRUM, MARCH 2013

The second article is a more in-depth opinion piece expressing serious criticism of the removal of the combat exclusion. David Frum is a contributing editor at the *Daily Beast* and a CNN contributor who had written several shorter pieces on women in combat on the *Daily Beast* before the publication of this feature post. Frum is blunt in his assessment of women in combat as a sign of "liberals . . . blinded by

[41] "Fang1944," October 27, 2012, comment on ibid.

ideology." He primarily relies on Kingsley Browne's book *Co-Ed Combat: The New Evidence That Women Shouldn't Fight the Nation's Wars* to support his list of reasons why women should not be allowed to fight on the "front lines." He focuses on the apparent instability of the arguments for women in combat, countering them with research and quotes from Browne's book. The arguments focus largely on the physical capabilities of women and the physical nature of combat (although the article also references sexual attraction and men's resistance to following female leaders). This article garnered significant attention; it was "shared" online more than 1300 times; it had more than 1000 "likes" on Facebook and was retweeted more than 100 times.[42]

Although the article garnered almost 600 comments, the vast majority fell into the categories of insult, irrelevant, or utterances. It is essential to note that one contributor, "joetheragman2," dominated – and arguably trolled – the discussion. This contributor posted a total of 85 times, and – in particular – cut and pasted a paragraph-long post on privacy 22 times. These contributions clearly influenced the focus of the discussions, with more than 42 contributors responding directly to his/her posts. In order to mitigate for this influence, "joethergman2"'s original post on privacy was included; however, subsequent reposts of exactly the same wording were excluded from the analysis (and were not counted in the content analysis). "Joetheragman2"'s other contributions were included, provided they did not fall into one of the excluded categories (utterance, insult, irrelevant, and divergent), which several did. It should also be noted that many of the responses to "joetheragman2" also fell into one of these excluded categories, as it seems that several contributors were frustrated with his/her reposting and repetitive comments. After removing these comments, as well as all other excluded comments, 236 remained. Table 3

---

[42] As of June 2, 2014. Determined using the tracking tool on http://muckrack.com/whoshared/ because the website does not publish the number of shares and retweets for older articles.

Table 3 *Frum Article Comments*

Supporting Comment Themes	Comment Count
Physical	44
Women are already on the front lines	30
Author's use of evidence/anecdotes	18
Courage is not tied to gender	6
Women should have equal rights	8
Rape prevalence is not grounds for exclusion	4
Privacy is irrelevant	3
Total	113
Opposing Comment Themes	Comment Count
Physical	86
Women in combat as a "leftist" agenda	8
Rape	6
Courage tied to gender	2
Issues with female leadership	2
Other	5
Total	109
Total Pacifist Comments	12
Total Comments Overall	234

provides an overview of the topics covered within the 236 comments; this is followed by an analysis of the themes.

Supporting themes

i. The physical   Similar to the comments opposed to women in combat, comments supporting the policy change largely focused on physicality. There were two types of comments within this category. The first made the general point that, if women can meet the same standards as men, they should be allowed to fight. This echoes comments made in response to the first and the third article among proponents of women in combat. The following comment is exemplary of this subtheme: "No one is saying women should be required to fight. There are standards. Plenty of men in the Army can't handle the infantry. Most women won't qualify. But you can't disqualify them on the basis of two X chromosomes."[43] Contributors seemed emphatic about the need for "the same physical and mental standards,"[44] "the same training and endurance tests as the men,"[45] and the military's commitment not to "lower standards for women."[46] In sum, similar to comments to the MacKenzie article, a significant portion of those who support opening combat roles to women also support equal standards. However, these contributors link equality to single, gender-blind standards.

A second subtheme in the physical category included comments promoting the idea that modern warfare does not require extreme physical capabilities, or the same physical capabilities as war might have had in the past. These contributors note that times have changed, resulting in military operations that are more sophisticated and driven by technology rather than "broadswords."[47] Contributors like "BFaul" directly criticize David Frum's point about the physically demanding nature of warfare, arguing, "[f]ools like [Frum] are still thinking that war is about battle axes and clubs and bows rather than rifles and machine guns and helicopters."[48] In both of these subthemes, contributors reaffirm the relevance and importance of male physical standards and the apparent physical superiority of men over women. Their support for women in combat hangs on the changing nature of warfare, and the fact that *some* women will be able to meet male physical standards. In this sense, few of the contributors radically challenge the existing standards, or the perception that war has

---

43 "debrouillarde," March 1, 2013, comment on David Frum, "The Truth About Women in Combat," *Daily Beast*, March 1, 2013, http://www.thedailybeast.com/articles/2013/03/01/the-truth-about-women-in-combat.html.
44 "Katstiles," March 1, 2013, comment on ibid.
45 "cookies23," March 2, 2013, comment on ibid.
46 "smcjane," March 1, 2013, comment on ibid.
47 "Primrose," March 1 2013, comment on ibid.
48 "Bfaul," March 2 2013, comment on ibid.

historically been a physically demanding job better suited to men. In fact one contributor, who voiced support for women in combat, simultaneously makes the case that men are superior soldiers:

> The question isn't what kind of homo sapien makes the best soldier. A huge, freakishly strong, highly-aggressive, extremely intelligent 21-year-old male is the ideal soldier. A million of them would make a great army. Ten million of them would make an even better army. Fifty million of them would make an even better army than that. We don't have fifty million such soldiers, so we have to work with what we have. Women are part of that equation.[49]

These contributors are pointing to the changing nature of warfare or to the exceptional women who can meet male standards as evidence that women should be included, not that women themselves have something unique to offer or that the institution itself should change.

ii. Women already there The position that "women are already in combat" represents a second theme to the comments in support of the policy change. Echoing comments to the first article, contributors pointed out the historic contributions of women to war and combat,[50] as well as indicators that "women are in combat situations right now."[51] What unites this theme is the effort to distract attention away from other arguments and draw attention to "reality" and proof of women's contributions, or "actual evidence of women performing direct ground combat tasks, and doing so well."[52]

iii. Poor evidence and courage The third and fourth themes included comments directly critiquing Frum's article. In particular, a significant number of comments expressed criticism of the author's

---

[49] "iowaclass," March 3, 2013, comment on ibid.
[50] "Insanity," March 1, 2013, comment on ibid.
[51] "Easton- Maria Houser Conzemius," March 1, 2013, comment on ibid.
[52] "jeffd85," March 1, 2013, comment on ibid.

use of anecdotes, poor evidence, or outdated evidence to support his arguments for keeping women out of combat roles. For example, "RLHotchkiss" retorts, "It would help if Frum provided you know some real science…But all Frum is providing is stories."[53] "Chuckster" also accuses Frum of using "sweeping assumptions – based mostly, it appears, on random anecdotal 'evidence.'"[54] In addition to concerns about his use of evidence, several contributors took issue with Frum's argument that "women's courage takes very different forms [from men's]." One contributor reacted with the following: "To say that women are incapable [of] courage in war is another way to say women are cowards and weak and as has been presented over the centuries (and in nearly every bleeping action movie that exists) that therefore men get to rule."[55] "Primrose" also pointed to what he/she called "the disgustingly sexist ramifications of such a statement by saying women have 'different' courage,'" arguing, "courage is courage…[it] is not actually an innate quality but something that must be nurtured and practiced."[56] Similar to comments related to Frum's choice of evidence, these comments are primarily aimed at showing weakness to Frum's article, rather than explicitly arguing why women should be in combat.

Opposing themes

i. The physical The most common theme in comments critical of women in combat was physicality. Contributors repeatedly made the point that women and men are different physically. More specifically, there was the consistent argument that men are more physically capable of combat, while "women just aren't built for combat"[57] and that, even if "some women can handle these demands,"[58] they

---

[53] "RLHotchkiss," March 1, 2013, comment on ibid.
[54] "Chuckster," March 1, 2013, comment on ibid.
[55] "KT_," March 1, 2013, comment on ibid.
[56] "Primrose," March 1, 2013, comment on ibid.
[57] "Montezia," March 1, 2013, comment on ibid.
[58] "best foot for'rd," March 1, 2013, comment on ibid.

remain "outliers."[59] "Best foot for'rd" took the argument further, stating that the military should not integrate the "statistical few"[60] women who can compete with men into the combat arms. These comments consistently reiterate three points: first, that male bodies are physically superior to female bodies; second, that this physical superiority translates into better performance in combat, or that male bodies are better equipped to serve in combat; and, third, that women who "equal" men physically, or are able to meet similar physical standards, are so rare that they should not impact military practice or policy.

Within these themes, there were consistent examples of contributors harnessing seemingly objective comments about physical standards to broader subjective claims about women and men's nature. For example, in response to a comment stating that women can be as strong as men, "ImadThisstupid" retorts, "women are on average, muscularly weaker than men (and this matters in non-routine miltary context, which is the context for which a military exists), women are not disciplined for cowardly behavior at the same standard as men, women are demonstrably divisive authority figures to men in the military – all these are extremely salient as strategic input to the military."[61] Here you have apparently objective claims about average women and their physical performance harnessed, or linked, to general assertions about whether women are brave or cowardly, and the response men have to women as leaders. Although they are completely separate issues, with divergent indicators and sources of support, harnessing such subjective statements to more objective claims about physicality gives them legitimacy.

A number of contributors highlighted their personal experience in the military, or discounted other contributors who seemed to lack such experience. For example, in response to claims that women can

---

[59] "joetheragman2," March 1, 2013, comment on ibid.
[60] "best foot for'rd," March 1, 2013, comment on ibid.
[61] "ImadThisstupid," March 1, 2013, comment on ibid.

compete physically with men, "Skullduggery" wrote, "Well you've obviously not got any experience in a infantry military unit." This contributor goes on to reference the previously mentioned "classic" image of a woman unable to carry her male comrade to safety in battle: "A fifeteen stone wounded man getting dragged to safety by a 9 stone female... LOl! Male soldiers should sue the political class in American for endangering their lives even further."[62] This comment is interesting because the contributor discounts alternative opinions and presumes that those who think women can "make the cut" are disconnected or lack experience in combat. At the same time, the contributor evokes the classic story of a weak and small woman unable to drag her heavier and stronger comrade as evidence that women should not be in combat. This contributor seems to be implying that those disconnected from combat "don't understand" what combat is really like, and also that dragging bodies across a field is "real" and a "true" experience of war.

ii. Rape As in the responses to the first article, a number of contributors mentioned the possibility of rape as evidence that women should not be on the front lines. "Joetheragman2" cites incidents of rape as evidence of women's inferior physical qualities: "Women are getting raped and if they are just as strong and as aggressive as men, then why are they getting raped? Does not compute."[63] Rather than acknowledging the responsibility of perpetrators or the role of military culture, such arguments blame women for sexual violence and point to the sexual assault and rape epidemic as further proof of women's physical inferiority. This further reiterates the significance of physical difference in the minds of those who feel women should not be in combat roles; secondary arguments, like sexual violence, or group dynamics, are continually linked back to the position that women are physically inferior. In other words, for many, the

---

[62] "Skullduggery," March 1, 2013, comment on ibid.
[63] "joetheragman2," March 1, 2013, comment on ibid.

apparent physical differences between women and men are at the root of several reasons why women should not be allowed to fight in combat roles.

There were impassioned responses to "joetheragman2"'s statements regarding rape and combat. Contributors contended that women should not be blamed for rape and the threat of sexual assault. For example, quoting an early post, "Taha" replied, "blaming women for men going from 'band of brothers' to 'pack of snarling primates' echoes eerily of the arguments made that try to blame sexual assault on the female victims for being there rather than on the male perpetrator who assaulted her."[64]

"END OF COMBAT BAN MEANS WOMEN FINALLY FULLY INTEGRATED INTO MILITARY," GAYLE TZEMACH LEMMON, JANUARY 24, 2013 (THE DAY OF THE ANNOUNCEMENT THAT THE COMBAT EXCLUSION WOULD BE LIFTED)

When this article was published, Gayle Tzemach Lemmon was a fellow at the Council on Foreign Relations who had written extensively on conflict and postconflict zones, including Afghanistan. The brief article compares the combat exclusion to former restrictions on homosexuals and African Americans in the military; she argues that the policy was antiquated and that the decision to remove the combat exclusion was long overdue. It can clearly be classified as a "positive" or supportive article because Lemmon references the unconventional nature of war, women's historic contributions to combat, and the value of equal opportunity as evidence that the policy change is a positive step forward for the military. This article was "shared" just under 250 times, had 197 "likes" on Facebook,[65] and elicited

---

[64] "Taha," March 1, 2013, comment on ibid.

[65] As of June 2, 2014. Determined using the tracking tool on http://muckrack.com/whoshared/ because the website does not publish the number of shares and retweets for older articles.

Table 4 *Lemmon Article Comments*

Supporting Comment Themes	Comment Count
Promotes Women's Equality	7
Will enhance troop numbers/recruitment	4
Physical	4
Women already on the front lines	2
Total	17
Opposing Comment Themes	Comment Count
Physical	9
Women in combat is misguided political correctness	5
Other	2
Total	17
Total Pacifist Comments	3
Total Comments Overall	36

70 comments. After exclusionary comments were removed, 37 comments remained (Table 4).

Supporting themes

i. Equality Perhaps because the original article focused on the opportunities that would be open to women, several of the respondents reiterated the importance of equality and equal opportunity for women in the military. The removal of the combat exclusion is described as a move that "opens up"[66] opportunities, removes "different standards"[67] in the workplace and tears down a barrier to equality between men and women in the military. Comments related to the second theme – troop numbers and the draft – often overlapped with the equality theme. Contributors argued that this new era of equality

---

[66] "Mike Kwan," January 24, 2013, comment on Lemmon.
[67] "Kate Whitaker," January 24, 2013, comment on ibid.

should mean that women will be required to sign up for selective service/the draft "like any man."[68]

Several of the contributors who felt women should not be in combat responded directly to this equality theme, noting that women in combat amounted to "equality" or "political correctness" "gone too far." These contributors lamented women's integration as a "social experiment" and a sign that equality and political correctness were being prioritized over the military mission and security. "AlanWeinraub" states, "anyone who serves (or at least has their priorities straight) understands that it is about 'the mission', not 'gender equality.'"[69] "Robert Elder" sarcastically adds, "[w]ell by all means, female careers are more important than combat readiness."[70] In response to comments about combat as a role that will open professional doors to women and as a sign of the military moving toward gender equity, "AlanWeinraub" offered the following contribution:

> Hate to argue with this who feel this is actually some sort of "great leap forward", but anyone who serves (or at least has their priorities straight) understands that it is about "the mission", not "gender equality" . . . that's just the nature of the game. Liberals can/will slam me for being old fashioned, but after 16+ years of service I'd like to think I know a thing or two from personal experience.[71]

This contributor focused on promotion rather than equal opportunity and seems to treat the removal of the combat exclusion as a form of affirmative action that will give women an undeserved career advantage.

---

[68] "MartinKileyMedved," January 24, 2013, comment on ibid.
[69] "Alan Weinraub," January 24, 2013, comment on ibid.
[70] "Robert Elder," January 24, 2013, comment on ibid.
[71] "Alan Weinraub," January 24, 2013, comment on ibid.

ii. Physical   Similar to the previous articles, contributors who were supportive of women serving in combat also addressed physical standards. Again, as with the previous two articles, these participants supported women's inclusion in combat roles provided the military does not "dumb down" or "lower" physical standards. Supporters responded to those skeptical of women's physical capabilities with reassurances that "women still need to prove themselves."[72] "MarkKohring" summarizes the overall argument: "[m]eet the standards, join the team and be welcomed to the club. Don't meet them, don't complain. An average of 25% of the men don't meet the standards either."[73] Finally, "Michael Schrier" reiterates, "[e]qual rights are fine but don't lower the standards to accommodate the females, if you want equality than live by the same standards that the males must live by." In turn, the contributors are clear that equality means that women will meet the male standard and that the military should not make institutional changes to accommodate women's their integration into combat roles.

Opposing themes

Physical   The comments opposed to women in combat mirror the themes in the previous articles. The dominant theme is a focus on the physical weaknesses of women. What distinguishes the critical physical arguments in this discussion is the emphasis on equality. This is likely because the author of the article focuses on equality, as do several of the other commenters. As indicated earlier, several of the contributors who are supportive of women in combat link women's ability to fight with their ability to meet equal standards. Conversely, several of those who argue that women should not be allowed into combat roles also focus on equality and physical standards. For example, "mos8541" states:

---

[72] "CarleyKleinhans," January 24, 2013, comment on ibid.
[73] "MarkKohring," January 24, 2013, comment on ibid.

Show me how a female of 5'4" weighing 120 lbs can carry a man
of 5'10" weighing 180 pounds over her shoulders from picking
him up and carrying him, not dragging him, 100 feet. Now lets add
on the combat gear that makes him weigh 210 to 230 pounds...
The standards will be lowered to allow women in. After all don't
you ladies do pushups differently than men on the Physical
Readiness Test (PRT)? If you had to do them to the same
CURRENT or PAST standard as a man you won't pass...I don't
care if you produce 10000 women that can kick a man's butt.
What we are talking about here is winning wars and that is NOT
what you ladies are built to do. Yes Men are different than women
and frankly it is about time women got over it. NO MORE PC.[74]

This contribution is striking because it points to the dual standards between male and female soldiers, references the image of a
weak woman trying to drag her male comrade, and then argues that
even if women can compete physically with men, they still should
not be allowed into combat. Interestingly, this contributor explicitly acknowledges that even women who can compete with men are
not "built" to win wars. This confirms criticisms that the physical
standards emphasis is not exclusively about standards but is an articulation of a sexist argument about the fundamental differences and
superiority of men over women.

Other contributions harness comments on physical standards
to broader conclusions about men and women. For example, echoing
the claim that women just do not belong in combat, "ollieo" states:

Most men do NOT want women at their side in war which is
evident by the higher military echelon's lack of action to end
sexual harassment and assault...Men I know want to fight with
other men they can depend on, not a less fit female. Jobs involving
brawn are not for women. I don't want to see male lives lost

---

[74] "mos8541," January 24, 2013, comment on ibid.

because there was not another male for support. Women are great in jobs involving brains but not brawn.[75]

This is another example of discussions about physicality bleeding into broader subjective comments about the nature of men and women. Here, "ollieo" implies that men do not want to fight along-side women because they are weaker; however, he/she harnesses this to the claim that "jobs involving brawn are not for women," which is clearly a much broader statement referencing the innate nature of women. Also, the author links the military's sexual violence problem with women's physical fitness, implying that the inaction related to sexual violence is driven by men's desire to rid the forces of women.

FEMINISM GONE TOO FAR?

As a result of the sheer quantity of comments, it was useful to organize the material according to the themes identified above. However, it is worth acknowledging that within these overarching themes there are several patterns to the way women in combat are discussed. One of the most surprising cross-cutting subthemes (cross-cutting articles and identified, dominant themes) included comments mentioning feminism. Across the three articles, feminism was mentioned twenty-one times. Strikingly, all but four of the references to feminism were hostile, sarcastic, or could generally be perceived as representing feminism or feminists negatively.

Feminists were consistently framed as out of touch, "leftists" who are focused more on a political agenda than acknowledging "realities" of war. This echoes van Creveld's infamous claim that "feminism is and always has been a peacetime luxury."[76] For example, "Mr.Wonderful_1" accuses another contributor of being "blinded by partisan Leftist feminist propaganda" that prevents him/her from "acknowledge[ing] the basic physiological differences between men

---

[75] "ollieo," February 11, 2013 comment on ibid.
[76] van Creveld, "Less Than We Can Be," 15.

and women . . . "[77] "Highcarry" concludes that "when the first woman dies in a real combat situation . . . the bleeding hearts and feminists will be up in arms hollering that we have to find better ways to protect them."[78] These comments characterize "leftist," "PC," and "socialist feminists"[79] as propagating "feminist fairytales, such as women being equal to men in combat potential and inclination."[80] In doing so, contributors seem to cast themselves as more connected to reality and in a position to discredit other contributors' points. This is illustrated in "mjmdmd19"'s statement "The average female individual can not perform physical endurance tasks as quickly and efficiently as the average male. That's the hard truth for all you feminists out there."[81] These comments show a general hostility toward the promotion of gender equality and women's rights with regard to the military. Arguments outlining why women could serve in combat units are framed as feminist ideals that have little or no relevance to everyday "realities" of combat units. Gender equality itself is treated as a luxury or a "fantasy" that defies innate and "true" qualities of men and women.

CONCLUSION

Conducting an analysis of the online comments to these three articles was interesting and challenging. The candor of the comments and the sheer volume of content was overwhelming at times. These comments make clear that women in combat is a topic that is incredibly divisive and evokes strong responses. The most clear-cut conclusion that can be drawn from these comments is that physical standards are the number one issue that contributors want to talk about when it comes to women in combat. Those opposed to women in combat particularly focused on this theme. These contributors

[77] "Mr. Wonderful_1," October 27, 2012, comment on MacKenzie.
[78] "highcarry," March 3, 2013, comment on Frum.
[79] "Tenet," March 6, 2013, comment on Frum.
[80] "Carney," March 2, 2013, comment on Frum.
[81] "mjmdmd19," October 27, 2012 , comment on MacKenzie.

consistently linked dual standards to double standards and made the general claim that dual standards *prove* women's inequality and weakness and therefore prove their inability to serve in combat. Even contributors who were supportive of women in combat made the case that women should be held to the same physical standards as men before they are permitted to fill these roles. In effect, although it is well established that military fitness tests are designed to measure fitness and not to measure combat-relevant skills, the public seems to associate male physical standards with equality and with job capability.

Another conclusion that can be drawn from the discussions of physical standards is that the image of men dragging their comrades across a battlefield looms large in the public imagination. Close to a dozen contributors expressed concern regarding women's ability to drag fellow soldiers to safety. This indicates that the ideal of war as man-to-man combat conducted across defined battle lines is alive and well in the public imagination.

The second most common theme in these discussions centered on rape and sexual violence. Contributors seemed divided as to whether the sexual violence epidemic plaguing the US military is a sign that women should be excluded from combat, or a symptom of sexist military culture that requires reform. The relationship between sexual violence and women's inclusion in the military requires further analysis. There are anecdotal claims that the combat exclusion reinforces a hierarchy that perpetuates misogyny and violence, yet it is impossible to measure a cause-and-effect relationship between the two. What can be garnered from this debate is that there is still a significant cohort of the public that treat sexual violence as "women's fault" and feel that the military is naturally a male space that women should enter at their own risk.

Although there were few explicit references to bands of brothers, the online comments echo the substantive themes outlined in the previous chapters. Moreover, the comments reiterated several themes that have been linked back to the band of brothers myth, including:

(i) the perception that war is a unique and privileged space that requires separate social rules and a unique social culture; (ii) the emphasis on male bodies as not only physically superior, but also more innately designed for combat duties; and (iii) the perception that women are not physically or emotionally capable of fulfilling combat duties. In addition, equal rights and feminist interventions were consistently treated as irrelevant, indulgent, and ultimately incompatible with the "realities" of warfare. This logic is important to locate and understand, because it seems to underpin arguments such as the claim that even if women meet physical standards, they cannot be included in combat. War is treated as a realm "beyond" the reach of equal rights.

Conclusion

The band of brothers myth is an enticing and destructive story. The romantic tale of men uniting to promote freedom, defend their nation, protect the weak, and enhance security is intoxicating. It is no wonder that countless war movies reproduce this myth. Watching men form bonds, make sacrifices for one another, and overcome extreme odds in defending their comrades and the nation makes for fantastic entertainment. However, these stories of war and soldiers must not be treated as accurate depictions of the "real" wars and violence being waged across the globe today. This leads to the destructive potential of the band of brothers myth. It is destructive in that it projects an idealistic image of war, "real" soldiers, combat operations, and the role of violence in achieving political objectives.

The band of brothers myth is so powerful that it influences military policy and shapes public perceptions of and emotional responses to war. Women have been excluded from combat within the US military largely because of this story. They have also been excluded because of a widely accepted set of emotional responses that loosely declare "women just don't belong." Imagine – a mythical story and gut reactions have been the accepted foundation of a major military policy that impacts military operations and women's career opportunities.

Reviewing the main arguments used to keep women from combat roles, it becomes clear that these debates have little to do with research, national security, or women's capabilities. Fears that menstruating women will attract sharks, claims that lesbians make the best soldiers because they don't fraternize and attract men, and conclusions that God would not have wanted women to serve in combat are simply ludicrous. Yet such arguments are regularly expressed by policy makers, military leaders, and the public. Moreover, such ridiculous claims are linked, or harnessed, to seemingly more objective claims about women's physical or social inability to serve in combat roles. These arguments would be less likely to be taken seriously if made in relation to women's ability to serve in other careers, including as physicians, professors, or engineers. Yet, despite the disparate, conflicting, and – at times – absent evidence to support the claims, conclusions that women are weaker, do not bond in the same way as men, and have different hygiene needs continue to persist. The story of the band of brothers has rationalized these irrational arguments.

This band of brothers myth is so powerful that even apparent counternarratives reproduce its messages. For example, one of the most common popular references used in discussions of women and combat is that of G.I. Jane. *G.I. Jane* is a now-iconic American movie starring Demi Moore. Moore's character attempts to defy the rule excluding her from the Navy SEALs and prove she can meet the physical requirements to serve alongside men. The movie avoids much of the politics around gender and the military, yet it acknowledges and capitalizes on existing emotional positions related to women and combat. We see this in the most iconic line of the movie: during a particularly grueling training session, Moore's character yells at another soldier to "suck my dick." The line marks the culmination of the physical changes she has undergone to compete with her male counterparts, including shaving her head and building significant muscle mass. The quote is also the moment when her character begins to be accepted – as one of the boys – by her male comrades.

Although Moore's character indeed is able to "make the cut" and complete the Navy SEALs training, the overarching message of the movie is not that women should be allowed to serve in any military role, or that the hypermasculine environment of the institution breeds discrimination and personal violence. The moral of the movie is that only extraordinary women can serve alongside men – and only in extreme circumstances. In other words, *G.I. Jane* is the story of exceptionalism. The *G.I. Jane* film and other stories of exceptional women, therefore, complement rather than challenge the band of brothers myth. Moore's struggle with the training, the physical changes she is required to make, and her acceptance of male aggression and culture conveys to audiences that women must become like men in order to serve with honor in infantry military units. Moreover, the movie valorizes masculine military culture and reaffirms the depictions of all-male units as exceptional and elite.

The combat exclusion has served a purpose similar to the G.I. Jane trope. The combat exclusion was used to reaffirm the centrality and exclusivity of the all-male unit. Moreover, the decision to remove the combat exclusion was framed largely in relation to *some* women's capacity to "make the cut" and serve alongside elite men. In other words, the removal of the combat exclusion does not indicate a marked shift in military culture, or a move away from the historic valorization of male bodies, male bonding, and male honor. Instead, it treats women's inclusion as a sign that there might be "a few good women" who are as physically fit and morally dedicated to combat as the average man.

At first glance the removal of the combat exclusion seems like a break from past practices; it was heralded as a positive step for women's rights and for equality within the military, and a sign of broader cultural change within the military. Unfortunately, this is not the case. When viewed through the lens of the band of brothers, the decision to remove the combat exclusion has very little to do with women. Instead, the policy change serves to recover a battered military image, rewrite the history of women's roles in Iraq and Afghanistan, and falsely portray the military as a gender-inclusive institution. Depicting the announcement as groundbreaking and as a watershed moment for women writes over the experiences of women who have served in hostile environments, been collocated with combat troops, contributed to all-female engagement teams, protected their comrades, and died in battle. The policy change also distracted attention from ongoing gender problems within the institution.

Removing the combat exclusion will do little to make the military a more attractive career option or a safer place for women to work. In particular, the policy does nothing to mitigate the existing sexual violence epidemic within the forces. The result is that women have more access to work within a military institution that – according to its own statistics – will almost guarantee their abuse, harassment, and assault.

HOW DO WE MOVE BEYOND THE BAND OF BROTHERS?

So what does it mean to go beyond the band of brothers? First, it requires declaring that the band of brothers myth is a useful, popular, well known, but unrealistic story about men and war. Second, it requires critical reflection about how this myth has mystified, romanticized, and justified warfare and political violence. The starting point for thinking beyond the band of brothers, therefore, is to question the embedded message that war is necessary, natural, and "the maker of men." This is not a call to demonize individual soldiers, or to question their integrity, their choices, or their commitment to serving. Rather, it is a demand that we ask difficult questions about the military and the impact of wars – that we face the less romantic aspects of war and militarization.

Without the sheen of the band of brothers myth, war looks far less attractive, easy, clean, and just. War is destructive, costly, traumatic, chaotic, demoralizing, disillusioning, and never-ending. For the USA, the wars in Iraq and Afghanistan alone have drained at least $6 trillion from the national economy. This was during a period when citizens in Detroit fought for their human right to water, and the public debated whether access to health care was a public good. The wars have left hundreds of thousands of soldiers with PTSD, 50 percent of whom will never seek treatment.[1] Nearly 50,000 veterans of Iraq

---

[1] U.S. Department of Veterans Affairs, "How Common is PTSD?" Last Updated November 10, 2014, http://www.ptsd.va.gov/public/PTSD-overview/basics/how-common-is-ptsd.asp

and Afghanistan are also reported to be at risk of homelessness.[2] One in three women serving in the military experiences military sexual trauma, with a reported 86 percent of victims of MST never reporting the crime.[3] The thousands of men and women who have experienced sexual harassment or trauma continue to struggle to access resources within the military system. The cost of dealing with sexual assault in 2012 alone was estimated at $3.6 billion.[4] In 2014, Veterans Affairs faced a troubling scandal as news broke of unreasonable waitlists, mismanaged files, and at least 35 veterans who died while waiting for care. These statistics contrast sharply to an image of an "army of one" and of an institution that will protect its own.

Resistance to the destructive capabilities of war and militarization requires a shift in the way we think about war and the stories we tell about war. Cynthia Enloe has long argued that "if ideas of 'manliness' and 'respectable woman' are not profoundly changed, we have left the seedbed for the next war."[5] Enloe reminds us that remilitarization depends on ideas of masculinity. I have argued that the band of brothers myth, along with the messages it conveys about manliness, good men, and real soldiers, is central to militarization and to the romanticization of perpetual war. Thus, unraveling the band of brothers myth is essential to demystifying and ending wars. My objective is not simply to see more women join the US military, or to make a case as to whether women are "good" or "bad" soldiers. My objective for this book has been to deconstruct the band of brothers myth in order to change the conversation about war, and to make it more difficult to romanticize and legitimize war.

The band of brothers myth presents men as elite, essential, and exceptional and depicts warfare as romantic, natural, necessary, just,

---

[2] http://www.usatoday.com/story/news/nation/2014/01/16/veterans-homeless-afghanistan-iraq-wars/4526343/

[3] http://harvardpolitics.com/united-states/quest-military-sexual-assault-reform/

[4] http://now.org/resource/will-military-sexual-assault-survivors-find-justice-issue-advisory/

[5] Enloe, "Women and Militarization."

and clean. Two of the main messages of the myth – that men are born soldiers, and that war is natural and inevitable – are closely intertwined. These characterizations of war are so embedded in the public imagination that they have begun to be treated as truths, and as common sense. However, these "truths" can be untangled, and pulling at the threads of one quickly unravels the other. This partially explains the intense effort to keep women out of combat units. The reality of women serving in combat defies, destabilizes, and challenges these foundational myths about war and "real" soldiers. In turn, paying attention to the role of myth and emotion in debates about women in combat encourages the public to rethink broader claims about military culture, romanticized depictions of war, and gendered representations of heroes, victims, and ultimately the protection of the nation.

Bibliography

Ablow, Keith Dr. "Why I Don't Ever Want to See Women in Combat, on the Front Lines." Fox News, May 19, 2012. http://www.foxnews.com/opinion/2012/05/19/why-dont-ever-want-to-see-women-in-combat-on-front-lines/.

Allen, Andi, Gina Ladenheim, and Katie Stout. "Training Female Engagement Teams: Framework, Content Development, and Lessons Learned." Center for Army Lessons Learned, July 2011. http://usacac.army.mil/cac2/call/docs/11–35/ch_3.asp.

Allen, Andi, Gina Ladenheim, and Katie Stout. "Training Female Engagement Teams: Framework, Content Development, and Lessons Learned." *Army Marine Integration* III (n.d.): 15–19.

Alvarez, Lizette. "G.I. Jane Breaks the Combat Barrier." *New York Times*, August 16, 2009, sec. US. http://www.nytimes.com/2009/08/16/us/16women.html.

Androutsopoulos, Jannis. "From Variation to Heteroglossia in Computer-Mediated Discourse." In *Digital Discourse: Language in the New Media*. New York: Oxford University Press, 2011.

Armor, David J. "Race and Gender in the U.S. Military." *Armed Forces & Society* 23, no. 1 (October 1, 1996): 7–27. doi:10.1177/0095327×9602300101.

"Army Marine Integration Volume III: Observations, Insights, and Lessons." Newsletter, Center for Army Lessons Learned, July 2011. https://call2.army.mil/toc.aspx?document=6695&filename=/docs/doc6695/11–35.pdf.

Baldor, Lolita C., and Russ Bynum "'Half My Body Weight': Women Get Taste of Combat Tasks in Army Study." Associated Press, February 26, 2014. Accessed June 13, 2014. http://www.cbsnews.com/news/half-my-body-weight-army-study-gives-women-taste-of-combat-tasks/.

Baldwin et al. v. Panetta et al. (District of Columbia District Court 2012).

Bartov, Omer. "The Conduct of War: Soldiers and the Barbarization of Warfare." *Journal of Modern History* 64 (December 1, 1992): S32–45.

Belkin, Aaron. *Bring Me Men: Military Masculinity and the Benign Façade of American Empire, 1898–2001*. New York: Columbia University Press, 2012.

"Don't Ask, Don't Tell: Is the Gay Ban Based on Military Necessity?" *Center for the Study of Sexual Minorities in the Military*, July 1, 2003. http://escholarship.org/uc/item/0bb4j7ss.

Ben-Shalom, Uzi, Zeev Lehrer, and Eyal Ben-Ari. "Cohesion during Military Operations: A Field Study on Combat Units in the Al-Aqsa Intifada." *Armed Forces & Society* 32, no. 1 (October 1, 2005): 63–79. doi:10.1177/0095327×05277888.

Bishop, P., K. Cureton, and M. Collins. "Sex Difference in Muscular Strength in Equally-Trained Men and Women." *Ergonomics* 30, no. 4 (April 1987): 675–687. doi:10.1080/00140138708969760.

Blair, Jane. "Five Myths about Women in Combat." *Washington Post*, May 27, 2011. http://www.washingtonpost.com/opinions/five-myths-about-women-in-combat/2011/05/25/AGAsavCH_story.html.

Boland, Barbara. "Female Marines Not Required To Do 1 Pull-Up." *CNS News*, August 20, 2013. http://cnsnews.com/news/article/barbara-boland/female-marines-not-required-do-1-pull.

Bottici, Chiara, and Benoît Challand. "Rethinking Political Myth: The Clash of Civilizations as a Self-Fulfilling Prophecy." *European Journal of Social Theory* 9, no. 3 (August 1, 2006): 315–336. doi:10.1177/1368431006065715.

Boykin, Jerry. "New Policy Ignores Biological Realities." *USA Today*, January 25, 2013.

Brett, Kate McKay. "Are You As Fit As a World War II GI?" *The Art of Manliness*. Accessed June 13, 2014. http://www.artofmanliness.com/2011/09/12/are-you-as-fit-as-a-world-war-ii-gi/.

Browne, Kingsley. *Co-Ed Combat: The New Evidence That Women Shouldn't Fight the Nation's Wars*. 1st edition. Sentinel HC, 2007.

Bumiller, Elisabeth. "For Female Marines, Tea Comes with Bullets." *New York Times*, October 2, 2010, sec. World/Asia Pacific. http://www.nytimes.com/2010/10/03/world/asia/03marines.html.

Bureau, David S. CloudWashington. "Pentagon to Ease Restrictions on Women in Combat." *Los Angeles Times*, February 9, 2012. http://articles.latimes.com/2012/feb/09/nation/la-na-pentagon-women-20120209.

Burrelli F, David. "Women in Combat: Issues for Congress," May 9, 2013. http://www.fas.org/sgp/crs/natsec/R42075.pdf.

Canadian Human Rights Commission. "*Annual Report*." Minister of Supply and Services Canada, Ottawa, 1994.

Carreiras, Helena, and Gerhard Kümmel. "Off Limits: The Cults of the Body and Social Homogeneity as Discoursive Weapons Targeting Gender Integration in the Military." In *Women in the Military and in Armed Conflict*, edited by Helena Carreiras and Gerhard Kümmel (Verlag für Sozialwissenschaften, 2008), 29–47. http://www.springerlink.com/content/n437m33q28q88gk3/abstract/.

Women in the Military and in Armed Conflict. Springer Science & Business Media, 2008.

Cawkill, Paul, Alison Rogers, Sarah Knight, and Laura Spear. "Women in Ground Close Combat Roles: The Experience of Other Nations and a Review of the Academic Literature." *Defence Science and Technology Laboratory UK*, September 29, 2009.

Chapman, Anne W. "Mixed-Gender Basic Training: The U.S. Army Experience, 1973–2004." *Library of Congress Cataloging-in-Publication Data*, 2008.

Chief of Naval Operations. *OPNAV Instruction 6110.1J: Physical Readiness Program.* Washington, DC, July 11, 2011. http://www.navy-prt.com/files/6110.1J_--Physical_Readiness_program.pdf.

Christopher, Leslie A., and Leslie Miller. "Women in War: Operational Issues of Menstruation and Unintended Pregnancy." *Military Medicine* 172, no. 1 (January 2007): 9–16.

Cirucci, Johnny. "GENDERCIDE: How Women And Gays Are Destroying the U.S. Military." *Before It's News*, June 27, 2013. http://beforeitsnews.com/blogging-citizen-journalism/2013/06/gendercide-how-women-and-gays-are-destroying-the-u-s-military-2448232.html.

Claudetta, Roulo. "Defense Department Expands Women's Combat Role." US Department of Defense, January 24, 2013. http://www.defense.gov/news/newsarticle.aspx?id=119098.

Cohn, C. "Wars, Wimps, and Women: Talking Gender and Thinking War." In *Gendering War Talk*, edited by Miriam Cooke and Angela Woollacott, 227–46. Princeton, NJ: Princeton University Press, 1993.

Cohn, Carol. "'How Can She Claim Equal Rights When She Doesn't Have to Do as Many Push-Ups as I Do?' The Framing of Men's Opposition to Women's Equality in the Military." *Men and Masculinities* 3, no. 2 (October 1, 2000): 131–51. doi:10.1177/1097184×00003002001.

——— ed. *Women and Wars: Contested Histories, Uncertain Futures.* 1st edition. Cambridge, UK: Polity, 2012.

Coll C, Anna. "Evaluating Female Engagement Team Effectiveness in Afghanistan." *Wellesley College Digital Scholarship Archive*, 2012. http://repository.wellesley.edu/cgi/viewcontent.cgi?article=1068&context=thesiscollection.

Commandant of the Marine Corps. *Marine Corps Order 6100.13 W/CH 1: Marine Corps Physical Fitness Program.* Washington, DC, August 1, 2008. http://www.marines.mil/Portals/59/Publications/MCO%206100.13%20W_CH%201.pdf.

Committee on Armed Services. *Inquiry into the Treatment of Detainees in US Custody.* Committee Findings. Washington, DC: United States Senate, November 20, 2008. http://www.armed-services.senate.gov/imo/media/doc/Detainee-Report-Final_April-22–2009.pdf.

"Corps: Urination Video Was 1 of 12 Marines Made." *Marine Corps Times*. Accessed May 15, 2014. http://www.marinecorpstimes.com/article/20130116/NEWS/301160308/Corps-Urination-video-1-12-Marines-made.

Creveld, Martin van. *Men, Women & War: Do Women Belong in the Front Line?*. Cassell, 2002.

Cushman, John. "History of Women in Combat Still Being Written Slowly." *New York Times*, February 9, 2012. http://www.nytimes.com/2012/02/10/us/history-of-women-in-combat-still-being-written-slowly.html?ref=us.

Datnow, Amanda. *Gender in Policy and Practice*. New York: Routledge, 2002.

Decew, Judith Wagner. "The Combat Exclusion and the Role of Women in the Military." *Hypatia* 10, no. 1 (1995): 56–73. doi:10.1111/j.1527-2001.1995.tb01353.x.

DeGroot, Gerard J. "A Few Good Women: Gender Stereotypes, the Military and Peacekeeping." *International Peacekeeping* 8, no. 2 (2001): 23–38. doi:10.1080/13533310108413893.

Dvorak, Petula. "Will We One Day Mourn Female Combat Veterans?" *The Washington Post*, May 29, 2012. http://www.highbeam.com/doc/1P2-31456233.html.

Eager, Paige Whaley. *Waging Gendered Wars: U.S. Military Women in Afghanistan and Iraq*. New edition. Farnham , UK: Ashgate, 2014.

Eden, Jude. "The Problems of Women in Combat – From a Female Combat Vet." *Western Journalism*, January 26, 2013. http://www.westernjournalism.com/the-problems-of-women-in-combat-from-a-female-combat-vet/.

Eichler, Maya. "Women and Combat in Canada: Continuing Tensions between 'difference' and 'equality.'" *Critical Studies on Security* 1, no. 2 (August 2013): 257–59. doi:10.1080/21624887.2013.814855.

Elshtain, Jean Bethke, and Sheila Tobias, editors. *Women, Militarism, and War*. Rowman & Littlefield, 1990.

Enloe, Cynthia. "Combat and 'combat': A Feminist Reflection." *Critical Studies on Security* 1, no. 2 (2013): 260–63. doi:10.1080/21624887.2013.814857.

Maneuvers: The International Politics of Militarizing Women's Lives. 1st edition. University of California Press, 2000.

Enloe, Cynthia H. *Globalization and Militarism: Feminists Make the Link*. Rowman & Littlefield, 2007.

Maneuvers: The International Politics of Militarizing Women's Lives. University of California Press, 2000.

Erwin, Stephanie K. *"The Veil of Kevlar An Analysis of the Female Engagement Teams in Afghanistan."* Thesis, Monterey, California: Naval Postgraduate School, 2012. http://calhoun.nps.edu/mgmt/handle/10945/6792.

Exum, Andrew. *This Man's Army.* New York: Gotham Books, 2005.

Eys, Mark A., and Albert V. Carron. "Role Ambiguity, Task Cohesion, and Task Self-Efficacy." *Small Group Research* 32, no. 3 (June 1, 2001): 356–73. doi:10.1177/104649640103200305.

"Fallen Soldiers, Declining Support for War." Accessed June 12, 2014. http://www.psychologytoday.com/blog/polarized/201205/fallen-soldiers-declining-support-war.

Fenner, Lorry, and Marie deYoung. *Women in Combat: Civic Duty or Military Liability?.* Washington, DC: Georgetown University Press, 2001.

Ferran, Lee. "Marine Who Urinated on Dead Taliban Says He'd Do It Again." *ABC News,* July 17, 2013. http://abcnews.go.com/Blotter/marine-urinated-taliban-dead-hed/story?id=19687916.

Fischer, Hannah. *United States Military Casualty Statistics: Operation Iraqi Freedom and Operation Enduring Freedom,* March 25, 2009.

"Five Myths about Women in Combat." *Washington Post.* Accessed June 13, 2014. http://www.washingtonpost.com/opinions/five-myths-about-women-in-combat/2011/05/25/AGAsavCH_story.html.

Flood, Christopher. *Political Myth: A Theoretical Introduction.* Psychology Press, 1996.

Francke, Linda Bird. *Ground Zero: The Gender Wars in the Military.* New York: Simon and Schuster, 1997.

Freud, Sigmund. *Totem and Taboo.* Psychology Press, 1999.

"From Representation to Inclusion: Diversity Leadership for the 21st-Century Military (Final Report)." United States, Military Leadership Diversity Commission, 2011. https://www.hsdl.org/?abstract&did=1139.

Frum, David. "The Truth about Women in Combat." *The Daily Beast,* March 1, 2013. http://www.thedailybeast.com/articles/2013/03/01/the-truth-about-women-in-combat.html.

Fullerton, Howard N. Jr. "Labor Force 2006: Slowing Down and Changing Composition." *Monthly Labor Review* 120 (1997): 23.

Fulton, Lawrence V., Matthew S. Brooks, Timothy K. Jones, Matthew J. Schofield, and Hershell L. Moody. "Policy Implications for Female Combat Medic Assignment: A Study of Deployment and Promotion Risk." *Armed Forces & Society,* November 3, 2011. doi:10.1177/0095327x11426253.

Gabbatt, Adam. "US Marines Charged over Urinating on Bodies of Dead Taliban in Afghanistan." *The Guardian,* September 25, 2012, sec. World news. http://www.theguardian.com/world/2012/sep/24/us-marines-charged-dead-taliban.

Gartner, Scott Sigmund. "Secondary Casualty Information: Casualty Uncertainty, Female Casualties, and Wartime Support." *Conflict Management and Peace Science* 25, no. 2 (April 1, 2008): 98–111. doi:10.1080/07388940802007215.

Gillibrand, Kristen. "Gender Equality in Combat Act." Senate of the United States, May 2012.

Goldin, Claudia. "The Role of World War II in the Rise of Women's Work." *National Bureau of Economic Research*, no. 3203 (December 1989). http://www.nber.org/papers/w3203.pdf?new_window=1.

Goldstein, Joshua S. *War and Gender: How Gender Shapes the War System and Vice Versa*. Cambridge: Cambridge University Press, 2001.

Goodell, Maia. "Physical-Strength Rationales for De Jure Exclusion of Women from Military Combat Positions." *Seattle University Law Review* 34, no. 1 (August 31, 2010): 17.

"GOP Retreats on Women-in-Combat Bill." *Washington Times*. Accessed July 24, 2014. http://www.washingtontimes.com/news/2005/may/26/20050526-121729-8305r/.

Graham, Bradley. "Coed Training, Army Revisiting Basic Strategy." *Washington Post*, November 21, 1994.

Greenhouse, Linda. "JUSTICES, 6–3, RULE DRAFT REGISTRATION MAY EXCLUDE WOMEN." *New York Times*, June 26, 1981, sec. U.S. http://www.nytimes.com/1981/06/26/us/justices-6-3-rule-draft-registration-may-exclude-women.html.

Grice, Robert L., and Lawrence C. Katz. "Cohesion in Military and Aviation Psychology: An Annotated Bibliography and Suggestions for US Army Aviation," 2005, Arlington VA, United States Army Research Institute for the Behavioral and Social Sciences (http://hqda.army.mil/ari/pdf/TR1166.pdf)

Griffin, Steve. "Fighting for Gender Equality on the Battlefield; At War." *New York Times*, January 31, 2012. https://global-factiva-com.ezproxy2.library.usyd.edu.au/aa/?ref=NYTB000020120131e81v008n9&pp=1&fcpil=en&napc=S&sa_from= .

Griffith, James. "Further Considerations Concerning the Cohesion-Performance Relation in Military Settings." *Armed Forces & Society* 34, no. 1 (October 1, 2007): 138–47. doi:10.1177/0095327×06294620.

"Multilevel Analysis of Cohesion's Relation to Stress, Well-Being, Identification, Disintegration, and Perceived Combat Readiness." *Military Psychology* 14, no. 3 (2002): 217–39. doi:10.1207/S15327876MP1403_3.

Gruber, Helmut. "Analyzing Communication in the New Media." In *Qualitative Discourse Analysis in the Social Sciences*, edited by Ruth Krzyzanowski and Michael Krzyzanowski, 54–77. Houndmills: Pelgrave, 2008.

Gutmann, Stephanie. "Sex and the Soldier." *The New Republic*, February 24, 1997.

The Kinder, Gentler Military: Can America's Gender-Neutral Fighting Force Still Win Wars?. Simon & Schuster, 2000.

Hansen, Christine. "A Considerable Sacrifice: The Costs of Sexual Violence in the US Armed Forces." *The Baldy Centre for Law and Social Policy*, no. Military Culture and Gender (September 15, 2005).

Hansen, Lene. *Security as Practice: Discourse Analysis and the Bosnian War.* 1st edition. London: Routledge, 2006.

Harding A, Tyra. *Women in Combat Roles: Case Study of Female Engagement Teams.* United States Army War College, 2012. www.dtic.mil/docs/citations/ADA561195.

Haring, Ellen L. "What Women Bring to the Fight." *Parameters* 43 no. 2 (2013): 27–32.

Harrell, Margaret C., and Laura L. Miller. "New Opportunities for Military Women." *Product Page*, 1997. http://www.rand.org/pubs/monograph_reports/MR896.html.

Harrell, Margaret C., National Defense Research Institute (U.S.), United States. Dept. of Defense. Office of the Secretary of Defense, and RAND Corporation. *National Defense Research Institute.* RAND Corporation, 2002.

Harrell, Margaret C., Laura Werber, Peter Schirmer, Bryan W. Hallmark, Jennifer Kavanagh, Daniel Gershwin, and Paul Steinberg. "Assessing the Assignment Policy for Army Women." *Product Page*, 2007. http://www.rand.org/pubs/monographs/MG590-1.html.

Haskell, Sally G., Kirsha S. Gordon, Kristin Mattocks, Mona Duggal, Joseph Erdos, Amy Justice, and Cynthia A. Brandt. "Gender Differences in Rates of Depression, PTSD, Pain, Obesity, and Military Sexual Trauma Among Connecticut War Veterans of Iraq and Afghanistan." *Journal of Women's Health* 19, no. 2 (February 2010): 267–71. doi:10.1089/jwh.2008.1262.

Healy, Melissa. "Poll Finds Split Over Women's Combat Role: Military: 47% Oppose Ban, While 44% Back It. Public Sentiment Will Be a Key in Determining Future Duties." *Los Angeles Times*, September 12, 1992. http://articles.latimes.com/1992-09-12/news/mn-276_1_public-sentiment.

Hegar et al. v. Panetta (California Northern District Court 2012).

Hegar, Mary Jennings. "Women Warriors Are on the Battlefield. Eliminate Outdated, Unfair Military Combat Exclusion Policy." *American Civil Liberties Union*, November 27, 2012. https://www.aclu.org/print/blog/womens-rights/women-warriors-are-battlefield-eliminate-outdated-unfair-military-combat.

Herbert, M. S. *Camouflage Isn't Only for Combat: Gender, Sexuality, and Women in the Military.* New York: New York University Press, 1998.

Hoge, Charles W., Julie C. Clark, and Carl A. Castro. "Commentary: Women in Combat and the Risk of Post-Traumatic Stress Disorder and Depression." *International Journal of Epidemiology* 36, no. 2 (April 1, 2007): 327–29. doi:10.1093/ije/dym013.

Holland S, David. "Women Marines Need Endurance More Than Strength." *Wall Street Journal*, November 20, 2012.

Holmstedt, Kirsten. *Band of Sisters: American Women at War in Iraq*. Stackpole Books, 2008.

"Internet World Stats." *Internet World Stats*, August 11, 2014. http://www.internetworldstats.com/stats.htm.

Irby, Ida. "'FET' to Fight: Female Engagement Team Makes History," April 18, 2013. http://www.army.mil/article/101111/.

Jacinto, Leela. "Girl Power: Women Join the Boys in Combat, But Not without a Fight." *ABC News*, January 14, 2011, online edition, sec. Original Report. http://www.realnews247.com/girl_power.htm.

Jacinto, Lella. "The Cost of Women in Combat." American Broadcasting Corporation, 2014. http://abcnews.go.com/International/story?id=79646&page=1&singlePage=true.

Jarecki, Eugene. *Why We Fight*. Documentary, History, War, 2005.

Kang, Han, Nancy Dalager, Clare Mahan, and Erick Ishii. "The Role of Sexual Assault on the Risk of PTSD among Gulf War Veterans." *Annals of Epidemiology* 15, no. 3 (March 2005): 191–95. doi:10.1016/j.annepidem.2004.05.009.

Kier, Elizabeth. "Homosexuals in the U.S. Military: Open Integration and Combat Effectiveness." *International Security* 23, no. 2 (October 1, 1998): 5–39. doi:10.2307/2539378.

King, Anthony. "The Existence of Group Cohesion in the Armed Forces: A Response to Guy Siebold." *Armed Forces & Society* 33, no. 4 (July 1, 2007): 638–45. doi:10.1177/0095327×07301445.

"The Word of Command: Communication and Cohesion in the Military." *Armed Forces & Society* 32, no. 4 (July 1, 2006): 493–512. doi:10.1177/0095327×05283041.

"Women in Combat." *The RUSI Journal* 158, no. 1 (2013): 4–11. doi:10.1080/03071847.2013.774634.

Kirkwood, R. Cort. "Women in Combat: War for and against Women," April 12, 2013. https://www.thenewamerican.com/culture/item/15012-women-in-combat-war-for-and-against-women.

Knapik, Joseph J, and Whitfield B East. "History of United States Army Physical Fitness and Physical Readiness Training." *U.S. Army Medical Department Journal*, June 2014, 5–19.

Knight, Robert. "Deceitful Debate over Women in Combat." *Washington Times*, November 30, 2012. http://theacru.org/acru/deceitful_debate_over_women_in_combat/.

Lemmon, Gayle Tzemach. "End of Combat Ban Means Women Finally Fully Integrated Into Military." *Daily Beast – Women in the World*, January 24,

2013. http://www.thedailybeast.com/articles/2013/01/24/end-of-combat-ban-means-women-finally-fully-integrated-into-military.html.

Levi, Michelle. "Abu Ghraib Head: We Were Scapegoated." April 22, 2009. CBS News. Accessed May 12, 2014. http://www.cbsnews.com/news/abu-ghraib-head-we-were-scapegoated/.

Lohrenz, Carey D. "Time for Some Fearless Leadership." *Time Magazine*, January 20, 2013. http://nation.time.com/2013/01/30/time-for-some-fearless-leadership/.

Londoño, Ernesto. "A Decade into War, Body Armor Gets Curves; Female Troops Have Often Been Encumbered by Body Armor Designed for Men. This Fall, a New Generation of Body Armor for Women Will Be Tested." *Washington Post*, September 21, 2012.

Lunen, Kelly Von. "FEMALE ENGAGEMENT TEAMS Built Trust in Iraq." *VFW, Veterans of Foreign Wars Magazine* 99, no. 6 (March 1, 2012): 28.

MacCoun, Robert J., Elizabeth Kier, and Aaron Belkin. "Does Social Cohesion Determine Motivation in Combat? An Old Question with an Old Answer." *Armed Forces & Society* 32, no. 4 (2006): 646–54. doi:10.1177/0095327×05279181.

MacKenzie, Megan H. "Overdue: Why It's Time to End the U.S. Military's Female Combat Ban." *Daily Beast – Women in the World*, October 26, 2012. http://www.thedailybeast.com/articles/2012/10/26/overdue-why-it-s-time-to-end-the-u-s-military-s-female-combat-ban.html.

Mackenzie, Megan H. "The Pentagon Still Needs a Facelift." *American Review*, May 2013.

Maginnis, Robert L. *Deadly Consequences: How Cowards Are Pushing Women into Combat.* 1 edition. Washington, DC: Regnery, 2013.

Maninger, Stephan. "Women in Combat: Reconsidering the Case against the Deployment of Women in Combat-Support and Combat Units." In *Women in the Military and in Armed Conflict*, edited by Helena Carreiras and Gerhard Kümmel, 9–27. Verlag für Sozialwissenschaften, 2008. http://www.springerlink.com/content/l883735108×76p2r/abstract/.

Manning, Frederick J. *An Investigation into the Value of Unit Cohesion in Peacetime.* U.S. Army Medical Research and Development Command, 1983.

Martin, Rachel, and Kayla Williams. "Female Troops: Combat Ban out of Step with Reality: NPR." NPR.org. Accessed March 21, 2013. http://www.npr.org/2011/03/01/134168091/Female-Troops-Combat-Ban-Out-Of-Step-With-Reality.

McBreen, Brendan. "The Strength of the Wolf Is the Pack." *Marine Corps Gazette*, February 2004, 88:2 edition.

McBride, Keally, and Annick T. R. Wibben. "The Gendering of Counterinsurgency in Afghanistan." *Humanity: An International Journal of Human Rights, Humanitarianism, and Development* 3, no. 2 (2012): 199–215.

McCullough, Christopher. "Female Engagement Teams: Who They Are and Why They Do It," October 2, 2012. http://www.army.mil/article/88366/.

McManus, Otile. "Women in Harm's Way: Is America Really Ready to See Female Soldiers Die?" *Boston Globe*, January 24, 1991, online edition, sec. Special sections.

McSally, M. "Women in Combat: Is the Current Policy Obsolete?" *Duke Journal of Gender Law & Policy* 14, no. 2 (2007): 1011–59.

Meeker, Meg. "Moms, Body Bags, and Combat." *Meg Meeker, M.D*, January 28, 2013. http://www.megmeekermd.com/2013/01/moms-body-bags-and-combat/.

Michaels, Jim. "Marines Experiment Puts Women on Infantry Course for First Time; Rigorous Program Tests Officers' Mental, Physical Endurance." *USA Today*, October 3, 2012.

"Strength Key in Women-in-Combat Debate; Services Look at Physical Demands of Certain Jobs." *USA Today*, February 4, 2013.

Military.com. "PTSD Frequently Asked Questions." Text. *Military.com*. Accessed June 13, 2014. http://www.military.com/benefits/veterans-health-care/ptsd-frequently-asked-questions.html.

Military Leadership Diversity Commission. *Women in Combat: Legislation and Policy, Perceptions, and the Current Operational Environment*. Arlington, VA: Military Leadership Diversity Commission, November 2010. https://www.hsdl.org/?view&did=716213.

"Military to Ease Rules on Women in Combat." usatoday.com. Accessed May 28, 2012. http://www.usatoday.com/news/washington/story/2012–02–08/war-women-pentagon/53017764/1.

"Military Women Get (Slightly) More Access to Abortion." *Mother Jones*. Accessed June 13, 2014. http://www.motherjones.com/mojo/2012/12/military-women-get-slightly-more-access-abortion.

Mills, Scott. *Women in the Army – Review of the Combat Exclusion Policy*. U.S. Army War College, March 24, 2011.

Mitchell, Brian. *Women in the Military: Flirting With Disaster*. 1st edition. Washington, DC: Regnery, 1997.

Mohanty, Chandra Talpade, Minnie Bruce Pratt, and Robin L. Riley, editors. *Feminism and War*. 1st edition. London: Zed Books, 2008.

Moore, Brenda L. "A Time to Reassess: The Intersection of Race and Class." *Critical Studies on Security* 1, no. 2 (August 1, 2013): 246–48. doi:10.1080/21624887.2013.814843.

———. *To Serve My Country, to Serve My Race: The Story of the Only African-American WACS Stationed Overseas during World War II*. New York: NYU Press, 1997.

Morden, Betty Colonel. "The Women's Army Corps during the Vietnam War." Vietnam Women's Memorial. Accessed January 22, 2014. http://www.vietnamwomensmemorial.org/pdf/bmorden.pdf.

Mullen, Brian, and Carolyn Copper. "The Relationship between Group Cohesiveness and Performance: An Integration." Army Research Institute for the Behavioral and Social Sciences, February 1995.

Myers, Greg. *The Discourse of Blogs and Wikis*. Chippenham , UK: Continuum International, 2010.

Nagl, John A., and Brian M. Burton. "Dirty Windows and Burning Houses: Setting the Record Straight on Irregular Warfare." *Washington Quarterly* 32, no. 2 (2009): 91–101. doi:10.1080/01636600902772836.

Nantais, Cynthia, and Martha F. Lee. "Women in the United States Military: Protectors or Protected? The Case of Prisoner of War Melissa Rathbun-Nealy." *Journal of Gender Studies* 8, no. 2 (1999): 181–91. doi:10.1080/095892399102698.

Nasaw, Daniel. "Report Vindicates Soldiers Prosecuted over Abu Ghraib Abuses, Lawyers Say." *The Guardian*, April 23, 2009, sec. World news. http://www.theguardian.com/world/2009/apr/22/abu-ghraib-iraq-torture-senate.

National Center for Veterans Analysis and Statistics. "America's Women Veterans: Military Service History and VA Benefit Utilization Statistics," November 23, 2011. http://www.va.gov/vetdata/docs/specialreports/final_womens_report_3_2_12_v_7.pdf.

———. "National Centre for Veterans Analysis and Statistics: Selected Research Highlights." December 2010. www.va.gov/vetdata/docs/quickfacts/reports-slideshow.pdf.

Nexon, Daniel H. *Harry Potter and International Relations*. Lanham, MD: Rowman & Littlefield, 2006.

Norris, Jeffrey. "Gender Differences in PTSD Risk May Be due to Heightened Fear Conditioning in Women." *UCSF*, November 19, 2012. http://www.ucsf.edu/news/2012/11/13155/gender-differences-ptsd-risk-may-be-due-heightened-fear-conditioning-women.

Office of the Inspector General. *Tailhook 91: Part 2, Events at the 35th Annual Tailhook Symposium*. Washington DC: US Department of Defense, February 1993. http://hdl.handle.net/2027/mdp.39015029525204.

O'Hanlon, Michael. "A Challenge for Female Marines: The Grueling Infantry Officer Course Was Too Much for Women Who Volunteered." *Wall Street Journal*, November 13, 2012. https://global-factiva-com.ezproxy2.library.usyd.edu.au/aa/?ref=WSJO000020121113e8bd0002u&pp=1&fcpil=en&napc=S&sa_from= .

O'Keefe, Ed, and Jon Cohen. "Most Americans Back Women in Combat Roles, Poll Says." *Washington Post*, March 17, 2011, sec. Politics. http://www.washingtonpost.com/wp-dyn/content/article/2011/03/16/AR2011031603861.html.

Oliver, Laurel W., Joan Harman, Elizabeth Hoover *et al.* "A Quantitative Integration of the Military Cohesion Literature." *Military Psychology* 11, no. 1 (1999): 57–83. doi:10.1207/s15327876mp1101_4.

OMelveny, Sean. "Army Announces First Woman in Combat Support Role." Text. *Stars and Stripes*. Accessed July 16, 2012. http://www.military.com/daily-news/2012/07/03/army-announces-first-woman-in-combat-support-role.html.

Parashar, Swati. "What Wars and 'War Bodies' Know about International Relations." *Cambridge Review of International Affairs* 26, no. 4 (December 1, 2013): 615–30. doi:10.1080/09557571.2013.837429.

Parker, Kathleen. "Parker: Military Is Putting Women at Unique Risk." *Washington Post*, January 28, 2013. http://www.washingtonpost.com/opinions/parker-military-is-putting-women-at-unique-risk/2013/01/25/33d9eca6-6723-11e2-9e1b-07db1d2ccd5b_story.html.

Parrish, Karen. "DOD Opens More Jobs, Assignments to Military Women." U.S. Department of Defense, February 9, 2012. http://www.defense.gov/news/newsarticle.aspx?id=67130.

Peach, Lucinda J. "Women at War: The Ethics of Women in Combat." *Hamline Journal of Public Law and Policy* 15 (1994): 199.

Pew Research. "Politics Fact Sheet." *Pew Research Center's Internet & American Life Project*, November 14, 2012. http://www.pewinternet.org/fact-sheets/politics-fact-sheet/.

Phipps, Jeremy J. J. *Forward, Unit Cohesion: A Prerequisite for Combat Effectiveness*. National Security Affairs Issue Paper. National Defence University, 1982.

Pinch, Franklin C. Alison MacIntyre, Phyllis Browne, and Alan Okros, editors. *"Challenge and Change in the Military: Gender and Diversity Issues*. Canadian Defence Academy Press, 2006.

Quinn, Sally. "Mothers at War: What Are We Doing to Our Kids?" *Washington Post*, Section C-1, February 23, 1991. http://www.highbeam.com/doc/1P2–1050933.html.

Ramsay, Debra. "Television's 'True Stories': Paratexts and the Promotion of HBO's Band of Brothers and The Pacific." *InMedia. The French Journal of Media and Media Representations in the English-Speaking World*, no. 4 (November 12, 2013). http://inmedia.revues.org/720.

Ricks, Thomas E. "Knocked up and Deployed: An Army Captain's View." *Foreign Policy Blogs*, December 22, 2009. http://ricks.foreignpolicy.com/posts/2009/12/22/knocked_up_and_deployed_an_army_captains_view.

Risen, James. "Former Air Force Recruit Speaks Out about Rape by Her Sergeant at Lackland." *The New York Times*, February 26, 2013, sec. U.S. http://www.nytimes.com/2013/02/27/us/former-air-force-recruit-speaks-out-about-rape-by-her-sergeant-at-lackland.html.

Roan, Shari. "Women on War Front More Likely to Get Post-Traumatic Stress Disorder than Men, Study Finds." *Los Angeles Times*, May 19, 2011. http://articles.latimes.com/2011/may/19/news/la-heb-ptsd-women-military-20110519.

Scales, Robert H. "Can a Band of Brothers Include Women?" *Wichita Eagle*. Accessed March 26, 2014. http://www.kansas.com/2012/12/10/2595960_robert-h-scales-can-a-band-of.html.

Rollins, Angela. "Act Like a Lady!: Reconsidering Gender Stereotypes and the Exclusion of Women from Combat in Light of Challenges to 'don't Ask Don't Tell." *Southern Illinois University Law Journal* Winter (2012).

Rona, Roberto J, Nicola T. Fear, Lisa Hull, and Simon Wessely. "Women in Novel Occupational Roles: Mental Health Trends in the UK Armed Forces." *International Journal of Epidemiology* 36, no. 2 (April 2007): 319–26. doi:10.1093/ije/dyl273.

Rosen, Leora N. "Cohesion and Readiness in Gender-Integrated Combat Service Support Units: The Impact of Acceptance of Women and Gender Ratio." *Armed Forces & Society* 22, no. 4 (1996): 537–53.

Rosen, Leora N., Doris B. Durand, Paul D. Bliese, *et al.* "Cohesion and Readiness in Gender-Integrated Combat Service Support Units: The Impact of Acceptance of Women and Gender Ratio." *Armed Forces & Society* 22, no. 4 (July 1, 1996): 537–53. doi:10.1177/0095327x9602200403.

Rostker v. Goldberg, 435 U.S. 57 (U.S. Supreme Court 1981).

Rudy, Paul, and Philippa Gates. "Sound Shaping and Timbral Justification in the 'Moral Realist Combat Film' Black Hawk Down." Accessed February 5, 2014. http://oicrm.org/wp-content/uploads/2012/03/RUDY_P_CIM05.pdf.

Sadler, Anne G., Brenda M. Booth, Brian L. Cook, and Bradley N. Doebbeling. "Factors Associated with Women's Risk of Rape in the Military Environment." *American Journal of Industrial Medicine* 43, no. 3 (March 1, 2003): 262–73. doi:10.1002/ajim.10202.

Saros, Bethany. "My Shameful Military Pregnancy," November 14, 2011. http://www.salon.com/2011/11/13/my_shameful_military_pregnancy/.

Sasson-Levy, Orna. "Feminism and Military Gender Practices: Israeli Women Soldiers in 'Masculine' Roles." *Sociological Inquiry* 73, no. 3 (2003): 440–65. doi:10.1111/1475–682X.00064.

Schneider, Marcie B., Martin Fisher, Stanford B. Friedman, Polly E. Bijur, and Patrick A. Toffler. "Menstrual and Premenstrual Issues in Female Military Cadets: A Unique Population with Significant Concerns." *Journal of Pediatric and Adolescent Gynecology* 12, no. 4 (November 1999): 195–201. doi:10.1016/S1083–3188(99)00025-X.

Seal, K. H., D. Bertenthal, C. R. Miner, S. Sen, and C. Marmar. "Bringing the War Back Home: Mental Health Disorders among 103 788 Us Veterans Returning from Iraq and Afghanistan Seen at Department of Veterans Affairs Facilities." *Archives of Internal Medicine* 167, no. 5 (March 12, 2007): 476–82. doi:10.1001/archinte.167.5.476.

Service Women's Action Network. "Women in Combat," March 2011. http://servicewomen.org/media/publications/#factSheet.

"Sexual Assault in Military 'Jaw-Dropping,' Lawmaker Says." *CNN*, July 31, 2008. http://edition.cnn.com/2008/US/07/31/military.sexabuse/.

Sharp, Marilyn. "Physical Fitness and Occupational Performance of Women in the U.S. Army." Occupational Physiology Division, U.S. Army Research Institute of Environmental Medicine, October 2, 1994. http://www.google.com.au/url?sa=t&rct=j&q=&esrc=s&source=web&cd=4&ved=0CHUQFjAD&url=http%3A%2F%2Fwww.dtic.mil%2Fcgi-bin%2FGetTRDoc%3FAD%3DADA285676&ei=CAHDT_KFNbCYiAfgtoi-Cg&usg=AFQjCNEi9YkMYn95_whgmEC_P8N2qO2Hnw.

Shils, Edward A., and Morris Janowitz. "Cohesion and Disintegration in the Wehrmacht in World War II." *Public Opinion Quarterly* 12, no. 2 (1948): 280–315.

"Should More Veterans Get P.T.S.D. Benefits?" *Room for Debate*. Accessed June 13, 2014. http://roomfordebate.blogs.nytimes.com/2010/07/08/should-more-veterans-get-p-t-s-d-benefits/.

Siebold, Guy L. "The Essence of Military Group Cohesion." *Armed Forces & Society* 33, no. 2 (January 1, 2007): 286–95. doi:10.1177/0095327×06294173.

Siebold, Guy L., and Dennis R. Kelly. *Development of the Combat Platoon Cohesion Questionnaire*, October 1988.

Siegel, Neil S., and Reva B. Siegel. "Struck by Stereotype: Ruth Bader Ginsburg on Pregnancy Discrimination as Sex Discrimination." *Duke Law Journal* 59 (2010): 771–98.

Simons, Anna. "Women Can Never 'Belong' in Combat." *Orbis* 44, no. 3 (June 22, 2000). https://global-factiva-com.ezproxy2.library.usyd.edu.au/aa/?ref=orbs000020010809dw6m0000x&pp=1&fcpil=en&napc=S&sa_from=.

Sindoni, Maria Grazia. *Spoken and Written Discourse in Online Interactions: A Multimodal Approach.* New York: Routledge, 2013.

Sjoberg, Laura. *Gender, War, and Conflict.* 1 edition. Polity, 2014.

Sjoberg, Laura, and Caron E. Gentry. *Mothers, Monsters, Whores: Women's Violence in Global Politics.* Zed Books, 2007.

Sjoberg, Laura, and Sandra E. Via, editors. *Gender, War, and Militarism: Feminist Perspectives.* 1st ed. Santa Barbara, CA: Praeger, 2010.

Skaine, Rosemarie. *Women at War: Gender Issues of Americans in Combat.* Jefferson, NC: McFarland & Co., 1999.

Sohn, Emily. "Why Can't Women Serve at the Front?" *DNews*, November 28, 2012. http://news.discovery.com/human/psychology/women-military-front-120213.htm.

Solaro, Erin. *Women in the Line of Fire: What You Should Know about Women in the Military.* 1st ed. Berkeley, CA: Seal Press, 2006.

"Staff NCO to Lose Rank in Urination Video." *Marine Corps Times.* Accessed May 15, 2014. http://www.marinecorpstimes.com/article/20121220/NEWS/212200321/Staff-NCO-lose-rank-urination-video.

Stiehm, Judith. *Arms and the Enlisted Woman.* Temple University Press, 1989.

Street, Amy E., Dawne Vogt, and Lissa Dutra. "A New Generation of Women Veterans: Stressors Faced by Women Deployed to Iraq and Afghanistan." *Clinical Psychology Review* 29, no. 8 (December 2009): 685–94. doi:10.1016/j.cpr.2009.08.007.

Stur, Heather Marie. *Beyond Combat: Women and Gender in the Vietnam War Era.* New York: Cambridge University Press, 2011.

Sweeney, Heather. "PT Standards in Question for Women in Combat." Text. *Military.com.* Accessed June 13, 2014. http://www.military.com/daily-news/2013/11/14/pt-standards-in-question-for-women-in-combat.html.

Sylvester, Christine. "The Art of War/The War Question in (Feminist) IR." *Millennium – Journal of International Studies* 33, no. 3 (June 1, 2005): 855–78. doi:10.1177/03058298050330030801.

War as Experience: Contributions from International Relations and Feminist Analysis. 1st edition. New York: Routledge, 2012.

Taguba, Antonio. *The "Taguba Report" on Treatment of Abu Ghraib Prisoners in Iraw.* FindLaw, January 19, 2004. http://news.findlaw.com/cnn/docs/iraq/tagubarpt.html#ThR1.8.

Terhakopian, Artin. "Time to Curb Unintended Military Pregnancies." *Time Magazine*, January 31, 2013. http://nation.time.com/2013/01/31/time-to-curb-unintended-military-pregnancies/.

"The Castration of the U.S. Military." Forum. *Leatherneck.com*, June 2002. http://www.leatherneck.com/forums/showthread.php?16930-The-Castration-of-the-U-S-Military.

The Presidential Commission on the Assignment of Women in the Armed Forces: Report to the President, November 15, 1992. Washington, DC:, 1992. http://hdl.handle.net/2027/umn.31951d00277676f.

Thompson, Mark. "Women in Combat: Shattering the 'Brass Ceiling.'" *Time*. Accessed September 8, 2014. http://nation.time.com/2013/01/24/women-in-combat-shattering-the-brass-ceiling/.

Tyson, Ann Scott. "Amendment Targets Role of Female Troops." *Washington Post*, May 19, 2005, sec. Politics. http://www.washingtonpost.com/wp-dyn/content/article/2005/05/18/AR2005051802094.html.

United States General Accounting Office. *GENDER ISSUES: Information on DOD's Assignment Policy and Direct Ground Combat Definition*. Washington, DC, October 1998.

"*Gender Issues: Information to Assess Servicemembers' Perceptions of Gender Inequities Is Complete. Report to Congressional Committees*." United States General Accounting Office, November 1998.

University of Virginia School of Law. "Students, Professor Help File Lawsuit on Behalf of Plaintiffs Seeking to Overturn Military Ban on Women in Combat." *University of Virginia School of Law*, May 24, 2012. http://www.law.virginia.edu/html/news/2012_spr/combat_exclusion.htm.

"Unplanned Pregnancies May Be on Rise in Military." *CNN*. Accessed June 13, 2014. http://www.cnn.com/2013/01/23/health/unplanned-pregnancies-military/index.html.

US Commission on Civil Rights. *Sexual Assault in the Military*. Statutory Enforcement Report. Washington, DC, September 2013. http://sapr.mil/public/docs/research/USCCR_Statutory_Enforcement_Report_Sexual_Assault_in_the_Military_SEP2013.pdf.

US Marine Corps. "Timeline: Engaging Afghan Women on the Front Lines." *US Marine Corps*, n.d. http://www.marines.com/history-heritage/timeline?articleId=TIMELINE_FEMALE_TEAMS#2000.

"USMC 4-Star: Women to Attend Infantry School." *Marine Corps Times*. Accessed July 16, 2012. http://www.marinecorpstimes.com/news/2012/04/marine-corps-women-infantry-combat-dunford-amos-041812/.

Van Creveld, Martin. "Less than We Can Be: Men, Women and the Modern Military." *Journal of Strategic Studies* 23, no. 4 (2000): 1–20. doi:10.1080/01402390008437809.

Men, Women & War: Do Women Belong in the Front Line?. London: Cassell, 2002.

"The Great Illusion Women in the Military." *Journal of International Studies* 29, no. 2 (2000): 429–42.

Van Den Bossche, Piet, Wim H. Gijselaers, Mien Segers, and Paul A. Kirschner. "Social and Cognitive Factors Driving Teamwork in Collaborative Learning Environments Team Learning Beliefs and Behaviors." *Small Group Research* 37, no. 5 (October 1, 2006): 490–521. doi:10.1177/104649640629-2938.

Wardell, Diane Wind, and Barbara Czerwinski. "A Military Challenge to Managing Feminine and Personal Hygiene." *Journal of the American Academy of Nurse Practitioners* 13, no. 4 (April 2001): 187.

Weber, Cynthia. *International Relations Theory: A Critical Introduction.* Psychology Press, 2005.

Weinstein, Laurie Lee, and Christie C. White. *Wives and Warriors: Women and the Military in the United States and Canada.* Greenwood Publishing Group, 1997.

Whitlock, Craig. "4 Women Sue Over Pentagon's Combat-Exclusion Policy." *Washington Post*, November 28, 2012. http://global.factiva.com.ezproxy1 .library.usyd.edu.au/aa/?ref=WP00000020121128e8bs0001c&pp=1&fcpil=en& napc=S&sa_from=.

"Will Abortion Law Change Help Female Troops?" *Stars and Stripes.* Accessed June 13, 2014. http://www.stripes.com/news/will-abortion-law-change-help-female-troops-1.209513.

Wilson, Jacque. "Unplanned Pregnancies May Be on Rise in Military," January 24, 2013. http://edition.cnn.com/2013/01/23/health/unplanned-pregnancies-military/.

Wilson, John. *Compensation Owed for Mental Health Based on Activities in Theatre Post-Traumatic Stress Disorder Act.* US Government Printing Office, 2009. http://www.gpo.gov/fdsys/pkg/CHRG-111hhrg49911/pdf/CHRG-111hhrg49911.pdf.

Wiltrout, Kate. "Suffolk Reservist Sues over Ban on Women in Combat." *The Virginian-Pilot*, May 25, 2012. http://hamptonroads .com/2012/05/army-reservist-assigned-suffolk-sues-pentagon-over-combat-exclusion.

Winslow, Donna, and Jason Dunn. "Women in the Canadian Forces: Between Legal and Social Integration." *Current Sociology* 50, no. 5 (September 1, 2002): 641–67. doi:10.1177/0011392102050005003.

Witschge, Tamara. "Examining Online Public Discourse: A Mixed Method Approach." *Javnost – The Public* 15, no. 2 (2008): 75–92.

"Women and Militarization: Before, During, and After Wars" with Cynthia Enloe, 2012. http://www.youtube.com/watch?v=lfCktWyARVo&feature=youtube_gdata_player.

"Women at War: Pentagon Is Easing Its Job Limits." *The Guardian*, sec. World News, January 23, 2008. http://www.guardian.co.uk/world/feedarticle/10086205.

Women Content in Units Force Development Test: (MAX WAC). U.S. Army Research Institute for the Behavioral and Social Sciences, 1977.

"Women Feel Pain More Than Men." *BBC*, July 4, 2005, sec. Health. http://news.bbc.co.uk/2/hi/health/4641567.stm.

"Women in Combat." *CultureWatch*. Accessed June 12, 2014. http://billmuehlenberg.com/2011/04/12/women-in-combat/.

"Women in Combat: Army to Open 14K Jobs, 6 MOSs." *Army Times*. Accessed July 10, 2012. http://www.armytimes.com/news/2012/05/army-to-open-14000-jobs-6-mos-women-in-combat-050212/.

Women in Military Service for America Memorial Foundation. "Highlights in the History of Military Women." Women in Military Service For America Memorial Foundation, n.d. http://www.womensmemorial.org/Education/timeline.html.

"Women in the Battlefield." *New York Times*, January 24, 2013, sec. Opinion. http://www.nytimes.com/2013/01/25/opinion/women-in-the-battlefield.html.

"Women in War Zones Take Risks but Don't Reap Rewards." *USA Today*, December 12, 2012.

Wong, Leonard, Thomas A. Kolditz, Raymond A. Millen, and Terrence M. Potter. *Why They Fight: Combat Motivation in the Iraq War.* Strategic Studies Institute, U.S. Army War College, July 2003.

Yanovich, Ran, Rachel Evans, Eran Israeli, *et al.* "Differences in Physical Fitness of Male and Female Recruits in Gender-Integrated Army Basic Training." *Medicine and Science in Sports and Exercise* 40, no. 11 Suppl (November 2008): S654–59. doi:10.1249/MSS.0b013e3181893f30.

Zaccaro, Stephen J., and Charles A. Lowe. "Cohesiveness and Performance on an Additive Task: Evidence for Multidimensionality." *Journal of Social Psychology* 128, no. 4 (1988): 547–58. doi:10.1080/00224545.1988.9713774.

Zucchino, David. "Female Soldiers Fight Pentagon in Court for Combat Positions." *Los Angeles Times*, October 11, 2012. http://articles.latimes.com/2012/oct/11/nation/la-na-women-combat-20121012.

Index

CPSIA information can be obtained
at www.ICGtesting.com
Printed in the USA
LVHW02s2035271217
560946LV00011B/285/P